LITERARY NASHVILLE

edited by

PATRICK ALLEN

foreword by

MADISON JONES

HILL STREET PRESS   ATHENS, GEORGIA

A HILL STREET PRESS BOOK

Published in the United States of America by
Hill Street Press LLC
191 East Broad Street, Suite 209
Athens, Georgia 30601-2848 USA
706-613-7200
info@hillstreetpress.com
www.hillstreetpress.com

Text and cover design by Anne Richmond Boston.

Printed in Canada.

Library of Congress Cataloging-in-Publication Data

Literary Nashville / edited by Patrick Allen : foreword by Madison Jones.
      p.   cm.
  ISBN 1-892514-11-7 (alk. paper)
   1. American literature—Tennessee—Nashville. 2. Nashville (Tn.)—Social life and customs. 3. Nashville (Tn.) Literary collections. I. Allen, Patrick (James Patrick), 1965– .
  PS559.N3L58 1999
  810.9'03276855—dc21   99-37701
                          CIP

10 9 8 7 6 5 4 3 2 1

First edition

Contents

CONTENTS

Foreword

Nashville, like virtually all American cities, has greatly changed in the fifty years since I resided in and near it. The city has acquired a skyline, infinitely burgeoning suburbs, and all the other familiar and doubtful consequences of modernity. Through the haze of memory, though, I am yet able to see it as a town of middling size enfolded in a great bend of the Cumberland River, the venerable and handsome capitol building high on a hill at its center. Downhill from the face of it is old Church Street, long since become too narrow for the convenience of a motor-driven world, and beyond this, Broad Street, quite broad enough, sloping gently downhill to where it abuts on the river. There, in form somewhat elaborated since my youth, stands the replica of old Fort Nashboro, reminder of early days when Native Americans were considered a threat by settlers. Happily, the city has taken, and continues to take care that the many surviving evidences of its history be preserved and memorialized. Fort Negely, built by the Yankee army, offers another example, recalling the Federal occupation under which the city suffered severely throughout the greater part of the Civil War. A sense of history is a sure enrichment to imagination, and Nashville's constancy in this regard deserves the gratitude of its writers.

Among Nashville's historic sites (this one not in fact so very historic) I would for particular personal reasons mention the old Ryman Auditorium. Though it has other claims to fame, for me its role as the original home of the Grand Old Opry takes precedence. In those days the building was considerably run-down and fast approaching a condition of structural peril (it has since been renovated) but it had, and has, perhaps the best acoustics in the country. I remember it with special affection because of the many Saturday nights when I, with several good friends, was present for the performances of genuine (which is to say "folk-derived") country music. For those old performers were the real thing, illustrious progenitors of a vulgarized musical horde now grown amazingly popular. I remember best of all one performer, Uncle Dave Macon, who, along with the songs he played and sang, is virtually forgotten. Who remembers "From Jerusalem to Jericho," or "Bully of the Town," or "The Woman with the Red Dress On," much less the rollicking sound of the old man's grinding country voice? He was the essence of colorful. He was also quotable. Once, asked how he had happened to become a performer, he replied, "Son, I started out to make a preacher, but I found out there was more money in foolishness." Any kinship between that old man and today's much publicized performers is all but imperceptible.

It used to be and perhaps still is the case that Nashville, because of its many schools and colleges, advertised itself as the "Athens of the South." Among others, there long have been under various names Belmont, Fisk, Lipscomb, and Vanderbilt universities, and Scaritt and Peabody colleges, as well as numerous, though mostly now defunct, college preparatory schools. Typical was Wallace School, the one I attended until my senior year in 1942 when it finally closed. By this time it was quite small, with fifty or so students and a faculty of four, two of whom were part-time members. The building (now replaced with something like a hamburger joint) was a large old residence house on West End Avenue, fairly shabby and, like most of Nashville in those days, darkened with soot. In the light of modern hygienic requirements, it amuses me to recall the physical conditions under which we were educated—dirty windows, dust everywhere, a stinking bathroom that no one would willingly enter. We students barely noticed, being accustomed to the assumption that our sole business there was education. To this end, old Mr. Wallace, owner and headmaster, in the face of degenerating educational expectations, labored mightily. Until the school's demise, students were required, though with exceptions in increasing number, to take four years of Latin, two of French, Bible History, and so on according to the classical idea of proper curriculum. Clarence

Wallace, eighty when he closed his school, meant business, and enforced it with penalties of attendance at Saturday school and of corporal punishment. The latter of these consisted of licks with an arrow shaft on the bare hand of the offender. This discipline worked, though as always there were exceptions. One exception was the case of a certain country boy with a hand like an anvil, to which Mr. Wallace quite in vain applied and often broke, his arrow shafts.

There was almost nothing in my growing up to suggest that I would have a literary career. I don't recall being conscious of any Nashville writer except Alfred Leland Crabb who made something of a name for himself in the 1940s with *Dinner at Belmont*, *Supper at the Maxwell House*, *Lodging at the Saint Cloud*, and other books similarly titled. It was somewhere along in my days at Vanderbilt that I was introduced in a serious way to literature and the idea of writing it. The particular agent of this introduction was Donald Davidson, the one literature professor still on hand who had been a part of the illustrious group of Vanderbilt and Nashville-connected poets and fiction writers known as the Fugitives. Among these were John Crowe Ransom, Allen Tate, Robert Penn Warren, and Andrew Lytle. Later I came to know these men, and others related, more or less well, but it was the encouragement of Davidson that put me on my way. A brilliant teacher and more than that only, he pointed me to my origins, which became the groundwork of my fiction overall.

So, Nashville, figures here, as cocoon or, maybe better, paradigm. And I suspect that at least in some degree this has been so for other writers associated with the city, including more recent ones. Altogether they are not a few, as this book demonstrates. And to mention names like Randall Jarrell, James Dickey, Peter Taylor, Walter Sullivan, and, most recent, Madison Smartt Bell is only to begin the list. Many must agree with what Robert Penn Warren wrote in his 1979 essay "A Reminiscence": "How

Preface

Through his exuberant interpretations of individuals both central and secondary to Nashville history, locally born artist Red Grooms gives us the vibrant sweep of the city's history in his Fox Trot Carousel housed at Nashville's Riverfront Park. All of the working carousel's renderings both of figures important in civic history, such as Anne Dallas Dudley, Rabbi Isadore Lewinthal, and Sequoia, and of subjects ephemeral to, but known by all Nashvillians, such as the catfish, the chigger, and the Purity Milk Truck, are finely detailed works of art. But when the figures are considered alongside his carved panels depicting scenes from Tennessee history and the whole pageant of color and form revolves, Grooms's approximation of the city as a diverse, polyglot panorama is revealed. *Literary Nashville*, although more modest in scale, comes from the same impulse. Nashville is too diverse, too historically rich, too contradictory to be distilled into an essence by a single writer. In a fashion not unlike Grooms's carousel, this book attempts to present a portrait of the city not through a single icon, but through the assemblage of many writers' perspectives, observed details, and anecdotes.

Because the pieces herein come from writers born in, transplanted to, and merely visiting the city, not to mention from different eras, in varying forms, and from different races and both genders, many contradictory views emerge. The city, slowly evolved from the home of ancient peoples and from white settlement of the eighteenth century, is now a center of digitally-based business looking to the next millennium. Music City holds the promise of star power and even though most of those who seek it find only obscurity, Nashville's temptress quality frequently entraps newcomers and convinces them that no other place will do. It is home to both Belle Meade Brahmins and down-home pluckers, the Old South and the newly rich. Everywhere in Nashville are the contradictory faces of hard luck and easy money, Bible Belt values and fast-living musicians.

Nashville, a city which benefits mightily from the energy and ideas of newcomers and transients, has a proudly rooted populace.

The city's contradictions have inspired writers in many forms: poetry, essay, fiction, memoir, diary, and journalism. All those are included here with preference throughout given to the literary. Nashville has been portrayed countless times in lyrics from Appalachian ballads to countrypolitan hits but, since it would be impossible to even survey the rich body of Nashville song here, I have chosen to exclude this literary form.

As much as possible, I have selected pieces from an author's work in which the city, more than a passive backdrop, is felt as a character or force. The contradictions highlighted above are rarely resolved in the city itself, and I make no attempt to do so here. Therefore, I rely on simple chronology of publication date, rather than thematic divisions to order this book. I have sought a balance between the familiar and the obscure, both among the mix of artists themselves and the pieces chosen to represent them.

Although I intend this volume as a literary record, not as a documentary history, I have attempted to represent the "Athens of the South" in many different eras. It should be noted that some of the language and attitudes, particularly as they relate to people of color, will trouble many readers. Knowing that such attitudes are unfortunate historical realities in some sections of the city, as they have been throughout the whole of American society, I have made no effort to hide or eliminate them. I rely on the historical understanding and conscience of the reader to put them in the proper perspective.

In the process of deciding which artists and what pieces to include in his book, the anthologist challenges himself to a one-person tug-of-war, an exercise the end result of which inevitably inspires defensiveness or surprise in some readers. Simple space considerations prohibit all the fine work in all literary forms being included here. A list of recommended further reading, itself admittedly incomplete, would be extensive. Antebellum

poets Virginia French and Clara Cole are noteworthy. Late nine-
teenth- and early twentieth-century writers of Nashville birth or
residence include Maria Thompson Daviess, Francis Perry
Elliott, Harriett Malone Hobson, Kate Sharber, Kate Vaughn,
and Thomas Lee Woolwine. Will Allen Dromgoole, literary editor of the *Nashville Banner*, first Nashville woman to enlist in the
Navy in World War I, and author of the well-known poem "The
Bridge Builder," achieved popular success in her day. Clarkesville,
Tennessee-born Evelyn Scott writes interestingly of market days in
turn-of-the-century Nashville in her *Background in Tennessee*
(1937). Among writer and long-time Fisk University librarian and
administrator Arna Bontemps's many publications is *Chariot in
the Sky* (1951), a children's book about the Fisk Jubilee Singers.
Numerous writers and poets have passed through Fisk's gates, far
more than could be represented here. Many figures associated
with the Fugitives and Agrarians are absent from this book, not
the least of which are Cleanth Brooks, Caroline Gordon, and
Mildred Haun. Their omission here is recognition that although
their personal ties to Nashville were strong, their work was not
often set there. Other noteworthy writers who have studied in or
practiced their writing in Nashville include William Cobb, John
Egerton, Jesse Hill Ford, Elizabeth Spencer, James Summerville,
and Elizabeth Dewberry Vaughn.

Tony Earley and Ann Patchett are writers of acclaim who
make their homes in Nashville, but do not often write of their
adopted cities. Nashville and environs are also home to Kate
Daniels, Cathie Pelletier, and Michael Lee West, all of whose
work has received popular and critical attention. Karen Kijewski,
Cecelia Tishy, and Edgar Award-winner Steven Womack set their
detective stories and thrillers in the Music City.

Many important writers and poets have resided in Nashville,
sometimes briefly, sometimes for extended periods, but left no literary record of their stay which I am able to locate. James Weldon
Johnson taught at Fisk University for nearly a decade. John O.
Killens was writer-in-residence at Fisk for three and a half years
and wrote *'Sippi* (1967) there. Nikki Giovanni attended Fisk in

the late 1960s. Kingsley Amis taught at Vanderbilt University for a semester in 1967-1968. Shotaro Yasuoka's *Amerika kanjo ryoko* (*Sentimental Journey to America*, 1962) is an account of the important Japanese writer's American travels, including his stay in Nashville, which has never been translated.

I wish that space would permit me to include some ephemera or bits of literary trivia. Ogden Nash is known as the consummate New Yorker, but his Nashville roots run deep. Nashville was named for his ancestor General Francis Nash. The humorist and poet described his own accent as a "clam chowder" with bits of New England and Southern dialect mixed together. O. Henry visited the city when his daughter attended the Belmont Academy and he set a story in Nashville called "A Municipal Report."

This volume is only a starting point in the study of the literature of the city. No better places to continue the study of Nashville letters exist than the impressive collections of Nashville's libraries. The first lending library was established in the city in 1844, and present day institutions with impressive collections of Nashvilliana include the Jean and Alexander Heard Library at Vanderbilt University with its excellent collection of the papers of Brainard and Frances Cheney, Alfred Leland Crabb, Edwin Mims, Frank Owsley, Peter Taylor, Jesse Ely Wills, and others; and the Fisk University Library which houses a collection of papers of W. E. B. DuBois, Chester Himes, Langston Hughes, and Zora Neale Hurston, to name a few; as well as the Nashville Room of the Ben West Library and the Tennessee State Library and Archives. Many Nashvillians fondly remember Mills Bookstore, which closed in 1990 just short of its hundredth anniversary, but many quality bookstores such as Bookstar, Barnes and Noble, Books-a-Million, Out Loud, Magical Journey, Walden, and Doubleday as well as the local chain Davis-Kidd Booksellers remain to serve Nashville readers. Sources for rare books and reprints of Nashville interest include Elder's Bookstore or, for modern first editions and antiquarian books related to the city, Bodacious Books, Bookman, and the Nashville House of Books. The liveliness of Nashville's reading community can be experienced at the Tennessee Humanities Council's annual Southern Festival of the Book, under the direction of Robert Cheatham and Galyn Glick Martin, and the Sewanee Writers' Conference. The city had its first reading group, the married women-only Review Club, as early 1893, and is home to many such groups today. There is wonderful coverage of books on Sue McClure's book page in the *Nashville Banner,* as well as in *Nashville Scene* and other local publications. For rounding out my own education on the literature of the city, I must acknowledge the thoughtfulness and expertise of the staffs of the special collections departments of the Fisk and Vanderbilt libraries, Carol Kaplan and the staff of the Nashville Room of the Ben West Library, Bob Summer, Ron Watson, and Haywood Moxley. I would also like to thank M.fred at Hatch Show Print, a division of the Country Music Foundation, for kindly providing a cover image for *Literary Nashville* as complex and energetic as the city itself.

Patrick Allen
Editor

from *A Narrative of the Life of David Crockett, of the State of Tennessee*

DAVID CROCKETT (1786–1836)

David Crockett was born near present-day Rogersville, Hawkins County, Tennessee, the son of a tavern owner. He received little formal schooling before trying his hand at farming and managing a gristmill, a gunpowder manufactory, and a distillery. Crockett found success in the military where he served under General Andrew Jackson in the Creek Wars of 1813. He served in the Tennessee legislature and for two terms in the United States House of Representatives. He moved twice to the Tennessee frontier. After losing his congressional seat to Jackson when he opposed the latter's land policies, Crockett left politics and moved to Texas. He was killed at the Alamo on March 6, 1836. In his *Narrative* (1834), written with Thomas Chilton, Crockett is seen as an earthy backwoodsman. He was, in reality, a sober, genteel man with a gift for humorous, if sometimes highly exaggerated anecdote.

But the reader, I expect, would have no objection to know a little about my employment during the two years while my competitor was in Congress. In this space I had some pretty tuff times, and will relate some few things that happened to me. So here goes, as the boy said when he run by himself.

In the fall of 1825, I concluded I would build two large boats, and load them with pipe staves for market. So I went down to the lake, which was about twenty-five miles from where I lived, and hired some hands to assist me, and went to work; some at boat building, and others to getting staves. I worked on with my hands till the bears got fat, and then I turned out to hunting, to lay in a supply of meat. I soon killed and salted down as many as were necessary for my family; but about this time one of my old neighbours, who had settled down on the lake about twenty-five miles from me, came to my house and told me he wanted me to go down and kill some bears about in his parts. He said they were extremely fat, and very plenty. I know'd that when they were fat, they were easily taken, for a fat bear can't run fast or long. But I asked a bear no favours, no way, further than civility, for I now had *eight* large dogs, and as fierce as painters; so that a bear stood no chance at all to get away from them. So I went home with him, and then went on down towards the Mississippi, and commenced hunting.

We were out two weeks, and in that time killed fifteen bears. Having now supplied my friend with plenty of meat I engaged occasionally again with my hands in our boat building, and getting staves. But I at length couldn't stand it any longer without another hunt. So I concluded to take my little son, and cross over the lake, and take a hunt there. We got over, and that evening turned out and killed three bears, in little or no time. The next morning we drove up four forks, and made a sort of scaffold, on which we salted up our meat, so as to have it out of the reach of the wolves, for as soon as we would leave our camp, they would take possession. We had just eat our breakfast, when a company of hunters came to our camp, who had fourteen dogs, but all so poor, that when they would bark they would almost have to lean up against a tree and take a rest. I told them their dogs couldn't run in smell of a bear, and they had better stay at my camp, and feed them on the bones I had cut out of my meat. I left them there, and cut out; but I hadn't gone far, when my dogs took a first-rate start after a very large fat old *he-bear*, which run right plump towards my camp. I pursued on, but my other hunters had heard my dogs coming, and met them, and killed the bear before I got up with him. I gave him to them, and cut out again for a creek called Big Clover, which wa'n't very far off. Just as I got there, and was entering a cane brake, my dogs all broke and went ahead, and, in a little time, they raised a fuss in the cane, and seemed to be going every way. I listened a while, and found my dogs was in two companies, and that both was in a snorting fight. I sent my little son to one, and I broke for t'other. I got to mine first, and found my dogs had a two-year-old bear down, a-wooling away on him; so I just took out my big butcher, and went up and slap'd it into him, and killed him without shooting. There was five of the dogs in my company. In a short time, I heard my little son fire at his bear; when I went to him he had killed it too. He had two dogs in his team. Just at this moment we heard my other dog barking a short distance off, and all the rest immediately broke to him. We pushed on too, and when we got there, we found he had still a larger bear than either of them we had killed, treed by himself. We killed that one also, which made three we had killed in less than half an hour. We turned in and butchered them, and then started to hunt for water, and a good place to camp. But we had no sooner started, than our dogs took a start after another one, and away they went like a thunder-gust, and was out of hearing in a minute. We followed the way they had gone for some time, but at length we gave up the hope of finding them, and turned back. As we were going back, I came to where a poor fellow was grubbing, and he looked like the very picture of hard times. I asked him what he was doing away there in the woods by himself? He said he was grubbing for a man who intended to settle there; and the reason why he did it was that he had no meat for his family, and he was working for a little.

I was mighty sorry for the poor fellow, for it was not only a hard, but a very slow way to get meat for a hungry family; so I told him if he would go with me, I would give him more meat than he could get by grubbing in a month. I intended to supply him with meat, and also to get him to assist my little boy in packing in and salting up my bears. He had never seen a bear killed in his life. I told him I had six killed then, and my dogs were hard after another. He went off to his little cabin, which was a short distance in the brush, and his wife was very anxious he should go with me. So we started and went to where I had left my three bears, and made a camp. We then gathered my meat and salted, and scaffled it, as I had done the other. Night now came on, but no word from my dogs yet. I afterwards found they had treed the bear about five miles off; near to a man's house, and had barked at it the whole enduring night. Poor fellows! many a time they looked for me, and wondered why I didn't come, for they knowed there was no mistake in me, and I know'd they were as good as ever fluttered. In the morning, as soon as it was light enough to see, the man took his gun and went to them, and shot the bear, and killed it. My dogs, however, wouldn't have any thing to say to this stranger; so they left him, and came early in the morning back to me.

We got our breakfast, and cut out again and we killed four large and very fat bears that day. We hunted out the week, and in that time we killed seventeen, all of them first-rate. When we closed our hunt, I gave the man over a thousand weight of fine fat bear-meat, which pleased him mightily, and made him feel as rich as a Jew. I saw him the next fall, and he told me he had plenty of meat to do him the whole year from his week's hunt. My son and me now went home. This was the week between Christmass and New-year that we made this hunt.

When I got home, one of my neighbours was out of meat, and wanted me to go back, and let him go with me, to take another hunt. I couldn't refuse; but I told him I was afraid the bear had taken to house by that time, for after they get very fat in the fall and early part of the winter, they go into their holes, in large hollow trees, or into hollow logs, or their cane-houses, or the harricanes; and lie there till spring, like frozen snakes. And one thing about this will seem mighty strange to many people. From about the first of January to about the last of April, these varments lie in their holes altogether. In all that time they have no food to eat; and yet when they come out, they are not an ounce lighter than when they went to house. I don't know the cause of this, and still I know it is a fact; and I leave it for others who have more learning than myself to account for it. They have not a particle of food with them, but they just lie and suck the bottom of their paw all the time. I have killed many of them in their trees, which enables me to speak positively on this subject. However, my neighbour, whose name was McDaniel, and my little son and me, went on down to the lake to my second camp, where I had killed my seventeen bears the week before, and turned out to hunting. But we hunted hard all day without getting a single start. We had carried but little provisions with us, and the next morning was entirely out of meat. I sent my son about three miles off, to the house of an old friend, to get some. The old gentleman was much pleased to hear I was hunting in those parts, for the year before the bears had killed a great many of his hogs. He was that day killing his bacon hogs, and so he gave my son some meat, and sent word to me that I must come in to his house that evening, that he would have plenty of feed for my dogs, and some accommodations for ourselves; but before my son got back, we had gone out hunting, and in a large cane brake my dogs found a big bear in a cane-house, which he had fixed for his winter-quarters, as they sometimes do.

When my lead dog found him, and raised the yell, all the rest broke to him, but none of them entered his house until we got up. I encouraged my dogs, and they knowed me so well, that I could have made them seize the old serpent himself, with all his horns and heads, and cloven foot and ugliness into the bargain, if he would only have come to light, so that they could have seen him. They bulged in, and in an instant the bear followed them out, and I told my friend to shoot him, as he was mighty wrathy to kill a bear. He did so, and killed him prime. We carried him to our camp, by which time my son had returned; and after we got our dinners we packed up, and cut for the house of my old friend, whose name was Davidson.

We got there, and staid with him that night; and the next morning, having salted up our meat, we left it with him, and started to take a hunt between the Obion lake and the Red-foot lake; as there had been a dreadful harricane, which passed between them, and I was sure there must be a heap of bears in the fallen timber. We had gone about five miles without seeing any sign at all; but at length we got on some high cany ridges, and, as we rode along, I saw a hole in a large black oak, and on examining more closely, I discovered that a bear had clomb the tree. I could see his tracks going up, but none coming down, and so I was sure he was in there. A person who is acquainted with bear-hunting, can tell easy enough when the varment is in the hollow; for as they go up they don't slip a bit, but as they come down they make long scratches with their nails.

My friend was a little ahead of me, but I called him back, and told him there was a bear in that tree, and I must have him out. So we lit from our horses, and I found a small tree which I thought I could fall so as to lodge against my bear tree, and we fell to work chopping it with our tomahawks. I intended, when we lodged the tree against the other, to let my little son go up, and look into the hole, for he could climb like a squirrel. We had chop'd on a little time and stop'd to rest, when I heard my dogs barking mighty severe at some distance from us, and I told my friend I knowed they had a bear; for it is the nature of a dog, when he finds you are hunting bears, to hunt for nothing else; he becomes fond of the meat, and considers other game as "not worth a notice," as old Johnson said of the devil.

We concluded to leave our tree a bit, and went to my dogs, and when we got there, sure enough they had an eternal great big fat bear up a tree, just ready for shooting. My friend again petitioned me for liberty to shoot this one also. I had a little rather not, as the bear was so big, but I couldn't refuse; and so he blazed away, and down came the old fellow like some great log had fell. I now missed one of my dogs, the same that I before spoke of as having treed the bear by himself sometime before, when I had started the three in the cane break. I told my friend that my missing dog had a bear somewhere, just as sure as fate; so I left them to butcher the one we had just killed, and I went up on a piece of high ground to listen for my dog. I heard him barking with all his might some distance off, and I pushed ahead for him. My other dogs hearing him broke to him, and when I got there, sure enough again he had another bear ready treed; if he hadn't, I wish I may be shot. I fired on him, and brought him down; and then went back, and help'd finish butchering the one at which I had left my friend. We then packed both to our tree where we had left my boy. By this time, the little fellow had cut the tree down that we intended to lodge, but it fell the wrong way; he had then feather'd in on the big tree, to cut that, and had found that it was nothing but a shell on the outside, and all doted in the middle, as too many of our big men are in these days, having only an outside appearance. My friend and my son cut away on it, and I went off about a hundred yards with my dogs to keep them from running under the tree when it should fall. On looking back at the hole, I saw the bear's head out of it, looking down at them as they were cutting. I hollered to them to look up, and they did so; and McDaniel catched up his gun, but by this time the bear was out, and coming down the tree. He fired at it, and as soon as it touch'd ground the dogs were all round it, and they had a roll-and-tumble fight to the foot of the hill, where they stop'd him. I ran up, and putting my gun against the bear, fired and killed him. We now had three, and so we made our scaffold and salted them up.

from "Flirts and Their Ways"

MARY NOAILLES MURFREE (1850–1922)

Mary Noailles Murfree was born at Grantland, her family's plantation on Stone's River near Murfreesboro, Tennessee, descending from four generations of pioneers, landowners, lawyers, and legislators. Her father was a linguist and a published author; her mother is said to have brought the first piano to the state of Tennessee. After being stricken at age four with a malady which left her partially paralyzed, Murfree spent her summers at Beersheba Springs in the Cumberland Mountains. There she observed the folkways and learned the dialect she captured in her local color novels and short story collections, including *In the Tennessee Mountains* (1884), *Down the Ravine* (1885), *The Story of Keedon Bluffs* (1887), and *The Bushwhackers and Other Stories* (1899). With her family, she lived in Nashville from ages seven to seventeen and attended the Nashville Female Academy. Grantland was destroyed during the Civil War but was rebuilt as New Grantland. There she began her writing in earnest, most often using the pen name Charles Egbert Craddock. Rumor that Craddock was actually a woman began after the popular and critical success of her first two novels. Murfree, with her sister and father, traveled to Boston by train to reveal in person her identity to the editor of the *Atlantic*. Shortly before her death in 1922 in her patronymic home of Murfreesboro, she was awarded an honorary degree by the University of the South. The following is an excerpt from Murfree's first published article, a piece in the May 1874 *Lippincott's Monthly Magazine* which appeared under the name "R. Emmet Dembry," another Murfree pseudonym. In addition to the literary flirt described below, Murfree discusses several different types of flirts including the demure flirt, the pious flirt, and the sympathetic flirt.

The dictionary defines a flirt as "a young girl who acts with giddiness." Observe the incapacity of those who sit in high places!

The dictionary manifestly knows nothing about it. A flirt is not of necessity a young girl, and cannot in the nature of things be the least giddy. *Au contraire justement*, she acts with well-considered and deliberate purpose; she possesses great steadiness and force of character; her patience and perseverance are indomitable; and for years she keeps in view an object of comparatively trifling interest until it is *un fait accompli*. She assumes such moods and characteristics as she deems most efficient in pursuance of her designs, and plays a part with a verisimilitude which often deceives the most acute. She is a social Modoc, delighting in her cruel achievements, and rating her prowess by the extent of the wounds inflicted and the number of scalps taken.

As with early potatoes, there are several varieties of flirts, and it is difficult to decide which variety is preferable.

. . .

The literary flirt is, in her circle, a personage of great distinction; not that she has ever written anything, but her supposed capabilities are great indeed. Her friends frequently ask her, as respectfully as if addressing a being of a superior order, "Why don't you write a book?" to which she modestly replies, "I am not capable of that sort of thing." Yet she thinks she is capable of writing such a production as Bacon's *Essays* if she chose to give herself to the task. Her flirting material is somewhat scant, owing to the fact that numbers of young men are afraid of her. But those who bend at her shrine are of rather a higher type than the general class of beaux, with better acquirements, professions, ambitions, and withal more constant. She flatters them by her preference, for it is well understood she tolerates none but intellectual men; she delights with her ready appreciation of a *bon mot*, pleases with her sprightly and intelligent conversation, amuses with her charming little originalities, and has always read the newest books and criticisms; her society never fatigues, for her mind combines something of the strength of a man's with the alertness and vivacity of a woman's. Altogether, the stool at Minerva's feet is a most agreeable piece of upholstery. She is always eager to learn something new, to enter upon fields of knowledge hitherto untrodden, but unfortunately for acquirements of permanent value she is subject, like the rest of her sex, to whims, and constantly abandons one enterprise for another. Sometimes a votary undertakes to teach her German, and after months of patient labor, during which she makes considerable progress, he is thrown over in favor of a divinity student, who instructs her in the Hebrew language. She has been seen sitting on the lawn, a table before her, large and formidable folios scattered about, a broad hat on her head, a blue veil tied round her throat, her most serious expression on her pretty face, under the direction of a youthful neophyte of the law, pitching into Blackstone with enthusiastic ardor. The poor young gentleman, taking no precautions for the protection of his complexion, looked more like a ploughboy than a genteel young lawyer before the finale of his arduous labors. Alas for Judge Minerva's future eminence! She and her counsel learned in the law disagreed in a debate on the point of marrying and giving in marriage, he taking the affirmative and she the negative, and the juvenile Solon was dismissed before the completion of the first volume of the entertaining series.

She is often accused of writing and committing to memory her brilliant sayings previous to their delivery before a full audience. I can neither confirm nor contradict this statement, but certainly among the most stupid of her friends she practices deceptions which she does not attempt in the presence of the literati. How Softhead's dull eyes opened as she appropriated and glibly recited whole pages of that delectable text-book, Abercrombie's *Intellectual Philosophy*! The guileless youth afterward asserted to his friends, in the slang peculiar to his class, that she was a "stunner on the talk, anyway, and as pretty as a peach."

She looks down with great scorn from her elevation of Latin and logic upon the limited mental capacity and trifling pursuits of other young ladies, and induces a similar feeling in the breasts of her adherents, who desert all other damsels and walk with them no more. She is supposed to be very ambitious in the matter of her future husband. She aspires to a philosopher or savant of world-wide repute, and regards a United States Senator or general with much the same feelings as the dancing youth around her. Not that she scorns the giddy pleasures of galop or waltz. *Au contraire.* Listen! The band is playing the "Beautiful Blue Danube" waltzes: she breaks off in the most learned disquisition, with which she is entertaining an appreciative professor, on the subject of Aryan migrations and civilization, taps her little satin-booted foot in her eager anticipation, and delightedly whirls away with the most feather-pated popinjay in the room, leaving the professor to chew the cud of bitter meditation upon the fickle and unstable nature of woman in her best estate.

. . .

Although wise in my generation, it is utterly beyond me to give an opinion upon the relative merits of the foregoing varieties. Like the almanac that chronicles the transcendent virtues of each variety of early potatoes, my trumpet gives forth an uncertain sound, and like the almanac I shake my head and sagely opine all are good and none are best. Yet something of moment can I impart. Not long since I heard a retired flirt of great brilliancy say that she had during a long and successful career adopted each *rôle* in turn, and if she could recall the years of misdirected zeal and energy, she would reduce her former elaborate *modus operandi* to the following simple *régime*: Buy a hogshead of prayer-books and do the pious flirt.

"The Tear in the Cup"

OPIE READ (1852–1939)

Journalist, humorist, novelist, and lecturer Opie Read was born in Nashville. After working as a printer, reporter, and editor at various Southern newspapers, Read founded the *Arkansaw Traveller* in 1882 and built its circulation to 85,000, remarkable for its time. After moving the *Traveller* to Chicago in 1887 and resigning from the paper in 1891, Read spent the next decade and a half producing an extraordinary number of short stories and novels, many featuring the homespun humor of his part of the South and peopled with his stock cast of Southern colonels and drunken printers. His popular novels included *Len Gansett* (1888), *A Tennessee Judge* (1893), *On the Suwanee River: A Romance* (1895), *My Young Masters* (1896), and *The Waters of Caney Fork: A Romance of Tennessee* (1898). His novel *The Jucklins* (1896) sold over a million copies. His autobiography, *I Remember*, was published in 1930. Read stood six feet, three inches and weighed 250 pounds. When he died in 1939, *Time* magazine called him the "greatest literary shortstop of his time." Following is the titular short story from his *The Tear in the Cup and Other Stories* (1894).

I was in a Southern town, standing in front of a saloon—indeed, it would have been hard to stand elsewhere, unless the inside instead of the outside of the "doggery" had been selected—when my attention was attracted by several men who stood near. They appeared to be reminded of a good joke and were looking down the street.

"That was a great joke," said one of the men; and I, being somewhat on the look-out for great jokes, asked:

"What joke was that?"

"Joke on old Jasper—that old fellow coming along yonder. A man that don't know him wouldn't see the point very well, I don't reckon. Old fellow that edits a paper here, but he don't amount to much; he uster be pretty well up, though—married the handsomest girl in this town a long time ago; but I guess she's mighty tired of him."

Old Jasper came up, and the men began to laugh.

"How are your coppers this morning?" the fellow who had been explaining to me asked. "Reckon you'd like to down a bowl this morning, wouldn't you?"

The old man stopped, took off his hat, wiped his brow, and answered:

"You boys are privileged to guy me, I suppose. You thought you'd play a great joke on me, didn't you?"

"Come on in, old man, and have something."

"Wait," he said. "You boys got me drunk and thought it was a great joke. It was surely a very easy joke. Got me to go fishing with you and left me lying on the bank of the creek, drunk. That was a manly—a merciful joke, wasn't it? You slipped back to town and told it about the streets and laughed about it. My little boy heard you and went home and told his mother.

"Oh, what a night I passed! I was so sick that I couldn't raise my head. I heard the creek rippling with a reproachful murmur; a mocking-bird sang all night long—sang to his mate, the object of his tender care—and I, who had neglected every obligation, wished that the ground might swallow me. I dozed troublously toward morning, and when I awoke the sun was shining, and there, beside me, sat my wife, patching a pair of little trousers that she had brought with her. I did not dare to look up. I could not meet those patient eyes—eyes that told of years and years of suffering. I was burning up with thirst.

"'Mary, how long have you been here?' I asked.

"'Nearly all night,' she answered, with a sob.

"'I am nearly dead, Mary. Won't you please bring me a drink of water?'

"She had brought a cup with her. Ah, how well she had anticipated my wants! She went down to the creek, and I raised up and watched her as she dipped the cup into the shining stream. She came back slowly, and just before she handed me the water, she leaned over to hide her eyes, and I saw a tear fall into the cup. I reached forth my hand—I drank the water and the tear, and, throwing down the cup, I clasped my hands and said:

"'Mary, ever since you became my wife I have been drinking your tears. I have been drinking your tears and your anguish, and I swear, in the presence of the Eternal God, that I'll die before I ever do it again.'"

He put on his hat, looked at the leading joker, and said:

"No, I will not drink with you, and I warn you to keep out of my way. Good morning."

Foreword to "The Golden Mean and Other Poems"

MERRILL MOORE (1903–1957)

Merrill Moore was born to a family of writers and librarians in Columbia, Tennessee. His father, John Trotwood Moore, moved the family to Nashville in 1907 where he began editing the *Taylor-Trotwood Magazine*. Merrill's father served as the state librarian of Tennessee; and his mother, Mary Brown Daniel Moore, succeeded her husband in the position after his death in 1929. Upon graduation from Montgomery Bell Academy, Merrill entered Vanderbilt in 1920. While still an undergraduate, Moore joined the Fugitive group in 1922 and contributed often to the group's magazine. Moore was an energetic and prolific amateur poet. He rarely rewrote his sonnets, often a combination of loose free verse in a strict fourteen line form, preferring instead to simply write a new one. Robert Penn Warren often saw Moore jotting down lines of poems in a variety of situations, once observing him write lines of poetry in shorthand at a traffic light. Attesting to his prolificacy is his *M: One Thousand Autobiographical Sonnets* (1938). Moore went on to earn a medical degree from the Vanderbilt Medical School in 1928. After a year of residency in Nashville, Moore practiced psychiatry in Boston for the remainder of his life. Moore's publications include *The Noise that Time Makes* (1929), with a foreword by John Crowe Ransom; four books of poetry from and comment about *The Fugitive*; and *Clinical Sonnets* (1949). Following are three sonnets Moore wrote as a foreword to Ridley Wills's and Allen Tate's *The Golden Mean and Other Poems* (1923).

TO R. W.

Iconoclastic mortuary chapels
Hold incidental glories for the grave
That can be compared alone to the red apples
That are your pallid cheeks before you shave.

TO A. T.

Evenings the dawn breaks mordantly about
The fluted hillsides where we stand and shout
Eternal glories to your burnished name,
Burnished in silver, lucent with fine gold.
And when we wander farther we are told,
Simple our vices are but complex the shame
That handles with the graveness of a tout
The shrivelled tendons of a winter doubt.

PANEGYRIC TO THE ENTITY.
(To R. W. and A. T.)

Surely no good shall come of this ill union!
Shall velvet breed with silk to bring forth vesture?
I shall arise if this be true as pandemonium,
But so shall die my theistic cerebral gesture.

Let these men die of eating too much coffee,
So men may claim that Paul of Tarsus was
The sleeping sickness in its tendency
To show the consciousness of mankind's cause.

from *I'll Take My Stand: The South and the Agrarian Tradition*

TWELVE SOUTHERNERS

> The Agrarian symposium, *I'll Take My Stand*, is one of the more original and compelling documents of the cultural and social attitudes of the writers of the Southern Renascence. The humanistic refutation by the Nashville Agrarians of the mechanistic and materialistic values of industrial urbanism was the underlying foundation of the attitudes not only of their own work, but that of most of their important contemporaries. The contributors to the symposium, which was published in 1930, included poet Donald Davidson, poet John Gould Fletcher, journalist Henry Blue Kline, psychologist Lyle Lanier, novelist Andrew Nelson Lytle, political economist Herman Clarence Nixon, historian Frank Owsley, poet and novelist John Donald Wade, poet and novelist Robert Penn Warren, and drama critic and novelist Stark Young. The "Introduction: A Statement of Principle" was written by Ransom and critiqued and revised according to the other contributors' suggestions. In it many of the group's key concerns about the depersonalization and alienation of the modern industrial society and the value of the Southern tradition and social order are highlighted.

FROM "INTRODUCTION: A STATEMENT OF PRINCIPLES"

The authors contributing to this book are Southerners, well acquainted with one another and of similar tastes, though not necessarily living in the same physical community, and perhaps only at this moment aware of themselves as a single group of men. By conversation and exchange of letters over a number of years it had developed that they entertained many convictions in common, and it was decided to make a volume in which each one should furnish his views upon a chosen topic. This was the general background. But background and consultation as to the various topics were enough; there was to be no further collaboration. And so no single author is responsible for any view outside his own article. It was through the good fortune of some deeper agreement that the book was expected to achieve its unity. All the articles bear in the same sense upon the book's title-subject: all tend to support a Southern way of life against what may be called the American or prevailing way; and all as much as agree that the best terms in which to represent the distinction are contained in the phrase, Agrarian *versus* Industrial.

. . .

The tempo of the industrial life is fast, but that is not the worst of it; it is accelerating. The ideal is not merely some set form of industrialism, with so many stable industries, but industrial progress, or an incessant extension of industrialization. It never proposes a specific goal; it initiates the infinite series. We have not merely capitalized certain industries; we have capitalized the laboratories and inventors, and undertaken to employ all the labor-saving devices that come out of them. But a fresh labor-saving device introduced into an industry does not emancipate the laborers in that industry so much as it evicts them. Applied at the expense of agriculture, for example, the new processes have reduced the part of the population supporting itself upon the soil to a smaller and smaller fraction. Of course no single labor-saving process is fatal; it brings on a period of unemployed labor and unemployed capital, but soon a new industry is devised which will put them both to work again, and a new commodity is thrown upon the market. The laborers were sufficiently embarrassed in the meantime, but, according to the theory, they will eventually be taken care of. It is now the public which is embarrassed; it feels obligated to purchase a commodity for which it had expressed no desire, but it is invited to make its budget equal to the strain. All might yet be well, and stability and comfort might again obtain, but for this: partly because of industrial ambitions and partly because the repressed creative impulse must break out somewhere, there will be a stream of further labor-saving devices in all industries, and the cycle will have to be repeated over and over. The result is an increasing disadjustment and instability.

It is an inevitable consequence of industrial progress that production greatly outruns the rate of natural consumption. To overcome the disparity, the producers, disguised as the pure idealists of progress, must coerce and wheedle the public into being loyal and steady consumers, in order to keep the machines running. So the rise of modern advertising—along with its twin, personal salesmanship—is the most significant development of our industrialism. Advertising means to persuade the consumers to want exactly what the applied sciences are able to furnish them. It consults the happiness of the consumer no more than it consulted the happiness of the laborer. It is the great effort of a false economy of life to approve itself. But its task grows more difficult every day.

It is strange, of course, that a majority of men anywhere could ever as with one mind become enamored of industrialism: a system that has so little regard for individual wants. There is evidently a kind of thinking that rejoices in setting up a social objective which has no relation to the individual. Men are prepared to sacrifice their private dignity and happiness to an abstract social ideal, and without asking whether the social ideal produces the welfare of any individual man whatsoever. But this is absurd. The responsibility of men is for their own welfare and that of their neighbors; not for the hypothetical welfare of some fabulous creature called society.

Opposed to the industrial society is the agrarian, which does not stand in particular need of definition. An agrarian society is hardly one that has no use at all for industries, for professional vocations, for scholars and artists, and for the life of cities. Technically, perhaps, an agrarian society is one in which agriculture is the leading vocation, whether for wealth, for pleasure, or for prestige—a form of labor that is pursued with intelligence and leisure, and that becomes the model to which the other forms approach as well as they may. But an agrarian regime will be secured readily enough where the superfluous industries are not allowed to rise against it. The theory of agrarianism is that the culture of the soil is the best and most sensitive of vocations, and that therefore it should have the economic preference and enlist the maximum number of workers.

These principles do not intend to be very specific in proposing any practical measures. How may the little agrarian community resist the Chamber of Commerce of its county seat, which is always trying to import some foreign industry that cannot be assimilated to the life-pattern of the community? Just what must the Southern leaders do to defend the traditional Southern life? How may the Southern and the Western agrarians unite for effective action? Should the agrarian forces try to capture the Democratic party, which historically is so closely affiliated with the defense of individualism, the small community, the state, the South? Or must the agrarians—even the Southern ones—abandon the Democratic party to its fate and try a new one? What legislation could most profitably be championed by the powerful agrarians in the Senate of the United States? What anti-industrial measures might promise to stop the advances of industrialism, or even undo some of them, with the least harm to those concerned? What policy should be pursued by the educators who have tradition at heart? These and many other questions are of the greatest importance, but they cannot be answered here.

For, in conclusion, this much is clear: If a community, or a section, or a race, or an age, is groaning under industrialism, and well aware that it is an evil dispensation, it must find the way to throw it off. To think that this cannot be done is pusillanimous. And if the whole community, section, race, or age thinks it cannot be done, then it has simply lost its political genius and doomed itself to impotence.

from "The Migration"

ALLEN TATE (1899–1979)

Winchester, Kentucky-born Allen Tate first lived in Nashville at intervals in 1906–1908 while his brothers studied at Vanderbilt and Allen briefly attended the Tarbox School. Due to his family finances and frequent moves, his early education was erratic. He was specially admitted to his brothers' alma mater after he passed a third-year Latin examination. The end of his under-graduate career at Vanderbilt, during which he studied under John Crowe Ransom and Donald Davidson and roomed with Robert Penn Warren and Ridley Wills, was marked by his pseu-donymous publication (as Henry Feathertop) in the first issue of *The Fugitive* in 1922. He went on to help edit the magazine that launched the Southern Renascence and later edited anthologies of the Fugitives' best work, including *Who Owns America?* (1936). In 1924 Tate met and married writer Caroline Gordon. After residency in New York and a stint in Paris, Tate returned to Tennessee. He and Gordon set up housekeeping in an antebellum farmhouse near Clarkesville, about forty-five miles from Nashville, given to them by Tate's brother Ben. The house was named Benfolly in honor of the gift-giver and to rhyme with the title of Gordon's novel *Penhally* (1931). There the Agrarian group was founded from the nucleus of the earlier Fugitives: Ransom, Davidson, Tate, and Warren. Tate's theoretical and practical criticism, devel-oped in numerous publications in the 1930s and 1940s was fundamental to the school of New Criticism. Tate's illustrious teaching career including lecturing at Columbia, Harvard, Oxford, Princeton, and Vanderbilt. He died at his home near Nashville in 1979. The following short story, "The Migration," excerpted below, was published in 1938 in an edition with his only novel, *The Fathers*.

Early in April, 1798, all four families were ready to set out for the Cumberland country. It was a large cavalcade, each family being a group or company in what formed a kind of regiment;

strict order was to be preserved. For our part, we had six large wagons drawn by oxen, eight head of horses and three cows. My father had been chosen to lead. I can see him now, erect on his horse in a tight homespun jacket and buckskin breeches, his heavy black felt hat cocked neatly in military style; he carried in saddle holsters two large horse-pistols, loaded but not primed. Brother John and I rode in the rear.

It was agreed that all should leave their old homes the same day, in the morning, and meet at a deserted Episcopal church that stood in a forest of pines, and there encamp the first night. There were many of these deserted churches in Virginia and the Carolinas at that time.

Early in the April of 1798; according to appointment, all bade adieu to their old and kind friends, the scenes of early life, some of the graves of their fathers, and many objects besides around which memory will linger, and turned their faces towards the setting sun. It was a time of great tenderness of feeling; many, in taking leave, would not venture to speak; a tender embrace, a silent tear, a pressure of the hand in many cases would be all. But few of the aged men and women now living do not remember such parting scenes. In those early times the emigrants that left Carolina and Virginia to settle in Kentucky or Tennessee hardly expected ever again to see those from whom they parted, nor was there any hope in those who were advanced in years. They parted much as do those who part at the grave.

The children and the Negroes kept up their spirits by thinking and talking about Cumberland—the name of the beautiful new world we were to find at the end of our journey. We loved to hear the word pronounced, and on the journey towards it if a stranger asked us to what parts we were on our way, we answered proudly, "To Cumberland." We lost a little heart when we were told there were no herring, chincapins, huckleberries, or pine knots to kindle fires with, in all that beautiful country. The Negroes made a serious matter of the pine knots, and thought the lack of these a great drawback on any country however blest in other respects—even on Cumberland itself.

We took the direction from Halifax down to lower Edgecombe and crossed the Tar River at Tarboro on a long narrow bridge. The water under the bridge was still, black, and deep, and so dangerous looking I was glad we were safely by it. Then I remember Hillboro, a village in Orange County, and Guilford Court House where my father had fought in the battle seventeen years before, but of which there were no traces but a few cannon-scarred trees.

Some days after passing the battlefield I loitered behind the wagons, and upon catching up I found them all stopped on an elevated stretch of road. I asked the cause, and was shown what seemed to be a light blue cloud lying far away to the west on the verge of the horizon. It was to our young eyes a vision of beauty. In its vast outline not a rent or fissure could be seen. I gazed at it with mingled wonder and fear. So this, then, was the famous Blue Ridge about which we had heard so many tales and beyond which lay the land of our homes forever. Could wagons and teams ascend perpendicular walls or scale the clouds?

We went on and soon came near the base of the conical peak of Pilot Mountain in Surry County, around whose high summit some marvelling chap had seen shapes like men with wings flying in the clear blue sky. This was something to study about, and for many years the younger people talked about it, so deeply did it haunt our recollections.

As we approached the Blue Ridge it seemed to rise higher and higher towards the zenith like a gathering storm. At length we pitched our tents at its base. In vain we tried to believe that this was the same calm mountain that we had seen many days before. The vast masses of rock piled up in wild confusion. The sharp summits beaten and cracked by storms, the deep ravines worn in its side by descending torrents, bore no resemblance to the blue cloud of our first view which by distance had indeed been enchanted.

For some reason it was decided not to follow the Carolina road across the mountains to Jonesboro, but to cross farther north into Virginia, at a place, I think, called Ward's Gap. We reconnoitered the pass, and the ascent began. We took out the oxen, which were good for long regular pulls, and put the horses to the wagons because they were more responsive to unusual demands. In rough steep places we often had eight horses to a wagon and a man at each wheel to help turn it. When a few yards had been gained, these men, called scotchers, dropped a large stone behind each wheel to save what ground the great effort had won. In bad places we did well sometimes to make two miles in a day.

When we had crossed the great ridge we were in Virginia, and we made for the town of Abingdon which nestled between high ranges running northeast and southwest—the gateway to the Western States for the early ministries of Christianity bearing the Word to the new country. We had got to this place—the name Abingdon even now haunts my ears—and although my mother had been ill with a deep cold she seemed to be getting better. But only a day out of Abingdon she grew worse, and we began to fear that she could not finish the rest of the journey. I remember her pale and sorrowful face as she lay on her bed in the wagon, and her uncomplaining suffering as we moved over the uneven road. Then she died, and we halted for two days to make her a coffin and take the body to Abingdon, where it found a lonely grave.

I remember Bean's Station in East Tennessee, where the first white child west of the Ridge had been born. We were keeping steadily down the valley of the Holston River towards the Wilderness, an upland waste between Knoxville and Nashville and a hundred miles broad. It lay on the Cumberland Mountain between the Clinch River, which flowed into the Tennessee, and the Caney Fork, a tributary of the Cumberland River. It was necessary for the emigrants to get up food far ahead, as there were no stations on the Wilderness Road, and to forage for the animals lest they should not find much of the wild pea-vine that grew in such profusion in the low country.

After two days in the Wilderness we were descending a long hill, not far from a place now called Crab Orchard, and came at dusk to a pretty stream where we camped that night. It was called Daddy's Creek, a beautiful and romantic spot, and I began to understand why the Indians had fought so bitterly for that country. The hill we had passed over was called Spencer's Hill after an early hunter of that name, who with a man named Holiday had crossed the mountains and gone near where Nashville now stands. We knew his story—how a hunter, not knowing he was in the country, saw his huge footprints in the snow, became frightened, and reported the country full of giants; how Holiday lost his knife, and Spencer broke his in two and gave him half when they parted; and how, after he had finished his cabin, and fenced his little field, when on the way back home to bring his wife and children to the beautiful country he had found for them, he was killed by the Indians on the hill that bears his name.

The Indian troubles in that part of the West were nearly over; yet we heard stories of isolated outrages that made us apprehensive, especially in the Wilderness, whose ownership had been long disputed between Indian and white. At Daddy's Creek camp, at twilight, a lone Indian came to sell us fresh-killed venison, and said he was a "good Injun." Uncle William Maxey was very suspicious of him but at last the other men decided that if the Indian would stay with us all night, there would be no danger, since he could not get back to his companions and plot a massacre. The Indian stayed, and made no effort to escape after we were asleep, and left us next morning very pleased. We heard no more of Indians on the whole journey.

When we had crossed the Wilderness and were within thirty miles of Nashville, a party of three elegantly dressed gentlemen overtook us, and seeing so large a cavalcade of settlers, one of them began conversing with my father and urging him to settle south of Nashville in what he called "the Dutch River Country." My father heard him out very politely but remained unconvinced. After the gentlemen had gone he said that they were land speculators who, by offering advantageous trades to the settlers, soon took away all they had.

We were now in what was then called West Tennessee, but soon to be known as Middle Tennessee, after the western region nearer the Mississippi had been settled. And we were rapidly approaching Nashville, which we reached early in June after more than two months on the road. Doubtless I was expecting to see a town like those on the seaboard, settled and fixed-looking, but as we came to the south bank of the Cumberland, and I looked across that deep, slow-moving stream, I saw some twenty or thirty houses, mostly log houses but a few of them clapboarded and perhaps one or two of brick, straggling away from the waterfront as if they had been set up at random in a great hurry and only for a few days. We were ferried across the river, at a good price for each of the ten or a dozen trips and I saw how it was that the ferrymen in the West were the first men to get rich: This one was slow and unaccommodating, independent as a hog on ice. We stayed in Nashville that night and the next while my father had his patent papers examined by the land office and a surveyor appointed to accompany him to his land, which he was told lay to the northeast about thirty miles—another journey, before we could say we were there, of two days.

Hundreds of people came through the town every week. The craze for "Kentucky land" having to some extent given way to a better view of the western country, Tennessee was filling up fast, largely with families from North Carolina who brought with them very few slaves. I remember my father saying then, and I knew it was true even later, that there were four times as many Negroes in Kentucky as in Tennessee. He seemed to like this feature of Tennessee, and although we were still in the shadow of my mother's death, which bore its weight especially upon my father, we felt increasingly excited as we hourly reduced the miles to the new plantation. As we went slowly away from Nashville I did not know that I should see the town again only after ten years. I remember it seemed to my boyish perception that the tavern-keepers and the few traders in sugar and whiskey were the only permanent settlers, all the rest being Virginia lawyers with a great air of gentility, and land sharks with as great an air of benevolence.

About sundown of the second day out of town the surveyor called us to a halt, and said the tract of land lay along Station Camp Creek that we could see away in a rolling valley at a distance of about a mile. It was a lovely prospect, and yet it looked like other scenes that I knew, like other land that might be owned by other people. I felt a little dazed, and I could not think. The young children were suddenly quiet. My sister Emily's oldest, just four, asked: "Mammy, is this Cumber-land?" And I said to myself, This is Cumberland. We went on down the hill and camped by the creek, a deep stream broken at intervals by riffles and banked on both sides by tall sycamores and willows, with thick canebrakes here and there running off into the higher ground.

It was sobering to think that here we were, for better or for worse, in Cumberland, where now at last we should live forever. For some reason we broke our habit of cooking supper by families, and of pitching our tents by families, and all ate together by a big fire. The children threw cane stalks into the blaze, and the cane joints being hollow, full of air but air-tight, they crackled and sometimes blew up with a report loud as a pistol. It is mighty strange how people together will be moved by something trivial. It was the exploding cane that loosed our tongues, and the laughter of the children, and I knew before we had fairly seen it that we were reconciled to the land.

Somebody started singing, and nigger Willie got out his fiddle. Sister Emily and little Phoebe Wilkerson, who was about twelve years old, sang very prettily all the old songs. Emily had learned the old ballads from our mother and Willie scraped off the jigs and reels in a way to set everybody's feet going. It was indeed a special occasion, for old Henry Wilkerson, a religious man, made no objection. I remember one of the old favorites:

> O wha will shoe my bonny foot
> And wha will glove my hand?
> And wha will bind my middle jimp
> Wi' a lang, lang linen band?

When Phoebe had sung a little, Emily took it up, and then it would go the round till even the old men got off their dignity and began singing, and the old women too, for I remember old Aunt Phoebe Wilkerson, Henry Wilkerson's mother and the grandmother of my brother-in-law, John—how she would take her cob pipe out of her mouth and sing in a high cracked voice:

> O he's gane up yon high high hill,
> I wat he gaed wi' sorrow—
> And in a den spied nine armed men,
> In the dowie houmns of Yarrow.

It was too late to make much of a crop that summer, but we burnt off two big canebrakes and about seventy acres of wild grass to put corn in, to carry us over the next winter. This crop was raised in common by us all, and it was planted while we were still in our tents. My father chose the tract of land lying along the creek, as he was entitled to do by agreement; the Maxey tract touched the creek at one point; but the Wilkersons and the Peirces had to take high ground where they dug wells before they built cabins. Our Negroes and the two Maxey Negroes were lent them for the purpose, and towards the end of the summer every family in this way, by common effort, had ready for the winter a one-room hewn-log crib in which seven or eight people had to sleep in great congestion. Our own family lived this way until the next autumn, when we added another crib in the old style, with a dog-run between. In the next two or three years we had added upper rooms and an ell, and built two Negro cabins.

I was now, in about the year 1800, a tall strong lad of twenty-one, and because my father was still a vigorous man of fifty-eight—six-foot-two in his bare feet, with coal-black hair, large cold gray eyes, and an iron jaw—I felt that I would be a mere boy for years to come, and I grew restless, desiring to strike out in some way for myself. My brother John at this time decided to go to Kentucky, signing away his claim to our father's estate in consideration of one of the new Negro men, bought just before we left Edgecombe, and the sum of five hundred dollars to be paid to him gradually as the farm could make it. My father had married again, his wife being the widow Thomas, who had four children, and this I believe prompted brother John to leave more than anything else; for our stepmother in some roundabout way was kin to the Wilkersons and brother John conceived the notion that that family in time would get all our land by marriage and undue influence. I was sorry to see John go; I had for him a great affection, I had known only slightly my eldest brother Reuben and he had left us early to remain in Virginia. John was killed at the battle of New Orleans in the War of 1812.

Time passed and to make it profitable I got up a school which I taught for eight years, and had at various times as many as thirty scholars. At the outset of this undertaking the great religious revival of 1800 came on, and gave a more religious hue to education. I myself was affected by it, and a wonderful effect it had towards improving our lives. The West was a godless country; but the Lord stepped in when we needed Him and lifted us up. We had always had religious training; my father believed that a man's duty lay in two things—fear of God and the honorable improvement of man's earthly state, and twice a day, at daybreak and at bedtime, the family and the Negroes were assembled for prayer.

It was in the spring of 1801 that the great camp meeting was held in Logan County, Kentucky, about forty miles from our farm. We went to it, all of us, all our family but the Peirces, who were Calvinists, along with more than fifteen thousand other people. It was like a great army, covering hundreds of acres. This was the first time I had seen the jerks, and though I derived great spiritual benefit from the mighty sermons of many godly preachers, I looked upon this jerking exercise with astonishment. Many fell down under the burden of sin, as men slain in battle, and lay for hours in a nearly breathless and motionless state, sometimes for a moment reviving with symptoms of life, giving deep groans or piercing shrieks; and thus did they obtain deliverance from evil. Two or three of my particular acquaintance were struck down, and I patiently sat by one whom I knew to be a careless sinner, critically observing the contortions as they seized him. At one moment being still as death, he would begin to jerk in one arm, gradually and at regular intervals, till the motion spread over his entire body which heaved violently in all directions as if he were trying to tear himself apart. A grove of saplings had been cut down breast-high, and at each post a zealous Christian took his station, so that when the time came he would have something to jerk by. At these posts pretty girls and sober matrons waited, and it was wonderful to see my sister Emily Maxey jerk and kick so powerfully that the earth under her feet looked like a hitching place for horses in fly time.

Our lives were full; our large family connection numbered some forty people, not counting the Peirces, who were not yet intermarried with us; and we were enjoying a prosperity that we had never known. Our crops were enormous—eighty to ninety bushels of corn to the acre, against sixty, the best we had ever done in Edgecombe; we raised wheat and rye in large quantities. The Maxeys set up a still-house over a big cold spring on their land, and made a fine whisky, later known as Bourbon, out of a corn, barley, and rye mash. We fed most of our corn to the hogs, of which we had large droves. Every year the hog-drovers came through to take them to the East or to the new cotton country in the South; they sewed up the eyes of the hogs to keep them from running off into the fenceless country, and drove them for hundreds of miles in that way. But we raised no tobacco, and to that my father ascribed his prosperous turn in affairs.

We had come to the year 1806, and for some time I had been keeping company with Miss Phoebe Wilkerson, the sister of John who had married my sister Josephine, and so, on June twentieth of that year we were married, and I took her to live in our family. She was the only wife I could have found to please my stepmother, who was hard to please, for Phoebe was her distant cousin. Our first child, a son whom we named John Robert, John for my brother and Robert for a dead brother of Phoebe's, was born in Nashville on June 10, 1808, whilst we were in town for a few weeks on business.

In the ten years that had gone by since I had been there, the town had changed wonderfully. There were not more than six thousand people, but the constant bustle, the coming and going, the sudden appearance and disappearance of strangers who had tarried there a few days, gave the town an air of being a city. The new brick buildings along the waterfront, which was piled high with barrels of salt pork and lard, of whiskey and corn, and smaller quantities of tobacco, tended to give the scene a stability that impressed me greatly. We had friends there, and I call to mind one family whom we had known in Carolina, a family that in origin was like us in every respect, who now had a coach and four horses, and lived just out of town in a large brick plantation house amid a swarm of Negroes. The ladies came to town in flowered silk, the men of the family in tall hats and lace shirts; an outrider preceded the coach upon which was engraved a coat of arms. It was plain that the rich in the West had a desire to look richer than rich people in the East, for in a new country positions had to be maintained by appearance, at least for a time. It was commonly said that a prominent young lawyer of the town—Andrew Jackson, who was to be heard from later— had crossed the mountains in broadcloth, on horseback, with a Negro at his heels, but without a penny in his purse; and it turned out to be good business. He was already a rich man. I came to have a great reverence for him, but my father looked at him askance as a man who did one thing and talked another, and who was in all respects above his raising.

Now that the West had been conquered by the Scotch-Irish, and the Indians north of Alabama driven out or subdued, the Tidewater Virginians were coming in in great numbers. They had lived in Virginia more than a hundred years before they found the curiosity to climb to the top of the Blue Ridge, and to look westward; but looking was all that they did. They waited for men of my own blood to plunge into the wildernesses: Boone, the Lewises, and the Seviers, though it is true that John

Sevier, while not a Tidewater baron, was French, and Isaac Shelby was of English origin. Now the younger sons or the broken-down heads of the Tidewater families got into their coaches, and their ladies constantly in silk dresses and French shoes, drove politely into the new country to ruin that land also with tobacco.

At about this time, when the War of 1812 was coming on, Uncle William Maxey died, and the two boys, who had married my sisters, sold off their land, paying my father what was due him, and set out for the new cotton country in Alabama Territory. Our first ten years in Tennessee had been quiet; now it was known that the whole strip of country along the Kentucky border was great tobacco land; and another wave of settlers, not pioneers seeking new homes, but gentry bent on perpetuating their wealth, flooded the country. Men became restless again. William Maxey said the country was "filling up with tobacco-makers and Baptists"—the latter being, with some notable exceptions, however, the poor whites who follow blindly in the wake of any shift of population. I said good-bye to my dear sisters Emily and Drusilla, and I never saw them again. In my time and generation we were always saying good-bye, and the times we had together were not long enough to permit us to forget the sadness of family divisions and their farewells.

By the year 1816 my father was seventy-four, and I took over the farm, and managed it, and did very well. I now had six children, for my faithful consort had borne me nearly a child a year since we were wed. But I was convinced that the property would be left to my stepmother; what brother John had foretold was coming true. At this time the Peirces entered our family connection. My niece, Sally Wilkerson, who had been born a few weeks after our arrival in Tennessee in 1798—daughter of John Wilkerson and my sister Josephine—was, in 1818, twenty years old; old Jarvis Peirce, twice a widower in his forty-eighth year, and still a dour old Puritan for all his long absence from New England, succeeded in winning this young girl. The ground, not only the earth but the rock-bottom of our lives, was shifting a lit-

tle every day. The Peirces and the Wilkersons would never buy a
Negro, and now in 1819 they had heard that the Illinois Territory
had come in as a Free State, after a severe struggle of the pro-slav-
ery majority there to set aside the Ordinance of 1787 by which
Virginia, then the proprietor of all the Northwest Territory, had
abolished slavery in the new country. Slavery had been kept out
by one vote, and old Jarvis Peirce regretted that he had not been
there to cast it. These two families, in the summer of 1819 set out
for Illinois, having sold their quarter-sections at a good profit to
the tobacco planters, paying my father the original price of
twenty-five cents an acre, and keeping the difference.

Our community was broken up. My father was getting old.
About sundown of August 23, 1820, he took a fit of coughing,
followed by hard breathing. We got in the doctor, who bled him,
and the Methodist exhorter, Mr. Douglass, who prayed over him
continuously for eight hours, until at last he died, being then in
his seventy-eighth year and very feeble. I will always remember
the last thing he did and his last words. He called in Boy Jim, the
first Negro he owned, and his wife Mariah, and said, "By my
written will you are now free. Jim, take this old coat, and go over
to Nashville, and take the fifty dollars I have left you, get you an
old plug and a hack, and the fine coat with brass buttons will get
all the tobacco-makers riding behind you." The old coat was the
uniform he had worn as a captain in the Revolution. He asked
for my son, John Robert: "Chew tobacco if you will but never
grow it." In a little while he died. His thousand-acre farm went
to his wife, and on his tombstone, by the Methodist meeting-
house down on the creek, we carved by his express desire:

> Farewell my wife and children all
> I am gone away beyond recall
> Ask not for me it is in vain
> You call me to your side again.

"On a Replica of the Parthenon"

DONALD DAVIDSON (1893–1968)

Campbellsville, Tennessee-born educator and writer Donald Davidson entered Vanderbilt University in 1909, but withdrew after only one year due to financial troubles. After a series of teaching jobs at rural Tennessee schools, he returned to college in 1914 and studied there with Edwin Mims, John Crowe Ransom, and Walter Clyde Curry. Davidson quickly formed friendships with William Yandell Elliott and Stanley Johnson who introduced Davidson to a group of people who met at the apartment of the intellectual and Jewish mystic Sidney Mttron Hirsch. While a student, Davidson taught at the Wallace University School. He entered officer's candidate school in 1917 and earned his degree from Vanderbilt in absentia. He saw combat in France during the world war before returning to Nashville in 1919. By then the discussion group he had earlier left consisted of Hirsch, Ransom, Curry, William Frierson, and others and concerned itself with literary matters. Donaldson went on to co-found and edit the *Fugitive* magazine. In 1920, Davidson began working at the *Tennessean* and as an instructor at Vanderbilt while he started his master's degree, which he went on to earn in 1922. In 1924 Davidson became an assistant professor at Vanderbilt and, for the next six years, a book editor at the *Nashville Tennessean*. His first volume of poetry, *An Outland Piper*, was published in 1925. He contributed an essay to *I'll Take My Stand* (1930) and more of his essays were collected in *The Attack on Leviathan* (1938) and *Still Rebels, Still Yankees* (1957). The poem following appeared first in his *Lee in the Mountains and Other Poems* (1938). Poet Karl Shapiro, like Davidson, found a replica of the Parthenon out of place in a modern city. In his poem, "The Parthenon," Shapiro likens the replica to a "plane crash reconstructed."

Why do they come? What do they seek
Who build but never read their Greek?
The classic stillness of a pool
Beleaguered in its certitude
By aimless motors that can make
Only incertainty more sure;
And where the willows crowd the pure
Expanse of clouds and blue that stood
Around the gables Athens wrought,
Shop-girls embrace a plaster thought,
And eye Poseidon's loins ungirt,
And never heed the brandished spear
Or feel the bright-eyed maiden's rage
Whose gaze the sparrows violate;
But the sky drips its spectral dirt,
And gods, like men, to soot revert.
Gone is the mild, the serene air.
The golden years are come too late.
Pursue not wisdom or virtue here,
But what blind motion, what dim last
Regret of men who slew their past
Raised up this bribe against their fate.

from *The Big Sea*

LANGSTON HUGHES (1902–1967)

Joplin, Missouri-born Langston Hughes was raised by his grandmother in Kansas after his parents separated. His first major publication came in 1920 in the NAACP publication *Crisis* a year before he entered Columbia University. That poem, "The Negro Speaks of Rivers" has become one of the prolific poet's best known. After a short residency in Europe, Hughes returned to his university studies and to a volume of poetry, *The Weary Blues*, which launched his successful career as a poet upon its publication in 1926. Hughes went on to become one of the most influential members of the Harlem Renaissance. His best-known prose fiction is the 1950 *Simple Speaks His Mind*, featuring the shrewdly plainspoken character Jesse B. Simple. In 1931, Hughes and a friend set out from their home in Cleveland, Ohio, in a borrowed car to tour the American South. On the road to Florida, the travelers read newspaper accounts of the so-called "Scottsboro case," a highly volatile court case in which nine black youths were charged with the rape of two white women in Alabama. Hughes would write extensively of the case in essays and poems and even visited the accused in their Montgomery prison. He was particularly distressed by the relative silence on the issue he found in the halls of black colleges. The following excerpt from Hughes's 1940 autobiography relates his experience during an earlier visit to the South.

In the spring of 1927, I was invited to read my poems during commencement week at Fisk University in Nashville, Tennessee, and the week following at a Y.W.C.A. conference in Texas. I had never been in the South before, nor had I ever been offered such attractive fees for the reading of my poems, so I accepted both invitations, leaving Lincoln immediately after examinations.

I had heard of Fisk largely through the famous Fisk Jubilee Singers, and I was anxious to see that distinguished old institution of Negro learning in the Southland. My visit there was a delightful one. For the first time I stood before a large audience of my own people, reading my poems, and I was thrilled, because they seemed to like those poems—poems in which I had tried to capture some of the dreams and heartaches that all Negroes know.

While I was at Fisk, the headlines in the papers grew bigger and bigger about the Mississippi rising in flood. And then the river broke its banks. The Y.W.C.A. officials wired me that it was impossible to hold their conference in Texas, because too many of the delegates were from the flooded regions and could not come. With the fee from my Fisk engagement and the settlement the Y.W.C.A. made for their cancelled agreement, I decided to spend the summer traveling in the South. First I went to Memphis to see Beale Street.

On the train between Nashville and Memphis, a party of Fisk students with whom I was traveling played an amusing joke on me. They knew it was difficult for Negroes from the North to get used to the Jim Crow customs of the South, or to know exactly what one might or might not do. I learned, for instance, that in Nashville there were certain parks Negroes could not enter or cross. If a park lay between you and your destination, you could not walk through the park as a white person might do. Being colored, you had to go *around* the park. I knew, of course, that Negroes were compelled to use Jim Crow waiting rooms at the railroad stations, and ride in the Jim Crow car up next to the engine. And I rather expected to see a lynching every day; but about such subtleties as parks, I was ignorant.

However, the South is not entirely as bad as it is painted, although I did not know that my first week there. So on the way to Memphis, I sat in the dusty Jim Crow car and discussed my thoughts and apprehensions with the students. The sun was very bright and the cinders from the engine flew in the windows, so I put on a pair of smoked glasses that I carried to protect my eyes.

Shortly the train stopped at a small station to water the engine, and we had time to get out and stretch our limbs, and buy ice cream cones from a platform vendor. While I was standing on the platform, some of the Fisk students came cautiously up to me and whispered in my ear: "Mr. Hughes, don't you know the white folks down South don't allow Negroes to wear smoked glasses?" Quickly I snatched my glasses off and looked around to see if any white folks had noticed me wearing them!

The students laughed loudly, then I knew it was only a joke. But I had heard *true* stories of cities where colored people were permitted to drive only second-hand cars; and other cities where they had to step off the sidewalk when a white man passed; and towns with signs up:

> NIGGER DON'T LET THE SUN
> GO DOWN ON YOU HERE

so I thought maybe it might be possible that there was also a feeling against colored people wearing dark glasses to protect their eyes from the sun. But it was only a joke, like that famous Mississippi sign:

> DARKIE, READ AND RUN!
> IF YOU CAN'T READ, RUN ANYHOW!

which was probably invented in vaudeville.

I was disappointed in Beale Street, and it was not until several years later when I visited it in company with W. C. Handy that the feeling was somewhat removed. Portions of Fifth or Lenox Avenues in New York's Harlem were, I thought, equally tough, equally colorful, and quite as colored as the famous Memphis thoroughfare. So I went on down to Vicksburg, Mississippi.

By now, the waters of the river were raging, and it was possible to go to Vicksburg only by a roundabout way. The main thing I remember about the town is a river front cafe with marvelously misspelled signs on the wall:

from *At Heaven's Gate*

ROBERT PENN WARREN (1905–1989)

Guthrie, Kentucky-born Robert Penn Warren entered Vanderbilt University to study electrical engineering but soon changed his mind after an English class with John Crowe Ransom. Inspired by roommates Allen Tate and Donald Davidson, Warren joined the Fugitive group, named after the literary magazine of the 1920s. Warren taught at Vanderbilt from 1931–1934. As a founder and editor of *The Southern Review* from 1935–1942, Warren published the early work of Katherine Ann Porter and Eudora Welty. Warren achieved renown in both prose and poetry, winning Pulitzer Prizes for his novel *All the King's Men* (1947) and for his collection of poems *Promises* (1958). He married poet Eleanor Clark in 1952. Warren often wrote of Nashville during his nearly sixty years of writing which included fourteen volumes of poetry, a dozen books of nonfiction, eleven books of short and long fiction, and several textbooks and essay collections. *Understanding Poetry* (1938) and *Understanding Fiction* (1943), written with Cleanth Brooks, were classroom standards for two generations. In 1970 Warren was awarded the National Medal for Literature from the National Book Committee and in 1986 was designated the first official Poet Laureate of the United States. Warren's second published novel, *At Heaven's Gate* (1943), was suggested by the 1930s Nashville of financial wunderkinds Rogers Caldwell and Luke Lea. By the time they were barely thirty, both had built massive fortunes in banking, newspapers, insurance, and investment. When the two millionaires moved to ally their political and media power, the corrupt natures of their individual empires were revealed. Their collective and individual careers ended in indictment, humiliation, and financial ruin. In this scene, self-made Gerald Calhoun is released from jail where he, like his employer, the financier Bogan Murdock, is charged with financial fraud after the Murdock empire crumbles.

On the evening when Gerald Calhoun was released on bail, his father reached the jail some forty-five minutes after Duckfoot Blake had left to get Kahn. Jerry, sitting on the cot as he had sat before, hunching forward, his elbows on his knees, his wrists drooping forward, did not even look up when he first heard the sound of approaching feet. Even when the sound ceased, and he knew that someone stood before the cell, he did not look up until he heard the chink of metal as the key was applied to the lock. There, beside the man with the key, was his father, wearing jean pants and an old brown wool coat, and a white shirt, crudely starched but very clean, a button missing at the collar but the collar held almost together by the awkward knot of the black tie, which hung below the slight gap of the collar. Mr. Calhoun, holding his black hat in his hand, stood there, waiting for the manipulation of the lock, looking in through the bars, not saying a word. His breath came with a spasmodic heaviness.

Jerry, looking at him, felt, for the moment, nothing, nothing at all. He stared at him, noting with dispassionate clarity every detail of appearance; but the big old man, with the knotted hands clutching the black hat before him, might have been a stranger getting ready to say, "Mister—mister, I was just wondering if you'd—if you might be wanting to buy—" Or getting ready to say, "Mister, I musta got off the road—I was wondering if—"

The door swung open and Mr. Calhoun stepped into the cell, and stood there, as before, regarding his son but not able, yet, to find the words.

Then, after the door had clicked to behind him, he took one step forward, stopped, and with his face gathering itself for the effort, said: "Son." And then, again, said it: "Son."

Until that moment, the moment when the big old man said, "Son," and again, "Son," Jerry Calhoun had not seen his own situation as related to anything in the world except himself. His confusion, his apathy, his grief, his bitterness, and finally, his single flash of triumphant and releasing ferocity at the thought of Bogan Murdock—Bogan Murdock jailed, Bogan Murdock seized and flung into a cell, Bogan Murdock ruined-had been, simply, his own being, almost absolute in themselves, lacking relationship even to the events and persons of the tangible world which had caused his own situation. For those events and persons, from the time when he had opened a newspaper and seen the photograph of Sue Murdock above the savagely laconic statement, Slain Girl, had been as shadowy as frosted breath on the air. There had only been the flow of feeling which was himself.

But now, with his father's voice, his father was real, and demanding, demanding to break in upon that privacy of pain, which was himself, in which, now, he was almost jealously, preciously, at home. He looked at his father's face above the white shirt, the buttonless collar with the wisp of thread, the twisted tie. Looking at that wisp of thread, he saw with a horrible precision his father leaning over the open drawer, fumbling for the white shirt, dropping it in his haste, fumbling with the buttons, tearing off the button, his big knotted swollen hands shaking and his breath coming hard. And that scene was there before his eyes clearer than reality, and it was the last indignity, the last assault upon him, the last betrayal. No—it was more—it—

"I came as soon as I could, son," he was saying. "I saw the paper, and soon as I could, soon as I could get hitched up."

—it was more, it was the cause, the very cause of everything, of everything that had happened to him, of Sue Murdock dead, of himself in jail, of everything. And with that blaze of conviction and accusation in him, he stared at the man there before him, who was saying: "Why, son, why didn't you let me know—you ought to let me know, son, you ought—"

With a vindictive delight, he cut in, his voice rising in triumph: "You couldn't have done a thing—not a thing. And you can't do anything now!"

"Maybe not, maybe not, son—maybe I couldn't done a thing, but I could come. And they'd let me in—they let me in now and it's late and against the rules, but I told them how I'd come a long piece. and—"

"Oh, God damn it, God damn it" Jerry burst out, and watched the surprise come on the big, sagging, clay-colored face, as though it had been slapped, and then saw the surprise not there, the face as it had been, looking down at him, saying: "Son."

Mr. Calhoun took a step forward toward the cot.

Oh, God, if he put his hands on me, if he touches me, Jerry thought, and his muscles went tense as though to brace himself, for that was the one thing, the last thing, which he could not bear.

But Mr. Calhoun did not touch him. He took that single step toward the cot, then stopped, and merely looked at his son, not saying a word.

Then Duckfoot Blake was in the corridor, waiting for the man to unlock, and saying: "Well, Jerry, let's get going. It's all O.K." Then, inside, to Mr. Calhoun: "I'm mighty glad to know you. Jerry's been a buddy of mine for a long time. Yeah, I'm glad you turned up to help me take a hand with that loafer over there. Gawd, look at him, ain't he a sight?" And he wagged a long brittle forefinger toward the cot, where Jerry sat.

Duckfoot drove them out to the Calhoun place, in his car. He had proposed that they spend the night at his house, but Mr. Calhoun had said, "I'm much obliged, Mr. Blake, and I know Jerry's obliged, but I reckon we ought to be getting on home. You know how 'tis on a farm, you got to be getting home."

Home, Jerry had echoed in his mind, *home*, and had seen Lew's face and Aunt Ursula's face and his father's, and had felt the wild impulse to run across the square—for they were standing in front of the jail then—and run down the street under the murky lights, and keep on running, out where it was dark, where there wouldn't be anybody, where they would leave him alone, where everybody, everybody, would leave him alone.

So, over Mr. Calhoun's protest, they went in Duckfoot's car. Mr. Calhoun had said that he couldn't leave his horse and buggy standing out in the street all night. He said it used to be a man could put his horse in a livery stable, but he didn't know as there was one for a man now. But Duckfoot went to the telephone in the all-night restaurant on the square, and got hold of a Negro he knew to get the horse and bring him on out in the morning.

They didn't even have to wait for the Negro to come to the square, for the man at the restaurant said he'd attend to it. Duckfoot knew the man at the restaurant, too. Duckfoot knew everybody.

Jerry sat in the back seat of Duckfoot's old car, and his father in front. They rattled across the square, over the tangle of street-car tracks, out through the wholesale district, out through the suburbs where the few street lights showed the huddled, paint-less houses. There were no lights in the houses. Then they were in the country. On both sides, the fields, stripped, empty, dark, heaved toward the sky. The sky was starless, streaked with dark clouds. The woods beyond the fields were darker than the sky.

Duckfoot was talking to Mr. Calhoun. He was telling him some preposterous, endless tale of the time when he had been an auctioneer at a jewelry joint. He would release the wheel and gesture, and the car would swerve, then he would seize the wheel in the nick of time, and his high, nasal voice would go on and on. But Jerry did not follow the words. His body swayed and lurched with the motion of the car.

They turned off the highway at last, up the lane to the Calhoun place. He observed with some surprise that the house was white now, solid and serene among the leafless trees, under the dark sky. There was a new fence, a white fence. As the car drew up to the gate, he saw that the dead gum by the gate had been cut out. Even the stump had been dug out and the hole sod-ded over, he could make out even in that light. With a sardonic self-irony, he realized that everything was as he had planned to make it—oh, he had been going to paint the house white some day, oh, he had been going to put up a fence, oh, he had been going to take out that gum, he had been going to do all that when he got a little extra change. Oh, he had been going to fix up the Old Calhoun Place, and drive out Saturday afternoons and look at his herd of pure-bred Herefords—sure, he was going to have them, sure—and see how his setters were doing and maybe go down across the pasture beyond the wood lot, with a gun across his arm and a dog skirting the sage and some friend from town beside him, and knock down a couple of quail, and go back up to the house and sit in front of the fire with a glass in his hand and talk to that anonymous man from town whom he had brought out to the Old Calhoun Place. And where would Lew and Aunt Ursula have been? Gone—dead, perhaps— not in the picture. He had never said to himself, *After they are dead*. They simply were not in the picture. There was no place in the picture for them. Had there been a place in the picture for his father? The question flashed through his mind with its obscene candor. But he refused the question—he hadn't asked the question, nobody had asked the question, it was no question and nobody had a right to ask it. And the spasm of rejection in his mind transmitted itself to his limbs, so that he twitched as at the start of a rigor.

There was his father standing in the road now. So he got out and followed his father and Duckfoot through the white gate and up the brick walk to the glimmeringly white mass of the house beyond the dark trees.

Old Mr. Calhoun fumbled with his keys, found the right one, finally opened the door. "Just a minute," he said, "just a minute and I'll get some light."

The room was almost black dark. Jerry could see a few red chinks on the hearth, where Lew had banked the fire, red coals showing where the ashes had dropped off the chunks of wood. Mr. Calhoun struck a match, peered about with the tiny flame held up, and located the lamp. "We just never got the electricity turned back on since we got back," he said, in a voice of careful explanation, not apology. "And coal oil not costing nothing to speak of."

As the wick caught, the rays of the lamp flickered on the pale walls and on the high white ceiling; then steadied. Jerry stood by the door, staring at the clean room, which was so big and bare, dwarfing and devouring the old pieces of furniture, stripping them of their old meanings and functions, leaving them clearly and pitifully what they were, junk. His gaze traveled slowly around the room, which was familiar and yet so treacherously unfamiliar now, as in a dream.

"Shut the door, Jerry," his father was saying, "and I'll stir up the fire. And you, Mr. Blake, you just have a chair, and I'll get some coffee on. It's a ways for you to be going back in and the air's got some nip."

"I'm afraid it's no sale, Mr. Calhoun," Duckfoot said. "I'd sure like to have a cup and jaw a little, but it's late. How about fixing me a quart when I come out tomorrow or next day? That is—" he continued, and turned to Jerry, "if you want me to stop by your apartment and bring you anything out here?"

"You might get me some clothes," Jerry said.

"Sure," Duckfoot said, "I'll get your duds. I'll bring you your crate, too, if you'll give me the keys. Then you can drive me as far as the car line when I go back to town."

Jerry took the key pad from his pocket and detached his car keys and held them in his hand.

"You figure on staying out to supper, Mr. Blake," his father was saying, "when you come out with Jerry's stuff. We'd be proud to have you."

"Sure thing," Duckfoot said, and reached over and lifted the keys from Jerry's hand as though he were taking them off a shelf, "sure thing, Mr. Calhoun, and I'll plan on having an appetite. But now I got to shove."

Mr. Calhoun crossed the space toward Duckfoot, stood ponderously in front of him, seemed about to speak, then spoke. "Mr. Blake," he said, "Mr. Blake—you don't know how me and Jerry feel—what you did—" And he thrust out his hand.

"Aw, for Christ's sake." Duckfoot said, almost fretfully. Then he seized the hand and shook it, dropped it suddenly, and said: "I got to shove."

"I'll see you, pal," he called back to Jerry, as he stepped out of the door.

Mr. Calhoun had got to the door too late to open it for the guest. Now he held it ajar and looked out. After a moment Jerry heard the sound of the motor, then the grinding of gears. Mr. Calhoun closed the door. He crossed to the hearth, and spread his hands over the embers, which gave forth a little flame now. He seemed to be studying the flame.

Jerry still stood near the door. He stood there like a stranger who, neglected, waits to be asked his errand, and looked at the humped-over figure above the embers and the small flame. That figure would straighten up in a minute, it would straighten up and turn its face toward him. He knew that. He became aware of the ticking of a clock. He listened to the clock, and knew that in a minute that big, sagging, creased old face would turn toward him, not in accusation, not in rancor, not even in despair, but simply in recognition and acceptance, which would be most horrible of all. For against that there could be no defense.

Mr Calhoun turned from the fire.

"I reckon it's about time we went to bed, son," he said.

Jerry did not answer.

"You can sleep in your room, son," the man said. "The bed's not made up, but there's sheets and stuff up there."

"I'll make it up." Jerry said, and started to move across the room.

"Naw," his father objected, "naw, I'll help you," and followed him into the hall, and up the stairs, carrying the lamp, which threw Jerry's shadow enormously up the stairs ahead of him.

Jerry laid his hand on the iron latch, and in the light the room leaped from the chaos of darkness to its proper proportions, the pale, flowered walls, strange to him, the white ceiling here as below, the wide bare floor. The panes of the windows gleamed blackly, with the faintest iridescence, like a film of oil on black water, like a film laid over the coiling immeasurable depth of darkness outside.

The single flame of the lamp was reflected winkingly in the black glass.

Mr. Calhoun set the lamp down on the mantel shelf, over the cold, black square of the fireplace. Then he went to the walnut wardrobe, which seemed to lean perilously out from the flow-ered wall. The door of the wardrobe stuck; then under Mr. Calhoun's uncertain fingers, gave raspingly. He took out two folded sheets, and a blanket and a patchwork quilt, on which the colors had faded and run.

He stood on one side of the bed and Jerry on the other, and they spread the first sheet over the uneven mattress. Then the other sheet, then the blanket and quilt.

Mr. Calhoun went back to the wardrobe, and for some moments, leaning over, fumbled in the interior gloom. Then he straightened up, shaking his head. "A pillow slip," he said, "It looks like I don't find any pillow slip." He stood there seemingly lost in indecision, marveling and sad, holding in his hand a piece of cloth which was not a pillow slip. "It looks like there'd be a pillow slip," he said. He took a step toward the door. "Maybe," he said, "maybe I could—"

"Let it go," Jerry ordered, and seized a pillow from the chair where the two were piled, and thrust it under the lower sheet. Then he straightened up, and stood by the bed, which was ready.

Mr. Calhoun looked at the bed, then at Jerry, and moved a couple of steps toward the door. "I reckon I better let you get on to bed," he said, but, for the moment, he did not move, looking at his son, who stood by the bed, on the side toward the door, and did not answer. Mr. Calhoun seemed about to approach him; then, as though answering the unphrased impulse in himself, said: "Naw, naw—you better get on to bed, son."

He turned to the door, reached it, and laid his hand on the latch. He opened the door, and about to go out, hesitated on the threshold, again looking at his son's face. "Don't you take on and fret, son. Mr. Blake—" he paused, then continued, "Mr. Blake said he figured it would be all right. It's gonna be all right, son,"

"All right, all right," Jerry uttered. "What the hell does he know about it?"

"You go to bed, son," Mr. Calhoun said. "It's gonna be all right." Then he closed the door, and Jerry could hear him feeling his way down the stairs.

"All right," Jerry repeated out loud, bitterly, to the closed door. What the hell did Duckfoot know about it? What the hell did his father know?

He began to undress, flinging his clothes down across the foot of the bed, shivering a little as the air struck his bare flesh. When he had stripped to his underwear, he walked across, barefoot, to the fireplace, and blew out the lamp. Then, in the darkness which was absolute in the moment before his eyes had adjusted themselves, he felt his way to the bed, and laid himself down. The springs creaked painfully with his weight.

The springs had always made that sound when he got into this bed and shifted his body to find the position for comfort, always, ever since he could remember. Then, thinking that, he seemed to be sinking, not into the old mattress, which accepted his body now as it had years ago. But into those years themselves, into the self he had been. What had he been? And what did he share with that Jerry Calhoun who, long ago, had lain here?

He could make out objects now in the gloom—the chair and the table where once he had leaned over his books on Sunday afternoons when his father had come up to sit and watch with the absorbing, pitiless patience, the wardrobe, which was a pile of blackness against the pale paper of the wall. The objects were there in the same old places, waiting, and he had come. Under the paper there was the old wall, secret, aware, with eyes to see the old Jerry Calhoun under the new. And here he was, and they had received him, as the old self had received him, as the mattress had received him, as the past had received him, as he was drawn back into Aunt Ursula, and Lew, and his father, and the mother he had never known, and all the nameless people who were dead. Here he was, and the mattress was like a quicksand into which he would sink, imperceptibly, but steadily, forever, drawn down by the numberless, nameless fingers that plucked feebly but inexorably, ceaselessly.

He laid rigid, as though any motion, any struggle, might plunge him deeper. Oh, he had come back. He had come back, all right. *All right, all right*, he thought, and thought how his father had said it would be all right.

All right, all right—what right had his father to say "all right"?

He had stood by the door and had said, "All right," and he couldn't even know what *all right* was, for nothing had ever been all right for him, for he had always failed, the cord broke in his hands, the strap twisted in his fingers, the nail bent under his hammer, the dish slipped from his grasp. And he saw his father as he had seen him so many times, leaning over some small thing, some task too precise, breathing heavily with the sweat on his face; and the old sense of outrage and fury started in him. *All right, all right!* Nothing had ever been all right, and it wouldn't be now, and the old man would be alone in the house, alone with the old woman and Lew, and his son gone to prison and disgraced. Oh, that was part of the picture, that was the perfect ending. Thinking that, Jerry suddenly felt a kind of grim glee, a vindication, a vengeance.

He had come back. He had come back to have the old man stand there and say: "It's gonna be all right." He had come back to find out what he knew now. He had come back to lie in the old bed, in that dark which you couldn't tell from the old darknesses. He had left it for other beds, for other nights. He had gone a long way to come back to it. Something in the old self which had lain here had driven him out, but if you are going to come back, why do you leave?

What had driven him out? What had he wanted? Oh, the crowd had cheered in the autumn sunlight and the band had played and people had slapped him on the back and Bogan Murdock had smiled and money had been in his pocket and Sue Murdock—Sue Murdock had stood in the middle of her apartment that last night and had looked at him and had uttered that small, throaty cry, and he had known that she loved him. He had had those things and he had wanted those things. He had wanted so many things and had had all of them, and had had none of them, for what you had came wrong or too soon or too late, or it wore another face, and your three wishes always came true but the last undid all the rest, and you were where you had begun.

You get your wishes, all right, every one. You wanted to fix up the place that your great-great uncle had built. It was the Old

Calhoun Place. To paint it white and put on new shutters. To paper the walls and get the grime off the floors—oh, what beautiful floors, oh, yes, the original floors, oh, you don't see ten-inch flooring like that any more. To put up the white fence. To take out the dead gum by the gate. And you had your wish, all right. You came home, and found it all the way you had wanted, but it wasn't yours any more and you had come in the middle of the night. You came home from jail in the middle of the night.

You didn't come home in the middle of the afternoon and go out to look at your pure-bred Herefords and take your gun and your prize setter and go across the back pasture and knock down a couple of birds and sit by the fire with the glass in your hand and the smiling friend and nobody there but the friend and the nigger with the tray and no Aunt Ursula and no Lew and no—

Had you ever wanted your father dead?

No, you had never said that. You never said that. It's just that he isn't in the room. He is out somewhere. But where is he? Damn it, he just isn't here. Damn it, he's just out somewhere. There's nobody here but me and my friend and the nigger, in this beautiful room in the firelight. He just isn't in right now, that's all. And it's not my fault he's not here.

Why, there he is! Coming in the door. See, there is my father, and your suspicions were completely unjustified, but I'll accept your apology. See, there he is, wearing that beautiful new one-hundred-and-twenty-five dollar gray suit Larkinson made him in New York and looking unusually well and handsome and carrying his stick and smiling hospitably and looking at me with his fine eyes, which have large black pupils ringed with smoky-blue. I want you to meet my father. Father, this is Mr.——

But your friend stares at your father and bursts into extraordinary laughter. He laughs and laughs, and the terror grows in you. Then he controls his laughter a little, and points at your father, and says: That isn't your father, that's Bogan Murdock!

And you see that it is not your father. It is not your father at all. Where is your father? You better run, you better run quick and find him. Before they say you killed him. Before the police come and dig in the leaves in the woods and drag the river and look in the old well where you hit the drowning puppy with the brick and pry under the hay in the loft.

Jerry Calhoun heaved himself up in bed, and the springs creaked.

Did I want my father dead? he thought.

And said out loud: "No—no—"

He lay back down on the pillow, thinking, *No, no.*

Did I want my father dead?

No, no, he thought, lying there stiff on the mattress, with his eyes closed, and saw his father's face.

Father, father—I—I—

Yes, son.

I didn't really want to give her the blue shawl, father.

Yes, son.

I wanted Lew dead.

Yes, son.

Father, I wanted to sit by the fire, and they wouldn't be there—they wouldn't be there—and—and you wouldn't be there—

Yes, son.

I wanted you dead—I wanted you dead, father—I wanted to sit by the fire—

Yes, son.

You knew? Did you know?

Yes, son.

Oh, father—

Yes, son.

There was frost on the ground when Mr. Calhoun came out of the kitchen door, and moved across the backyard to the wood-pile. His feet cut through the white frost and left tracks where the dun color of the frozen mud showed through. He leaned above the woodpile, the breath puffing whitely from his mouth, and began to pick up stove-lengths. After he had placed three in the crook of his arm, he had some difficulty in picking more up, for his balance was bad and his hand was cold and unclever. But he finally managed.

While the fire caught and the water for Aunt Ursula's two eggs came slowly to a boil and her pan of milk began to simmer, he laid places for two on the kitchen table. Then he prepared the tray, broke the two eggs into a cup, poured the hot milk into a bowl, and went to feed the old woman, whom he had already propped up in bed on pillows, swathed to the chin in blankets, whose fire he had risen twice in the night to build, and whose face he had, that morning, already wiped with a cloth dipped in water heated in a kettle at her fireplace.

When he came back, Lew was hunched in a chair drawn up almost into contact with the stove.

"Good morning," Mr. Calhoun said.

"Yeah," Lew said, "ain't it, Mr. Astor?"

Mr. Calhoun put a skillet on the stove and in it two thick slices of shoulder meat. While the meat began to uncongeal and the grease to ooze from it on to the black iron, he broke four eggs into a bowl and stirred them. The odor of coffee was already beginning to drift in the air. The breath of the men now did not show white.

"Do you mind setting the bread on?" Mr. Calhoun asked.

"Naw," Lew said, and lurched up, clumping his foot on the hollow boards. He got a plate of cold biscuits and a pat of butter from the safe. As he leaned to place the objects on the table, he observed the plates there. "Ain't Jerry eating?" he demanded, eying Mr. Calhoun's heavy, curved back.

"He'll eat when he wakes up," Mr. Calhoun said, not turning from the stove.

"Yeah, yeah, he'll eat when he wakes up," Lew mimicked. "Yeah, and what'll he eat? Oh, he'll take a morsel of angel-food cake if you please, and a little peach ice cream."

"Being it's the first night," Mr. Calhoun said apologetically, "I figured I'd just not call him."

"Well, I'll call him," Lew announced, "him laying up there sleeping and it broad day. He ain't in no city now, he—"

"Naw, Lew, naw," Mr. Calhoun repeated steadily, occupied with the bowl, the eggs, the frying meat, "don't be bothering him this morning. Just let him sleep now. Tomorrow morning, that'll be different."

"Him laying up there, and work to do!"

"Tomorrow," Mr. Calhoun said. "Jerry, now—he never was no hand to slack, and the need there."

"Laying up there, laying up there!" Lew exulted bitterly, and swung from the table toward the door, and his boot rattled and clumped in victorious tattoo as he lurched and lunged toward the inner door.

"By God!" Mr. Calhoun uttered in a terrible voice.

In the moment of ensuing silence, Lew, his hand already on the knob, turned to confront the powerful, hulking figure, the working face and unsheathed, baleful eyes, the heavy hand lifted to heaven clutching the iron spoon, from which dripped a gout of egg.

He took his hand, almost surreptitiously, from the knob.

The place is the library of Bogan Murdock. The time is about eleven-thirty on a bright wintry morning.

A fire leaps and crackles cleanly in the big fireplace. On a table are set a siphon of soda, a bottle of Scotch whisky, a tray of glasses, and a box of cigars. At that end of the room four men are seated, nondescript men, with pads and pencils in their hands and cigars in their mouths. On the floor beside each of them is a partly filled glass. A fifth man stands behind the tripod of a camera, holding aloft the reflector and flash bulb. The camera is trained across the room.

There, directly in front of the camera, sits Bogan Murdock, erect, smiling, firm-jawed, with his eyes gimleted unflaggingly upon the black spot where, at the appropriate instant, will be exposed the flash of lens. On his right sits his father, who breathes heavily and observes nothing. On his left sits his wife, who, dressed in black, is beautiful and pale as wax. Behind him stands his son, dark-browed and sullen. One unruly lock on the son's head falls forward almost to his eyes. Now and then he twitches his head as though to free himself from that irritation.

The bulb gives its explosive, blinding, veracious flash.

"Thank you," the camera man says.

"Not at all," Bogan Murdock replies.

Bogan Murdock rises from his chair, and moves to the fireplace, moving with a controlled, tautened grace, which is as innocent as though he were alone. The eyes of the seated men follow him. He spreads his fine, brown hands to the blaze, then turns to face them.

"You have," he says, "asked me for a statement."

"Yes, sir," one of the men says, "if you don't mind."

There is a rustling sound as the men adjust themselves in their chairs and shift their pads of paper.

"You want me to make a statement about the failure of the firm of Meyers and Murdock, of which I have the honor to be president."

He looks at them with perfect candor.

There is no answer. So he smiles at them, slowly, in the security of strength and the melancholy of wisdom.

"I have only this to say," he says. "I say that I am completely responsible. I am responsible because I followed too faithfully my larger vision and trusted too much in friends, in subordinates in whom I thought I had found loyalty. But now—under these circumstances, which we need not discuss—I have found a loyalty which I never suspected to exist. In my friends, who have rallied round me. In my family, a great staunchness and loyalty in the midst of their bereavement." He pauses and regards the three people—the old man, the beautiful woman, the strong sullen boy. "So," he says, "in the confidence born of that loyalty, I look to the future. Courage—I hope that I may have a little of it. Courage—" he says, and nods to indicate the mountainous, wrecked old man, who wheezes slowly, "my father had courage. Courage, it is the heritage of all of us—of all citizens of this State. Courage," he says, and turns and indicates with a glance the portrait, as large as life, above the fireplace.

It is the portrait of a man who, more than a century ago, endured cold and hunger, who killed men with his own hand, who survived steaming malarial swamps and long marches, who was ruthless, vindictive, cunning, and headstrong, who was president of his country, who died in the admiration, or hatred, of millions of men. There is the painted face: the sunken flesh over the grim jawbone, the deep, smoldering eyes, the jutting beak of a nose, and the coarse crest of grayish hair, like an old cockatoo.

from *Home to the Hermitage*

ALFRED LELAND CRABB (1884–1980)

> Alfred Leland Crabb was born in Warren County, Kentucky,
> near Bowling Green. He taught at several Kentucky public
> schools before taking a degree from George Peabody College
> for Teachers in 1916. He received his M.A. from Columbia
> University and his Ph.D. from Peabody. He joined the faculty of
> the latter institution in 1927 and remained there until 1950
> when he became professor emeritus. Crabb set six of his histor-
> ical novels in his adopted home of Nashville, including *Dinner
> at Belmont* (1942), *Supper at the Maxwell House* (1943), and
> *Breakfast at the Hermitage* (1945), and wrote biographical
> novels for adults and children, including *Andrew Jackson's
> Nashville* (1966). He wrote a nonfiction portrait of Nashville,
> *Nashville: Personality of a City* (1960), and co-authored a his-
> tory of the Nashville Baptist Church, *Acorns to Oaks* (1972).
> The following is from his 1948 *Home to the Hermitage*.

Within her home Rachel Jackson walked ceaselessly from dining
room to kitchen and back again to the dining room. Food and
flowers and polished furniture; snow-white linen, and gleaming
silver, and the royal china bought in New Orleans a decade
ago—these were her concern. In the kitchen across the areaway
all was bustle and stir and tension. They were used to visitors at
the Hermitage. Visitors of quality afforded the home no novelty.
The Jacksons had entertained presidents, generals, statesmen and
high adventurers, and they had got along well enough with it. But
General Lafayette! He was something out of all familiarity.

In the kitchen four cooks moved under considerable excitement but held in poise by proper discipline. It would be to their
enduring glory if they prepared a dinner worthy of the day. In
the years to come they would talk about it in the quarters, and
their eyes would shine when they remembered. But if they had
failed—!

. . .

The visitors arrived. Rachel Jackson was ready for them. They went into the parlor, and a few minutes later into the dining room. They sat at the table and General Jackson spoke his ritual of grace. The waiters came in bringing bowls of the chicken soup. When the guests finished it the bowls were carried back into the kitchen.

It was time for the dramatic entrance of Uncle Cephas bearing the ham. He knew how to bring a ham into the dining room. He always reached his highest at that magnificent moment. The ham was placed on a spreading blue-flowered platter. Uncle Cephas knew how to hold that platter so as best to display with dignity and effect the ham resting on it.

He swung the platter with a ceremonial flourish and let it come to rest on the table just in front of General Jackson. The general bowed to him and the slave moved back a step and stood at his master's side. General Jackson arose and with grace and expertness carved from the ham ample slices for all the guests. Uncle Cephas carried the first plate served to General Lafayette, who turned and bowed to Mrs. Jackson and passed the plate to her.

Rachel Jackson, gifted with all the Donelson prescience as to hams, had chosen this one from the array that swung from the smokehouse rafters. It had not been an easy choice. She had made three trips to the smokehouse. Not only sight but smell helped direct her decision. With a large knitting needle she had punctured several hams along the side of the bone and whiffed the needle when withdrawn. Both sight and smell pointed to this particular ham. It had met all the tests. She chose it.

She had watched while Aunt Chloe trimmed away all its ragged and tasteless parts, while she encrusted it with a layer of spices, topped with a coating of New Orleans sugar. She had watched Aunt Chloe pour a thin depth of homemade wine into the great baking dish in which on a low rack she placed the ham. She covered it with a tightly tucked heavy cloth. For hours the process of baking went slowly ahead. At intervals the cloth was removed and the ham basted from the mixture of wine and drippings in the bottom of the pan. Time and again Chloe was cautioned to hold the fire down, not to hurry the approach of the ham toward edibility, to guard with care its gradual evolution into perfection.

Rachel Jackson cut a microscopic slice in the kitchen and when she tasted it she knew that her choice had been justified; she knew that Aunt Chloe's art had been without flaw.

When Lafayette tasted it a look of wonder and delight grew on his face. He turned to his hostess and made again that marvelous bow. "Oh, but, madame, one does not find even in France ham the equal of this!"

"I," said Francis Fogg, "can add territory to your comparison, sir. One does not find its equal even in Tennessee."

"My honor is enlarged," said Lafayette. He turned to Andrew Jackson. "Is it not true, General Jackson, that when we look at it closer the cloud may be found lined with pure silver? Three months ago you were defeated for the presidency of your country. Was that defeat not a victory? It gave you life here, life so lovely as this, with a companion so charming. The other, sir, is as tinsel compared with this."

Rachel was radiant. "Tell him that again," she said.

"I fear that our friend is greatly committed to his tinsel," said Governor Carroll. "Still which one of us wouldn't be?"

"Ah, the presidency!" said Lafayette. "It is noble, yes, but so heartbreaking."

"Tell my husband that again," said Rachel Jackson.

"I return to the food. How exquisite is this ham! I have observed, madame, that food fits itself to the home in which it is served. Would this ham, for instance, be as delicious if served elsewhere—Washington, for instance? Is it the ham alone that is so pleasing, or is it the ham in its proper setting. My countryman, Brillat-Savarin, thought so."

The satisfying cries of a plowman in the field next to the garden came in through the open window. A wood thrush in a paulownia tree in the front yard tuned its lovely trill without ceasing. The strain and excitement of Washington were far away. At the Hermitage there were the peace and beauty of a May afternoon.

When the dinner was eaten Rachel and Andrew Jackson took their guests for a walk in the garden. The clumps of peonies scattered about were fading, but the garden was rich with a profusion of blue flags. The heavy green of the cedars, the deep olive of the boxwoods and the lighter yellower green of the new leaves on the crepe myrtle trees touched the garden with variety. There was a long bed of peonies in full bloom at one end of the garden, and a bed of coreopsis whose buds were showing deep gold at the other.

Rachel Jackson looked among her blue flags until she found a perfect one, which she handed to Lafayette. He bowed. "Ah, madame, how exquisite! You bid me welcome with a lily of France gathered from your own garden."

She said in her commonplace phrase, "We are glad for you to see our garden."

"It is an exquisite garden. I shall remember it as your garden, madame. Doubtless you wished for these flowers, and so they bloomed."

"I did not wish alone," she said with her eyes on her husband.

"Not alone," said Andrew Jackson taking her hand tenderly in his. "You taught me how to wish, my dear."

They stood in the full light of midafternoon. Andrew Jackson was tall and straight and very thin. The rays of the sun glinted on his tousled reddish hair. His nose was long, his mouth thin and wide. A fire smoldered in his eyes ready to spring into full blaze. His face was narrow and sallow, but molded into severe distinction. His wife was short and plump. Her hair was coalblack, untouched by gray. Her face was saved from heaviness by eyes large, dark, and deep. The marquis stood near them, his hand toying with the blossoms of a mock orange bush. He was short and square, and his face seamed. The gray of his thin hair was shading into white. One who did not see his eyes or his hands or hear his voice might have passed him by with only a single glance. His eyes were blue and keen and their bright alertness never dimmed. His hands were sensitive, and their movements were as the flow of music.

The others stood about. General Jackson started to speak, but the distant call of a steamboat interrupted. Captain Hall of the *Mechanic* was tactfully reminding General Lafayette that time moved toward the dinner being prepared in his honor at the Nashville Inn.

"That Captain Hall, he is a tyrant, a most wicked tyrant. He commands me when I do not wish to be commanded. When I desire only the sound of friendly voices and the sight of a lovely garden he goes out on his deck and blows a whistle. Still, I am a soldier. When my commander blows a whistle I come."

"My wife is going to town with us," said Andrew Jackson.

"How inappropriate otherwise! But that Captain Hall, he should not hurry a lady."

"Oh, I am ready," said Rachel. "I am my husband's wife and I always expect to be hurried. I am used to it by now. I almost like it."

The whistle sounded again. "That Captain Hall! That tyrant!" said General Lafayette.

"The Carnegie Library, Juvenile Division"

RANDALL JARRELL (1914–1965)

Randall Jarrell was born in Nashville on May 6, the same birth-day as Sigmund Freud, a coincidence which delighted the poet who was intensely interested in psychoanalysis. Jarrell's first contribution to the arts of Nashville came when he posed at age eight for the Ganymede on the pediment of the replica Parthenon in Centennial Park. Soon thereafter, his family moved to California. After his parents' separation, he returned with his mother and brother to Nashville in 1926. He went on to gradu-ate from Hume-Fogg High School in 1931 and receive a B.S. in psychology from Vanderbilt University in 1935. During his undergraduate years he studied with John Crowe Ransom and was acquainted with Donald Davidson, Allen Tate, Peter Taylor, and Robert Penn Warren. Jarrell followed Ransom to Kenyon College and became an instructor of English there in 1937. He roomed with poet Robert Lowell in Ransom's house and continued working on his dissertation for a master's degree in English from Vanderbilt. His first book of poems, *Blood for a Stranger*, was issued in 1942 with a dedication to Allen Tate, and in the same year he enlisted in the Army Air Force. Upon his release from service in 1946, Jarrell took an instructor's position at Sarah Lawrence College, an experience he later sat-irized in his only novel, *Pictures at an Institution* (1954), and was named poetry editor of the *Nation*. In 1947, he began teaching at the University of North Carolina at Greensboro, a position he retained until his death in a car accident in Chapel Hill, North Carolina in 1965. Jarrell's poetry includes *Little Friend, Little Friend* (1945), *Selected Poems* (1955), and *The Woman at the Washington Zoo* (1960). His criticism includes *Poetry and the Age* (1953).

The soot drifted from the engines to the marble
The readers climbed to: stone, and the sooty casts
(Dark absent properties confused with crates
And rest-rooms in the darkness of a basement,
And constant in their senseless line, like dates:
A past that puzzles no one, or a child)
All overlooking—as the child too overlooked—
The hills and stone and steeples of the town
Grey in the pure red of the dying sun.

Here under the waves' roof, where the seals are men;
In the rhymes' twilight, where the old cup ticks
Its gnawing lesson; where the beasts loom in the green
Firred darkness of the märchen: country the child thought life
And wished for and crept to out of his own life—
Must you still isle such, raiders from a world
That you so long ago lost heart to represent?
The child tugs the strap tight round four books
To leave the cavern. And the cut-out ornaments
In colors harsh and general as names,
The dolls' scarred furniture, too small
For anything but pity, like the child—
Surely you recognize in these the hole
That widens from the middle of a field
To that one country where the poor see gold?
The woodman dances home, rich, rich; but a shade glides
Into the bright strange sunlight of the world
He owned once; the thaler blur out like a tear,

He knocks like a stranger and a stranger speaks,
And he sees, brass on the knocker, the gnome's joyless smile.

The books too read to ashes—for one owns
Nothing, and finds that there is no exchange
For all the uses lined here, free as air,
Fleeting as air: the sad repeated spell

Of that deep string, half music and half pain—
How many have believed you worth a soul!
How many here will purchase with a world
These words still smoldering for the perpetual
Children who haunt this fire-sale of the centuries.
Wandering among so many lives, they too will bear
The life from which they cannot yet escape;
And learn to doubt, with our sad useless smile,
That single universe the living share—
The practice with which even the books are charred.

We learned from you so much about so many things
But never what we were; and yet you made us that.
We found in you the knowledge for a life
But not the will to use it in our lives
That were always, somehow, so different from the books'.
We learn from you to understand, but not to change.

from *The Long, Long Love*

WALTER SULLIVAN (1924–)

Critic and novelist Walter Sullivan was born in Nashville and educated at Vanderbilt University and at the University of Iowa. He joined the faculty of Vanderbilt in 1949, where he currently teaches fiction writing and Southern literature. Sullivan's fiction includes *Sojourn for a Stranger* (1957) and *A Time to Dance* (1995). His criticism includes *A Band of Prophets: The Vanderbilt Agrarians after Fifty Years* (1982), *Allen Tate: A Recollection* (1988), *In Praise of Blood Sports and Other Essays* (1990), and *The War the Women Lived: Female Voices from the Confederate South* (1995). Sullivan is a frequent contributor to journals including *Hollins Critic*, *Southern Review*, *Southern Literary Journal*, and the *Sewanee Review*. Following is an excerpt from his 1959 novel *The Long, Long Love*.

I can remember very distinctly that when I was a child, I used to think often about life and about how I came to be where I was, doing whatever I was doing at a particular moment of the day or of the night. My family lived in a house on Russell Street in a section of Nashville that was then known as Edgefield; and it was a big house, three stories with turrets at the corners and as fancy as a river steamer with curlicues and gingerbread and stained glass transoms. Sometimes, if the day were dull, or if my only sister who is dead now had hurt my feelings, or if one of the servants had scolded me for being underfoot, I would climb up to one of the turret rooms—which was round as I imagined a dungeon room would be and dark with only a slit of sunlight through the narrow window and dusty from the desuetude of long years. I would sit down near the doorway—on a stool that I, in my vanity, had provided for myself as a kind of throne to sulk on—and I would listen to the coo of the pigeons that nested beneath the parapet or, if it were summer, to the sough and whir of the circling flies.

But I can truly say that I was not the type of child to pout for very long. Even now, after almost half a century, I can recollect how my mind would inevitably be diverted from the hurt or grudge it bore by a flight of fancy, by a cast of my imagination over the intricate connections that form the fabric of man's days. I would sit with my back against the wall, my eyes toward the window, my hands in my lap. And I would think, *I am Horatio Adams and I am nine years old and I have come upstairs because I am angry with Sister.* And then I would think, *But suppose I had left home right after luncheon to go fishing maybe with Wash Hamilton or to walk to town or down to the park where we might have played baseball. Then I would never have quarreled with Sister and I would not be here now. Or suppose I had been born before Sister, rather than after, then I would be her older brother, larger and wiser than she and she would not dare dispute me. Or, going back further, suppose Mother and Father had not married each other, would I be Father's son now or Mother's and in what ways would I be different and in what ways would I be the same?*

I tried, of course, to keep these thoughts carefully secret; knowingly, I disclosed them neither to my family nor to my friends. Yet my resolution was callow and the mark of its imperfection was the occasional question which I blurted out to Wash Hamilton or to Henry, our houseboy, or to my Aunt Irene. Once I asked Aunt Irene what she thought I would be like and what I would be doing if I had been born in Ohio rather than in Tennessee. My aunt was my father's sister, a tall woman with a sharp nose, who wore black dresses. She was an officer in the U. D. C. and her father had been a general in the Confederate Army; and she was very proud of the South and of herself for being a Southerner and of Grandfather Adams who had given his life for the Southern cause.

"Ohio!" she said when I asked her my question. "Ohio!" she repeated, her voice rising sharply. "Imp of Satan, don't you know where Ohio is?"

So I climbed, pouting, to my turret room and spent half an hour of a bright fall afternoon thinking of Ohio where I had never been and of how the days of my life might have fashioned themselves if I had been born there.

My aunt often said that I thought too much about myself.

Father had been very wealthy, richer I think, than even Uncle Billy and Aunt Irene had suspected. So there was no reason for the administrators of the estate to insist that the house on Russell Street be sold or rented. It was left intact. Dust covers were put on the furniture and Henry, who was getting up in years now, was retained to sleep there and guard the house and to keep it clean. At odd times during the summer and at other vacation periods when I was home from prep school or college, I would go from my uncle's place on West End Avenue across town to the house where once I had lived with my mother and father. After I had exchanged a few pleasantries with Henry, I would sit in the library or in the front parlor and watch the play of firelight on the polished andirons or, if the weather were warm, sip a cool drink and fan myself with my hat. I would remember the old time and how it used to be when I lived here and I would think of my mother and father who had died at sea.

Because it seemed to me that I owed them this much. It seemed somehow unnatural, not that they should die, but that all trace and memory of them should be so completely obliterated. Their bones drifted somewhere in the ocean, washed by what water no man could tell. Beyond a memorial window in the church on Woodland Street, there was nothing but this house—no monument to mark a final resting place, no grave where I might have placed a wreath of flowers. I grieved for my mother and father who were lost to the world of man. And I suppose I was aware, in some childish way, that my own life would have to end. I suppose, in a way, I was grieving for myself.

Yet, there was a comfort too in going to this house and conjuring up these images of the past. For after all, wasn't my memory of my parents a kind of monument to them, or better than a monument, emanating as it did from flesh and not from marble? And was not the fact that I cherished the recollection of Mother and Father a promise of sorts that in the future someone, perhaps yet unborn, would remember me?

I loved the house on Russell Street. And attenuated, devoted as I was to the shrines and relics of the past, I loved Adams' Rest perhaps even more. Adams' Rest was a part of my inheritance; a house thirty miles south of Nashville, a farm, a plantation really, on the outskirts of a little town called Van Buren, which had been built by my great-grandfather in 1821. It was a large house, red brick and white columns, and it sat on the top of a little eminence with a vast lawn that sloped gently toward the road. The land was under cultivation: tobacco and corn and pasture and orchards. There was stock in the stables and there were hands to work the fields and there was a skeleton house staff who took care of Uncle Billy and me when we went there to hunt quail or dove in the autumn.

The house at Adams' Rest was full of mementoes. The old ledger books from slavery days still lined the office shelves; the old tester beds remained in the bedrooms; and many of the windows were glazed with the old, greenish, bubbly, shimmering panes. The wardrobes contained relics of a romantic nature: there was a Freemason's apron and an old militia uniform, there were some dresses with hoop skirts and some military belts and an empty holster. On the walls there were portraits of my forebears, of my great grandfather who had built Adams' Rest and who was now buried in the cemetery beyond the house and of my grandfather who had been a general and a hero and who was buried in town in the Confederate graveyard.

According to the story that Aunt Irene told me, Grandfather had been killed in the Battle of Van Buren and had died almost on his own doorstep; but because he wished it with his final breath or because somebody thought he would have wished it or because the people who had seen the battle and considered him a hero thought it proper—for some reason that was not then entirely clear to me, Grandfather was buried beside his fallen men and after the War, his grave was marked with a shaft of marble. This, I believed, was the finest of all victories over death, the antidote to the depredations of time. Occasionally when I stood alone in the plot, reading the inscription of my grandfather's tomb, tears would sting my eyes and blur my vision. I would look at my grandfather's grave and cry. Such was the callowness of my sentient youth. Oh such, indeed, was my ignorance and folly!

Foolish was I, for of what use was fame, and how could it heal the broken heart or revivify the decaying flesh ere the day of judgement? But worse than this was the belief that the sight of Grandfather's tomb had led me into: that death, your own death, was the worst that time could do, the ultimate pain that the passing years could make you suffer.

My sister died of influenza during the epidemic of 1918 and I, too, contracted influenza that year and I was very much frightened. I remember more clearly than the aches and chills the great silence that would come over the house when Aunt Irene and Uncle Billy had gone to bed, and the nurse who was caring for me had left the room, and I was alone with only the wind beyond the glass, and inside, the night light's steady burning. I did not expect to live and I did not want to die, and many times during many nights I was frightened almost to the point of calling out that the nurse might come or Aunt Irene and hold my hand and touch cool fingers to my forehead. But I did not call out and, when I was well again, I recollected my behavior with pride. From that moment I believed that I, like Grandfather, was capable of dying bravely. I took comfort and—I must admit it—pride in the fortitude with which I had faced up to death. I congratulated myself on what I fancied to be my consummate courage.

And, indeed, in such a fashion are we all deluded, day by day. Men speak of the value of experience: the efficacy of experience brought to bear to solve life's problems, the comfort of experience which whispers that the worst must pass. But this is not true. Experience is a myth for men to cling to. It offers us too little. It is understood too late. The lessons that it teaches are often contradictory.

I emerged from my siege of influenza believing that I had faced up to the experience of death and that I knew now all that there was to know about dying. I had forgotten the lessons I had learned—no matter how vaguely learned—when, as a child, I hid myself in my turret room. I graduated from college. I went to work—if you can call it that, if I have ever worked—in a brokerage firm which had been founded by my father and which was being operated by the trustees for the beneficiary of the estate, who was I.

And one weekend in April when I should have been at the office, I was off at a house party near Lexington, Kentucky. There I met a girl named Nancy Henderson. I remember that on Saturday afternoon we had all been drinking a good deal. Everyone at the party had been drinking too much and Nancy Henderson and I decided to take a walk to clear our heads with the fresh air of April. We were at a farm which belonged to a college friend of mine and from the side veranda, we followed a flagstone path which was lined with iris just coming into flower. I remember how the sunlight caught the purple petals, glowed there softly and glowed on the soft new grass. And I recollect how we moved together—the slight, almost delicate girl and I—walked unsteadily hand and hand to a wrought iron bench that sat by a drained lily pool. We lighted cigarettes and I think we laughed about nothing; laughed in amazement, the way people who have been drinking will do, at the fact that the pool was bone dry now. We got up and walked around in the pool, hilariously pretending, I suppose, that like Our Lord we walked upon the water.

When we had resumed our places on the wrought iron bench, I looked at her for the first time in the full light of day or looked at her perhaps in the first stages of my returning sobriety, but looked at her, in any event, closely. I saw the dark hair cut short as was then the fashion; the very white skin; the face slender so that the features were almost, but not quite, sharp; and below the face, the limbs slender but not too skinny; the legs and arms fleshed out over the small bones to the bare point of a superb adequacy, the calves tapered to suit the eye but strong to carry the light body with grace. And at the same time, at the moment that I recognized her for the beautiful girl that she was, I heard in her voice the Northern accent.

At this distance, I cannot tell you what she said, though I recall distinctly the deep green of her dress. The glitter of a ring on her right hand, the snuff brown color of her pointed-toed, polished slippers. I recollect only the sudden strangeness of those sharply pronounced i's, the finality of the clearly enunciated r's coming at the end of a word or the close of a sentence. I listened for a while in bemused fascination. Then I said, "Nancy, where are you from?"

It was a rude thing to say, an ill-bred question to ask, but I did ask it and she did not seem to mind.

She smiled and said, "Cleveland. I live in Cleveland, Ohio. I was born there."

And oh, how the memories came rushing back of the days when I used to wonder what I would be like if I had been born not in Tennessee, but in Ohio. I remembered my Aunt Irene and how she had frowned and called me Satan's Imp, and my grandfather buried beneath his marble shaft, who for all I knew might have been killed by a man from Cleveland, Ohio. And perhaps even then I had made up my mind to marry this Yankee girl if she would have me.

At any rate, six months later, we were married in Cleveland, and we returned after Christmas to take up our lives in Tennessee. And was it the sight of Nashville and the old landmarks that turned my mind back to its familiar track and started from their slumber the ancient fears of my heart? I do not know; I cannot answer. I can only say that during all the long journey that Nancy and I took together, by ship and rail and carriage, sometimes up mountains and down into valleys, through good weather and beautiful country and through snow and rain, during the months of our honeymoon, I felt nothing but happiness.

The old depression which I used to feel did not come to haunt me or to suggest that time was passing, that even then fate was planning an end to our bliss. But when we got home and I once more discovered Nancy's beauty, tears came to my eyes.

Before our marriage, Nancy had come down to Nashville on a visit and we had purchased a lot of ground in Belle Meade and had plans drawn up and called in the builders. Nancy had consulted a decorator and hired servants, so when we returned from Europe we were met at the railroad station and taken to a house already furnished and staffed and waiting there bright and new against our occupancy.

We went through our house and admired its rooms. Nancy rejoiced in the richness of its carpets and draperies, caviled only slightly at the arrangement of the furniture. Then we returned to the foyer and went up the stairs to our bedroom suite where fires had been lighted. I remember that some of our baggage had already come out from the station and Nancy's maid was busy unpacking one of the trunks. We sat down in the sitting room, close together on a small couch, and in silence, we watched the play of shadows on the hearth. Then it occurred to me that this was our first time together in our own home and we ought to celebrate somehow. I rang for the butler and asked him to bring champagne.

It was afternoon of a cold January day. The yellow January sun sparkled at the windows and the glass of the windows was misting slightly, and inside was all warmth with the heat of the open fireplace and the house new and clean and very silent. The maid had gone now out of the dressing room and Nancy was beside me, her shoes off and her legs pulled up beneath her on the couch. I released her hand which I had been holding and put my arm around her shoulder and it was as if I had never been close to her, never touched her before. It was as if this were the first time, not only of marriage, but the first moment of courtship. The arm that I felt beneath the cloth of her dress was strange, mysterious in its slender shape and firmness, but tempting far beyond its simple mystery.

I moved closer to her, but I did not kiss her at once. I held off, my lips so near hers that I could feel the warmth and dampness of her breath against my face, and then I did kiss her gently on the corner of the mouth, easily as old people kiss or as you kiss a child. I drew back and kissed her again, and this time it was a lover's kiss. Her lips were as warm and as damp as had been her breath and the breath of her very life was present in our kiss, shaping it, and shaping our lips together. I put my hand beneath her dress and let it brush up along her thigh past the top of her stocking.

"Not here, darling," she said.

I smiled and said, "No. Not here."

I got up and I helped Nancy to rise, and I walked with her through the door into the bedroom.

from "Formaldehyde and Poetry"

RALPH MCGILL (1898–1969)

Ralph McGill was born equidistant from the east Tennessee farming communities of Soddy and Daisy, but as the former has a post office, official documents gave it as his birthplace. Using borrowed tuition money, McGill boarded at the McCallie brothers' new school in Chattanooga. As the reminiscence below from his *The South and the Southerner* (1963) discusses, McGill attended Vanderbilt University from 1917 to 1922, with a brief interruption to serve in the Marine Corps during the world war. While at school, McGill knew many of the Fugitives, specifically John Crowe Ransom, Robert Penn Warren, Allen Tate, and Merrill Moore. His poetry was of uneven quality and he was never closely associated with the group. Nevertheless, the seriousness and intensity of the writers inspired him to use his talents in journalism. He wrote for the school newspaper, founded the school humor magazine, and worked as a part-time copyboy and sportswriter for the *Nashville Banner*. He was suspended shortly before his planned graduation in 1922 for his part in a fraternity prank and his authorship of a satirical editorial which suggested the Vanderbilt administration had squandered a bequest. He never returned to the university. He soon became a sportswriter and then sports editor for the *Nashville Banner* and remained at the paper in various reporting positions for seven years. McGill served as the associate editor, editor, and publisher of the *Atlanta Constitution* from 1938 to his death in 1969. He was a reluctant crusader for black civil rights advocating for social change with a combination of high-mindedness, common sense, and good humor. In 1958 he won a Pulitzer Prize for his editorial on the bombings of a black church and a Jewish synagogue.

In the fall of 1919 with a loan of $125 in Chattanooga and another from the university loan fund, I was back at Vanderbilt. Then began two more fast-moving years. The football squad was heavy with returned veterans and stars of other years. I played at least part of all the games and won a letter. But already there were other interests. The campus was in a ferment of talk and new ideas about books and poetry. Some of us felt we were of the lost generation and if we could not be expatriates in Paris we would make do with what we had in Nashville and at Vanderbilt.

John Crowe Ransom, one of the younger members of the English faculty, whose poems had already been published in a number of magazines, began to attract about him students and teachers who were interested in poetry. Allen Tate, who was in my class, turned to poetry with an enthusiasm and a dedication rare and exciting. He always seemed to be writing poetry, or talking about it.

One evening as a group of us from the sophomore literary fraternity walked across the campus to a sorority house where poems were to be read and coffee served, Tate was reciting as he went. I recall the closing line of the poem, which was heavy with symbolism to have been: "They bore on high the phallic symbol bold."

One of the group protested. "Gee, Allen," he said, "don't you think you might embarrass them?"

"No," said Tate, "all these girls come from Middle Tennessee high schools. They won't have the vaguest idea what a phallic symbol is."

As far as one could tell, none did. Tate read the poem with fine dramatic effect. Even the housemother showed no sign of shock. It was a fine, exciting evening in the best sophomoric tradition with Tate's comment and poem symbolizing it perfectly.

There were at least a half dozen students whose pockets, like Tate's, were filled with copies of poems. Others were writing novels. Merrill Moore, later to become a distinguished psychiatrist in Brookline, Massachusetts, was even then producing sonnets at an unbelievable rate. It was a facility he never lost. My own energies, after bitter frustration with verse, turned to the weekly student newspaper, the *Hustler*. A column idea was submitted and accepted. It ran column one on page one and quickly involved me in discussion and controversy. Some of the latter led to blows, but it was fun. There was an excitement in getting the four pages ready for the paper. We made an all-night job of it, talking and arguing on a variety of unrelated subjects.

Two of the fraternity chapter alumni worked on the *Nashville Banner*. By spring I had begun to visit them in the city room when the late afternoon street edition was waiting on the baseball detail to conclude. One day, arriving earlier than usual, I found there was a great to-do because the young man who usually took the play-by-play as telephoned in from the park, had quit. I filled in. The detail came in slowly—"Smith struck out. Jones flied to right. Johnson singled to left," etc. A stranger to a typewriter could make out. This was my first newspaper job, and it was agreed it would be a regular one. I reported at 2 P.M. each day the ball club was in town, and worked from 3 P.M. to 3:30 A.M. on other days. On Saturdays I worked from noon until 2:30 Sunday morning. That summer I was also a part-time police reporter, and held minor assignments. The pay was seventeen dollars per week, I can still recall the intense excitement and the pleasure of those days. I knew then I had found what I wanted to do.

At Vanderbilt in the year of 1920–1921 the group which later called themselves "The Fugitives" was already the talk of the campus. Two of them, Merrill Moore and Stanley Johnson, were my close and valued friends. Johnson was in the English Department, and his wife, Will Ella, was university librarian. Their apartment in the old theological school dormitory attracted three or four of us almost nightly. Contemporary poetry was read aloud. I can yet remember the pleasure we had in Edwin Arlington Robinson. Johnson was writing a novel, later published and titled *Professor*.

Merrill Moore learned shorthand. He needed it for his notes and it was helpful, too, for writing sonnets. Frequently, Moore, at a party or dinner, not wishing to attract attention, would quietly write a sonnet in shorthand on his left shirt cuff.

John Crowe Ransom and Walter Clyde Curry, who taught courses in Shakespeare and Chaucer, were telegraphing sonnets by night letter to a young lady in Murfreesboro, Tennessee, forty miles away. The idea caught on and each Saturday evening at least a half dozen other poets began to telegraph sonnets to young ladies in distant cities. I know of one such custom which was halted abruptly. One tearful damsel telephoned to say that her father had said if he were awakened one more Sunday morning by Western Union he would take a cane to his daughter and also make the journey to Nashville to cane the idiot who was sending the poetic telegrams.

On the *Banner* four of us found an evening or so each week on which to read plays out loud, with the parts assigned. We discovered Eugene O'Neill. We read Russian plays, all of Ibsen's, and mixed in Broadway plays whose long runs had interested publishers in putting them in book form. The new novels were devoured and discussed. I can yet remember the impact of *Jurgen*, *Main Street*, and *Babbitt*. Most of us on the *Banner* and at Vanderbilt were from small towns or cities and though Gopher Prairie was in the Midwest, we were enchanted to find something of our own Tennessee home towns in *Main Street*, and were sure Lewis must, at one time or another, have seen our local Rotarians. Henry Mencken, of course, was our knight in shining armor who each month slew the dragons of dullness in the pulpits in Washington, the governor's office, the legislature and in the seats of the mighty generally. Who else could have written of President Warren Harding's prose: "It reminds me of a string of wet sponges."

Ellen Glasgow was a welcome relief in the flood of novelists. I read her slowly, not swiftly as with most of the new novelists, recognizing her for a pioneer and a writer with something to say. I still remember Judge Bland in *The Romantic Comedians*. Time has not used her well. Her novels are, in my opinion, quite the equal of Willa Cather's. Scott Fitzgerald's *This Side of Paradise* moved conversation to a higher pitch. The twenties were the American Renaissance—not, perhaps, in the classic sense of the word, but a renaissance just the same.

Years later Willa Cather was to say that the world broke in two in 1922, or thereabouts. In retrospect—it did. But those who lived it did not note it. There are many who have diagnosed the 1920'S, and most of them have been close to the mark. Students and young reporters had a vast contempt for Warren Harding, and, later, for Calvin Coolidge. They came along when the nation's elders, the voters, in substantial majority, wanted normalcy. But those who believed in the League of Nations, and those who saw in the corruption of Harding's years and the crass commercialism of Coolidge's a symbol of what it was they were in rebellion against, did not feel that normalcy was the answer. The young rebels were, perhaps, as charged, guilty of "Byronic self-consciousness" and of occasional posturing and excessive self-confidence. Even so, it was a mood more honest and nearer the verities than that provided and propagandized by the spokesmen for all that was represented by Harding and Coolidge. It is unrewarding to speculate on what direction the country might have taken, and what it and the world might have avoided, had James M. Cox and Franklin D. Roosevelt been elected in 1920. Cox was pledged to the League. He was a proved progressive.

We never thought deeply about these things on the campus at Vanderbilt, or in the city room at the *Banner* or the rival *Tennessean*. It was exciting to be alive. So we were stirred by the new ideas, the new poets and novelists. T. S. Eliot, Archibald MacLeish, Elinor Wylie, E. E. Cummings, Stephen Vincent, and William Rose Benét, each had their acolytes.

Countee Cullen was the first Negro poet I remember reading and discussing.

Dorothy Parker was, we all agreed, a healthy influence, debunking much of the pretense of the time. The twenties could laugh when she wrote:

> Authors and actors and artists and such
> Never know nothing, and never know much,
> Sculptors and singers and those of their kidney
> Tell their affairs from Seattle to Sydney
> Playwrights and poets and such horse's necks,
> Start off from anywhere, end up at sex.
> Diarists, critics, and similar roe

Never say nothing and never say no.
People Who Do Things exceed my endurance;
God, for a man that solicits insurance!

We in Nashville were, of course, provincial innocents. The
Marxist worm, for example, never bored into our lovely apple.
We read the New Masses and the hastily put-together proletarian
novels—they came late in the twenties—along with the others
and never felt a taint. They were all a part of the new freedom. As
Miniver Cheevy yearned for the grace of iron clothing, we
yearned for the garrets and fleshpots of Greenwich Village.
Occasionally, by dint of saving, one or two of us would go to
New York. Once I sold a story, based on an experience as police
reporter, to one of the confession magazines and made it to New
York for a weekend. Lonely and lacking any acquaintance in the
Village, I wandered there two afternoons and evenings, a naive
small-city reporter seeking some contact with the gods. Nor was
the journey a failure. I met no writer of note; saw the shabby and
the faking, but excused it utterly. Merely to walk there, and to eat
in one of the small candle-lit restaurants and see the tables of
arguing, eccentrically clad guests, was to touch, for a moment,
the hem of the garment of the goddess of Bohemia.

Vanderbilt's poets gave us a feeling of being in the main current by publishing, in April, 1922, the first edition of the magazine *The Fugitive*. They had, of course, been meeting to read and
criticize each other's poems for about two years. Noms de plume
were used and the campus buzzed with speculation for days
while those in the know smiled smugly. John Crowe Ransom,
whose volume, *Poems about God*, had already been published,
was the shepherd of the Fugitives. (His poems had been soundly
attacked in some pulpits as expressions of a man opposed to
God.) Henry Mencken rallied to the Fugitives, making them few
friends in other Tennessee cities and colleges, by writing that the
first issue "constitutes, at one moment, the entire literature of
Tennessee." This brought forth cries of rage and protest from a
number of papers and critics outside Nashville, but Vanderbilt

and the Fugitives loved it, and wrote letters of appreciation to the sage at Baltimore. The Fugitives purchased postcards and had an ad printed on the message side. It was headed "The Fugitive in the 'Sahara of Bozart.'" These appealed for circulation. *The Fugitive* was published from April, 1922, to December, 1925. Faculty members were John Crowe Ransom, Donald Davidson, Walter Clyde Curry, Stanley Johnson, and William Y. Elliot. Students were Merrill Moore, Allen Tate, Robert Penn Warren, Jesse Wills, and Ridley Wills. Nashvillians, of whom Sidney Hirsch—at whose home the group met—was the patron, completed the list. Most of the latter were Vanderbilt alumni.

Because the South for so long had been, in truth, a Sahara of the beaux arts, the Fugitives deserved, and had, national recognition. Louis Untermeyer, Christopher Morley, Robert Graves, and others contributed to, and hailed *The Fugitive* with generous praise.

After 1925 the university-connected Fugitives began to disperse. But their influence did not. For the next quarter century three of them, Ransom, Warren, and Tate, profoundly influenced, if indeed they did not dominate, American literary criticism. John Crowe Ransom left Vanderbilt for Kenyon College. He made the *Kenyon Review* a respected, and accepted, voice of criticism. Allen Tate, easily the most energetic, ambitious, and least disciplined of the talented Fugitives, produced a steady procession of competent critical essays. The phrase "The New Criticism" began to be widely used. Only three or four of Tate's poems gained any recognition. One of these, "Ode to the Confederate Dead," is a favorite of editors of anthologies. But Tate was a tireless correspondent, lecturer, and propagandist without equal. He taught, moving restlessly from job to job. He took a nondescript *Sewanee Review* and with an eye on Kenyon made it into one which rivaled the masters'. But he never really seemed to come to grips with himself or his work.

The "New Criticism" mothered, in the manner of a hen with new chicks, a closely knit group of poets. They indulged, perhaps, in too much praise of one another, but after all, the outlets for their criticism were few. They also began to strain after esoteric symbolism and learned metaphysical exercises. There were those critics who insisted that too many of their poems were written in a sort of Esperanto for which only the members of the club had a pony. The New Criticism mocked at Stephen Vincent Benét's *John Brown's Body*, for example, as third-rate stuff. There were a few hesitant moves toward putting Robert Frost in his place, but resolution was lacking.

Robert Penn Warren was, and is, the colossus of the Fugitives. A winner of a Pulitzer Prize for poetry and a novel, he continues to teach and produce first-rate novels and poems. As a young reporter I lived one summer in Vanderbilt's old West Side Row dormitories with Warren as a next-door neighbor. His light always was burning, no matter how late the hour. I marveled then at his discipline and have never ceased to do so.

In 1930 some of the Fugitives, with new recruits called to the colors, made an error which all but one or two die-hards regret. Proclaiming themselves Agrarians, they published a collection of essays titled *I'll Take My Stand*. It was a composite, posturing plea for a return to the economy and the culture of the plantation. *I'll Take My Stand* did not quite advocate slavery. It did, however, most earnestly recommend a return to a paternalistic system in which civilized planters would halt the writing of a poem to turn smiling faces to Uncle Tom, who, hat in hand, had a request to make. One essay began, "The Southern white man wishes the Negro well—he wishes to see crime, genial irresponsibility, and oppression replaced by an informed, productive Negro community." Tate seemed to apologize for any past criticism of a perfect culture and announced he would never criticize the South again. The year 1930 was to see the beginning of the end for what was left of the "Old South," the myth of which so gently drew the suddenly sentimental Agrarians. By 1933 the idle hookworm-and-pellagra-sick cotton sharecroppers, and the bankrupt "Big Houses" all testified eloquently that the one-crop economy was finished.

There was a determined effort to forget *I'll Take My Stand*. Only Donald Davidson stood on the burned-out deck.

Merrill Moore, youngest of the Fugitives, was in many respects unique in the group. He was the real individualist. He had no unusual eccentricities of manner or dress. He did not drink to excess. He was a quiet, wonderfully stubborn young man, with much courage and compassion in his make-up. He was a few years younger than I but we were close and enduring friends. The Moores lived a few miles out from Nashville in a large, two-story white clapboard house. The father, John Trotwood Moore, was a novelist of the old school, and a poet. The mother was a sweet, gracious, patient lady, who served, later, as state librarian. She had a wide knowledge of books and poems. There were, in those days, two pretty, very young sisters, twins.

John Trotwood Moore was a born talker and storyteller. There usually was a crowd at the Moores' on Saturday nights and Sunday afternoons. We went on possum hunts, and talked books and poems. John Trotwood would read some of his, or perhaps an excerpt from a story or a novel on which he was at work. This tall, kindly man was in demand throughout the South as a friend and speaker. He kept writing almost to the day he died.

Merrill Moore went serenely on through the academic years, and four more in medicine. It seemed odd to us that he wanted to be a doctor, but he did. As a medical student, he wrote sonnets about the cadavers, the professors, and diseased livers and hearts found in post-mortems. He early knew that he wanted to specialize in neurology and psychiatry. He did so at Boston City Hospital and the Boston Psychopathic Hospital. Merrill Moore possessed an unusually brilliant mind. Dr. T. L. Wells, assistant professor of psychology at Harvard Medical School, published an article about him in 1939 titled *The Mental Measure of Merrill Moore*—A Psychometric Study of the Author of *M, One Thousand Autobiographical Sonnets*.

Moore, Dr. Wells wrote, had scored astonishingly high in various tests of intelligence and various psychiatric experiments with language or non-language symbols. Merrill had, too, an uncanny intuitive grasp of things. He was, I am sure, seldom depressed, rarely melancholy. He was sentimental, but never gushing. He was a disciplined man. After he went to Boston, we kept in touch by mail and telephone. During the Second World War he did magnificent things in setting up an army hospital in China. He sent poems and rhymes, some bawdy, as an army is, from New Zealand, where he was before going to China. No mention of loneliness, unhappiness, weariness, or boredom ever crept into his letters. I doubt if he felt any of these emotions. I long have believed that he wanted to be a priest or minister, but somehow could not, and so went into medicine. He quickly saw that the really troubled persons were those who were mentally disturbed. This drew him. At least a hundred exceptional acts of kindness to disturbed persons, young and old, are known to me. Two classmates were saved from suicide by him—one a narcotics addict and the other an alcoholic. Both were fully restored to mental health and productive work.

His intuition often was a sudden thing. A friend in Boston recalled that one night after a dinner—which he and Robert Frost had attended together—Merrill said that something had just occurred to him. Would he, Frost, ride a few miles out in the country? They drove, with no explanation from Merrill, turning, at last, into the huge-pillared entrance of a large estate, and along a curving drive to a darkened house. Merrill went confidently to the door, a curious Frost by his side, and made the heavy knocker boom. After a bit lights came on, and a robed, slippered figure (the butler as it turned out) turned on an outside light and cracked the door.

"Why, Dr. Moore," he exclaimed.

"Come in, Robert," said Moore.

Frost, according to the narrator of the story, later said that in the big, deeply carpeted entryway he could see two or three faces looking over the upstairs railing where the stairway led.

Merrill inquired if a young lady, whom we here shall call Mary Anne, was in. She was. She was one of those peering down from above.

Merrill, familiar with the house, walked through an entry into the library. The young lady, about twenty, came hesitatingly in.

"This is Mr. Robert Frost, Mary Anne," said Merrill. He added they had been driving by and had decided to stop and talk for a while. The young lady, Merrill informed Robert Frost, was a poet.

So they talked. The enchanted girl, soon over her initial nervousness, was asking questions and talking of her favorite poems by Frost. After about a half hour Merrill said they would be going. Driving out, said the teller of this story, Merrill replied, in answer to Frost's demand for a postponed explanation, "Therapy, Robert, therapy. You are her hero. She has been wanting to meet you but was too frightened to try. It suddenly occurred to me tonight that if we came in as we did she would be in your presence before she knew who you were, and talking with you before she had time to become disturbed. It worked admirably, Robert, and I am greatly obliged."

Merrill Moore died of cancer in 1957. Until a few days before his death he was writing sonnets. His practice, which was large, did not halt publication, at frequent intervals, of the volumes called Clinical Sonnets. In them his compassion for troubled humanity, and his deep insight into its weaknesses and strength, come through.

One of his psychiatrically based sonnets will illustrate:

> Mrs. Broderick was a very unusual woman,
> But she was different from what most people thought.
> They called her a hard woman, sinister,
> But she was neither sinister nor hard;
> That was a grotesque reputation nearly
> Forgotten now by those who crossed her yard.
>
> Actually she was extremely sympathetic.
> Once when two Italian laborers were correcting
> A leak in her cesspool she had a pitcher of lemonade
> Sent out from her kitchen. They were not expecting
> Such thoughtfulness; their gratitude was pathetic.

And another time she got up in the middle of the night
To pour ice water over some lobsters that
Were waiting in a sack to be boiled (alive) the next day;
She was a very unusual woman that way.

Looking back from the sixties to the twenties, the Fugitives
are seen as the best symbol of the South's campus response to the
many motivations of rebellion, or flight, from the tyranny of the
Southern Brahmin. Poems were written in class, pages from proposed new novels were read along the paths between classes.
They were fine sunlit days. The cup of life seemed always running over. A poem by Richard Eberhart, titled "If I Could Only
Live at the Pitch That Is near Madness," reminded me of those
years. It begins:

If I could only live at the pitch that is near madness
When everything is as it was in my childhood
Violent, vivid, and of infinite possibility:
That the sun and the moon broke over my head.

from "False Youth: Two Seasons"

JAMES DICKEY (1923–1997)

James Dickey was born in Atlanta, Georgia. His early interest centered on sports, particularly football and track. After attending Clemson University for one year, Dickey became a fighter-bomber pilot in the Pacific during World War II. After the war, he attended Vanderbilt University and his interest turned for the first time to poetry. He published his first poems in the Vanderbilt student literary journal, the *Gadfly*. After his graduation in 1948, he worked at various jobs, particularly in advertising, for the next decade. His first book of poetry, *Into the Stone* (1960), won him a Guggenheim Fellowship in 1961. Dickey won the 1966 National Book Award for Poetry for *Buckdancer's Choice* (1966), and *Life* magazine dubbed him "The Unlikeliest Poet," referring to his good-old-boy persona. The publication of his *Poems 1957–1967* (1967) established him as a major voice in American poetry. He took the position of poet-in-residence at the University of South Carolina in 1968 and remained in that position until his death. His first novel, *Deliverance* (1970), was critically and popularly acclaimed and Dickey went on to write the screenplay, suggest the musical theme "Duellin' Banjos," and act the role of Sheriff Bullard in the Academy Award-nominated film version of 1972. Dickey practiced his art well into his seventies, producing his final collection of poetry, *The Eagle's Mile* (1990), and his third novel, *To the White Sea* (1993). Following is a section from his "False Youth: Two Seasons" (1965).

WINTER

Through an ice storm in Nashville I took a student home,
Sliding off the road twice or three times; for this
She asked me in. She was a living-in-the-city
Country girl   who on her glazed porch broke off

An icicle, and bit through its blank bone: brought me
Into another life   in the shining-skinned clapboard house
Surrounded by a world where creatures could not stand,
Where people broke hip after hip. At the door my feet
Took hold, and at the fire I sat down with her blind
Grandmother. All over the double room were things
That would never freeze, but would have taken well
To ice: long tassels banging from lamps   curtains
Of beads   a shawl on the mantel   all endless things
To touch   untangle   all things intended to be
Inexhaustible to hands. She sat there, fondling
What was in reach   staring into the fire with me
Never batting a lid. I talked to her easily   eagerly
Of my childhood   my mother whistling in her heartsick bed
My father grooming his gamecocks. She rocked, fingering
The lace on the arm of the chair   changing its pattern
Like a game of chess. Before I left, she turned and raised
Her hands, and asked me to bend down. An icicle stiffened
In my stomach   as she drew on my one lock of hair
Feeling the individual rare strands   not pulling any
Out. I closed my eyes as she put her fingertips lightly
On them   and saw, behind sight   something in me   fire
Swirl in a great shape like a fingerprint   like none other
In the history of the earth   looping   holding its wild lines
Of human force. Her forefinger   then her keen nail
Went all the way along the deep middle line of my brow
Not guessing but knowing   quivering   deepening
Whatever I showed by it. She said, you must laugh a lot
Or be in the sun, and I began to laugh quietly against
The truth, so she might feel what the line she followed
Did then. Her hands fell   and she said to herself, My God,
To have a growing boy. You cannot fool the blind, I knew
As I battled for air   standing   laughing a lot as she
Said I must do   squinting also as in the brightest sun
In Georgia   to make good   to make good the line in my head.
She lifted her face like a swimmer; the fire swarmed

On my false, created visage   as she rocked and took up
The tassel of a lamp. Some kind of song may have passed
Between our closed mouths as I headed   into the ice.
My face froze with the vast world of time   in a smile
That has never left me since my thirty-eighth year
When I skated like an out-of-shape bear to my Chevrolet
And spun my wheels on glass that time when age was caught
In a thaw in a ravelling room   when I conceived of my finger
Print as a shape of fire   and of youth as a lifetime search
For the blind.

"'Mystery Boy' Looks for Kin in Nashville"

ROBERT HAYDEN (1913–1980)

Robert Hayden was born and raised in the Paradise Valley ghetto of Detroit. Despite the extreme myopia that worsened throughout his life, he became an early and avid reader. While acting in a Langston Hughes play in his college years, Hayden showed Hughes his first attempts at poetry, only to be told by the elder poet that they were derivative. After work in the late 1930s researching local black folklore and history for the Federal Writer's Project in Detroit and his marriage in 1940, Hayden enrolled in the English master's program at the University of Michigan. After taking his M.A., he was offered a position as assistant professor of English at Fisk University in 1946. He remained at Fisk until 1969. In addition to teaching, Hayden also served as adviser to the student literary journal, the *Herald*, and saw the magazine publish the work of such writers as William Demby, Lonne Elder, and Julius Elder. Hayden was close friends with fellow writer Arna Bontemps, who served as the librarian at Fisk, and art curator Myron O'Higgins, with whom Hayden privately published a small volume of poetry, *The Lion and the Archer* (1948). That book, like his 1955 *Figure of Time*, was published by Nashville's Hemphill Press. In 1949, Hughes and Bontemps published the important anthology *The Poetry of the Negro* and several of Hayden's poems of black history were included, the best known of which is "Middle Passage." The 1950s were largely an unproductive time for Hayden, but the changing aesthetics and politics of the 1960s were a boost to his creativity. But because of his belief in the Bahá'í tenet of the unity of mankind and his appreciation of traditional poetic forms, the black political poets of the 1960s largely ignored or openly assailed Hayden and his work. The first Black Writers' Conference held at Fisk in 1966, organized by writer-in-residence John O. Killens, turned into a virulent attack upon Hayden by the followers of Ron Karenga's black nationalist philosophy. Hayden left Fisk in 1969 to teach at his alma mater, the University of Michigan. Hayden was elected to the American Academy of Poets in 1975 and in 1976 was the first African American to be appointed Consultant in Poetry to the Library of Congress. The following poem is from his *Words in the Mourning Time* (1970).

Puzzle faces in the dying elms
promise him treats if he will stay.
Sometimes they hiss and spit at him
like varmints caught
in a thicket of butterflies.

A black doll,
one disremembered time,
came floating down to him
through mimosa's fancywork leaves and blooms
to be his hidden bride.

From the road beyond the creepered walls
they call to him now and then,
and he'll take off in spite of the angry trees,
hearing like the loudening of his heart
the name he never can he never can repeat.

And when he gets to where the voices were—
Don't cry, his dollbaby wife implores;
I know where they are, don't cry.
We'll go and find them, we'll go
and ask them for your name again.

from *Milbry*

BOWEN INGRAM (1906–1980)

Bowen Ingram was born in Gordonsville, Tennessee. After graduating from Cumberland University in Lebanon, Tennessee in
1924 and moving to Nashville, she went on to become a frequent contributor to such magazines as the *New Yorker*,
Seventeen, and *Town and Country*. Her first novel, *If Passion
Flies* (1945), was published shortly after she ended her wartime
military service at the U. S. Army Maneuver Headquarters at
Lebanon, Tennessee. *Light as the Morning* followed in 1954.
Milbry, her 1972 novel from which the following excerpt was
taken, was serialized in the *New Yorker*.

We had always gone to Nashville in spring and fall, to stay at a
hotel a week or two while we shopped for new clothes, saw our
dentist, and went to theatres and other places of cultural enter-
tainment, for Nashville was a city my parents, from having gone
to college there, considered the culture capital of the world. We
had stayed at the old Tulane, and the new Hermitage, but this
time Father took two rooms in a house across the street from the
capitol, on the corner of Cedar Street and Seventh Avenue.
Mother said that living across from the capitol would be a fine
cultural experience for Virginia and me, and that she was sure
we would learn to love Nashville like she and my father did.

It was a very cultured neighborhood. Half a block down
Seventh Avenue was the governor's mansion, and a full block
away was the corner where President Polk had once lived. Also
on that corner stood the telegraph pole that Senator Carmack
had fallen against when the Cooper brothers shot him, but street
hoodlums threw fresh red paint on it so often, to look like fresh
blood, that after one walk past the telegraph pole Mother
stopped us from strolling down Seventh Avenue. She had found
a part-time nurse to take Virginia and me out, in the afternoon

only, but she instructed her also not to leave our block. I was soon so bored by walking from one corner to the other, beside Virginia's carriage, that I longed to back to the homeplace.

Our side of the block was lined with tall brick houses set close together, all with high mansard roofs, and windows rounded over the top like surprised eyebrows, and front lawns no bigger than little green aprons. Across the street there was no sidewalk and the capitol grounds rose so steeply from a rocky bluff that we couldn't even see the tower on the capitol building. I was beginning to dislike Nashville very much when our nurse discovered that all of the neighborhood children played on the capitol grounds in the afternoon, and asked me if we could go there. I asked my parents.

"It doesn't seem dignified," Mother said.

"There's no law against it," Father said, remembering he had once been a lawyer.

"If it is a neighborhood custom I suppose it is all right," she said. "But mind you don't romp through the flower beds."

The next afternoon we joined the group on the capitol grounds, and I began to love Nashville.

The grounds were beautifully kept. The trees were as fine as our trees at home, the shrubs were thick, and the flower beds full of bloom. The grass was everywhere thick and green, and not many grown people came on the grounds, with the legislature in adjournment, and those who did walked straight to the capitol building without leaving the cement walk. On the Sixth Avenue side the flower beds around Andrew Jackson's statue restricted playing, and higher up, near the esplanade, there were beds of blooming cannas, but the large area between Sixth Avenue and Cedar had only shrubs and grass, and it sloped gently to the retaining wall, so it was here that nurses and children gathered every afternoon.

The nurses left the baby carriages on the sidewalk below the wall and carried the babies up to lie on the grass in the shade, while they sat and gossiped with one another and the bigger children fanned out in play at their backs. We soon realized that unless one of us fell down and cried, or started a fight, our nurses would not pay us any attention, so more and more often we roamed farther away from them, feeling joyfully free of correction or admonishment. Naturally, with so much space and so many trees and shrubs to hide behind, our favorite game was hide-and-seek. Often, while crouched behind a tree or shrub near the esplanade, we saw gardeners stop weeding the canna beds to peer at us, frowning, but nothing was said to us, either to stop us or warn us off, and soon we were roaming boldly beside the canna beds in search of new hiding places.

One day I joined a group scouting a canna bed just below the esplanade. The big coral blooms had looked as solid as a roof, from a distance, but on this inspection we found the stalks grew far enough apart to let a child slip between them, and the big sword-shaped leaves were not at all as sharp to the touch as we had feared. I was feeling of a leaf, surprised by its tenderness, when a cross-looking gardener appeared from nowhere.

"Stop that!" he yelled at me. "Don't touch them flowers!"

I snatched my hand back from the leaf and stared at him. He went on yelling, "Don't you even get close to them blooms. They's fraygile!" I was so entranced by this pronunciation of fragile that I still stood and looked at him, although the other children had scampered away. He glared at me, repeating angrily, "I said, 'They's fraygile.' They crush easy! You leave 'em alone!"

He raised a threatening arm, and I scampered too.

But the temptation of the canna bed returned. Having long forgotten parental orders to leave the flowers alone, I sneaked back a few days later, to test their defense solo. Nobody yelled at me, this time. I didn't see the cross-looking gardener. My nurse was happily gossiping, with her back turned to me, and did not see me slip quickly in and out of the bed.

I went back again, a few days later, and slipped quickly in and out, without getting caught, and this convinced me that I could get by with hiding in the canna bed if only I hid alone. The next day when we began playing hide-and-seek, I slipped into the green gloom and crouched among the canna stalks, with my head carefully bent beneath the coral roof, and waited in gleeful silence for the "it" to give me up. Almost immediately, however, the cross- looking gardener gave furious tongue.

"I told you to stay out of there," he yelled. "You didn't mind! Now, I'm gonna stop you from coming here a-tall!"

I beat it hastily back to my playmates who, attracted by the noise, were watching the scene seriously, but we quickly went on with our game, unworried by his threat. The next afternoon, when the nurses and children started up the capitol steps, guards barred our way. They had orders, they said, to keep us off the grounds from this day forward. At once there was loud argument, protest, and enraged outcry from nurses and children, which, failing to move the guards, eventually recoiled on me.

"You're the cause of it! You're the one that hid in the cannas!" both children and nurses yelled at me. Even my own nurse denounced me bitterly as she rushed me home to report to Mother, furiously, that I was a bad child and nobody in our neighborhood would hereafter have anything to do with me.

"Nor me neither," she added. "I quit!"

"You're discharged," said Mother calmly. "You were supposed to look after the child and prevent this sort of thing. You neglected your duty."

After that she got another nurse to take Virginia out in the afternoons, and took me out herself. Usually, we went shopping. It was time I learned quality and value, she said, which I couldn't learn in Mr. James's store at home. We were only two blocks from the Nashville shopping section and I might never have such a fine opportunity again, she said.

The shopping area was all in a two-block loop beginning at the corner of Seventh Avenue and Church Street, down Church to Fifth Avenue, left, down Fifth to Union, and left back up to Sixth. This included four big department stores: Castner-Knott and Co., Lebeck Brothers, Cain and Sloan, and D. Loveman, Berger, and Teitlebaum, with many small specialty shops and restaurants between. When we went to a restaurant at night, Father took us to Skowlowski's, but in daytime Mother and I liked to go to The Ocean because it had imitation orange trees along its walls, with lighted glass oranges. Mother called the small shops Quality Shops and much preferred them to the big department stores, but I liked the big stores because there was so much more to see, so she allowed me to learn, first, in the department stores.

Her method of instructing me was simple. We did not actually buy a great deal, but she made me look at the same article in all of the four big stores and, by comparing the price and quality in each store, decide which was the better buy. Occasionally, to test my progress, she gave me a dollar and turned me loose to shop alone, and afterward asked how I had spent it and instructed me on why I had made a good buy, or bad. This adult treatment made me feel so important I didn't at all mind not playing with children on the capitol lawn, and I had completely forgotten the cross-looking gardener until, one day, as I prowled through the jewelry section of a department store while my mother tried on hats in the hat section, I saw a rope of beads that caused me to stop abruptly and stare.

It hung on a tall rack on the top of a glass counter, and inside the counter were several more like it, spread flat. I knew it was long enough to wind three times around my neck because, at home, in an old trunk, we had a rope of beads its length and exactly like it both in thickness and the way the little beads were woven over the rope. The difference was that these beads were of iridescent glass, and the beads at home were coral, and these were woven over new white cotton rope, and ours on brown Irish seaweed. These were new, and ours was an antique heirloom. I fingered the price tag. One dollar. The rope at home, Mother had told me, was priceless.

It was priceless because there was none other like it in America, she had told me. It had once belonged to Miss Maggie Murphey, who had brought it from Ireland when her husband came to fight with the Union Army, during the Civil War, and she came with him. Miss Maggie had said there was none other like it in America, and few in Ireland, because it was an heirloom in her family, woven on Irish seaweed, generations back, in an Irish folk art lost to the modern world. The story of Miss Maggie and the necklace was my favorite of all the homeplace stories, and I thrilled again at the memory of how she had said, as an old lady on her deathbed, handing the necklace to Mother, a little girl, "Ye must treasure it always, for there is none other like it in the whole world!"

When my mother repeated these words she rolled the r's in "treasurrre" and "worrld" like Miss Maggie had, and added that someday the necklace would be mine to keep and I must treasure it, too, and I felt sure that I would. Now the problem, after the shock of discovering the lost art had not only been found but was actually on display in a department store, was whether the glass beads were worth more than their price or our coral beads worth less. I fingered the price tag again. I had a dollar. Should I buy? Would Mother judge I had bought well or badly when I opened the package at home? Should I bring her to see the beads and let her decide? I tried to think what to do.

. . .

"Don't touch the beads, little girl, unless you intend to buy!"

From nowhere a lady clerk had sprung up behind the counter. I had forgotten I was still holding the price tag. I had forgotten the beads of glass. I snatched away my hand and, stung by the "little girl" tone, brought out my dollar to show that I could buy if I chose. But the problem of value was still not decided in my mind. I felt that Mother should know the truth about the corals and know their real worth, yet. . . . All at once the coral canna bed on Capitol Hill flashed into my mind, with the blooms looking as solid as a roof and the cross-looking gardener saying, ". . . fraygile, . . . fraygile. You leave 'em alone."

The clerk lifted the beads from the rack and spread them on the counter. They glittered like frost, although her voice had now turned warm.

"They would make a lovely gift for your mother," she said coaxingly. "Shall I wrap them for you?"

I looked in the direction of the hat section and saw Mother coming toward us. She was smiling with the inner pleasure that came when she had enjoyed a trying-on and resisted the temptation to buy. Suddenly, I stuffed the dollar back in my pocket.

"Oh, no!" I said to the clerk and ran fast to meet Mother and stop her before she saw the beads.

She paused, when we met, asking gaily, "Well! Did you have any luck?"

I caught her hand and tugged her around to face a side exit. "It's hot in here," I said. "Let's go to The Ocean and get a sherbet. This is the quickest way out." And, as she still hesitated and looked at me undecidedly, I added, "We can window-shop the quality shops on the way. These big stores have nothing but trash, Mother. Please, from now on, take me to the little shops that you like, so I can learn more about values." Surprised, pleased, and approving, she fell for it.

"I'm glad you realize that," she said, as we headed for the exit. "Quality is so important!"

With luck, I thought, if I kept her in the little shops from now on, she might never know about the glass beads and the lost folk art now found, and she would happily go on believing Miss Maggie's story the way Miss Maggie had told it. This would mean I had lapsed a second time from our family dedication to truth in art, and might suffer secret feelings of guilt about it like I had about loving our ugly house, but I owed my mother a return courtesy, I thought, for her serene conviction it had not been my fault that all the children in our neighborhood had been barred from playing on the capitol grounds.

from *A Wake for the Living*

ANDREW NELSON LYTLE (1902–1995)

Andrew Nelson Lytle was born in Murfreesboro, Tennessee. Before becoming a writer, editor, actor, and playwright, he was educated at Sewanee Military Academy and Vanderbilt University. His undergraduate studies under John Crowe Ransom and attendance at Fugitive meetings were inspiring. Influenced by literary classmates such as Robert Penn Warren and Allen Tate, whose first prose works were Civil War biographies, he published *Bedford Forrest and His Critter Company* in 1931. His novel, *The Long Night*, appeared in 1936. Later he taught at Southwestern University, the University of the South, the State University of Iowa, and the University of Florida. He was editor of the *Sewanee Review* from 1943 until 1948. Lytle was a regular contributor to the *Georgia Review*, the *National Review*, and a wide variety of other journals. He received a Guggenheim fellowship in 1941 which allowed him to live in New Orleans for six months to work on *At The Moon's Inn*. He wrote two more novels—*A Name for Evil* (1947) and *The Velvet Horn* (1957). The following excerpt was taken from his 1975 *A Wake for the Living: A Family Chronicle*. In a 1960 letter to Allen Tate, he describes his intention for writing the family story for his daughters: "I'm going to do this little memoir with the fable of instructing the three girls as to who they are."

It is inconceivable now with vacationers flying or driving half around the world, commuting between the great world cities or even the little cities, how much a part of our life the watering places filled. There were some ten in Franklin County. Those out in the country had to be reached by buggy or hacks which the proprietors had waiting upon the trains passing through Estill Springs. There were inns at Estill itself; or, if you were going to Winchester Springs, some five miles in the country, you got off at Winchester probably, although it was on the branch line to Huntsville, and rode out from there. Grandma preferred this watering place, as did Papa's mother, who lived in Nashville until Major Nelson bought the old Coulon place, Villa Rose, at Thibodaux.

She writes in her diary, so full of woes, Wednesday 7th of July, 1852, "We all, Ma, Major Nelson [her husband], Mary Jane Nelson [stepdaughter], and Price [a son by her first marriage], all left Nashville on the cars for Winchester Springs. I had a sick headache all the way. We got here at 12 o'clock yesterday. Found the Springs much crowded, quite common folks . . . Col Johnson's family, Sue Wheless came with us [all kin and connections] I was quite sick all day."

Papa, her son, was six months old at the time. No doubt part of her trouble was aftereffects of childbirth. She was frequently cauterized by Dr. Ford. "O! I suffer so much with my back—I feel so disheartened! So sad! Will I never know health again? I went to my meals stayed to see them dance—quite late. Felt much fatigued. Aunt Mary Johnson left for home."

After guests coming and going, "We left the springs at 2 o'clock got on the cars at 3—got to Murfreesboro at 6—found all well at Mr. Crichlow's. [He married Major Nelson's sister Sarah.] Brother Tom and Jim Wheless came up on the cars from Nashville. Johnny was sick all night last night had a hot fever. Mrs. Keeble, Miss Thomson, Miss Elliott, Mrs. Avent came to see us."

Tues. Aug. 10, 1852

Had a hard rain last night. Johnny sick all night. I feel very weak. Mrs. Williams and Mrs. Wade were to see me. Misses Curran were to see Mary and Ma.

Wed.

Kitty came staid all day and night. Mrs. Burton and Miss Donelson came in the evening. Mrs. Brady was to see me. I feel some better today. Johny not at all well.

Thurs.

Mrs. Horace Keeble and Mrs. Spence were to see me. We all went
to spend the day with Mrs. Helen Crichlow. Mrs. Spence was
there, too. We all went to see Cousin Nancy Lawing. Has a sweet
babe.

The next day the Nelsons return to Nashville. Either in town or
country there was this continual visiting. All of the family names
she mentions I know, but little about the persons themselves. What
I do know is that this is a community functioning by visits and conversation, where all the family news is told, all the good and bad
happenings, and the important matters of birth and death. No television to canker the minds and lull them into emptiness.

At Estill Springs there was the Beard House, a famous place in
my mother's day. It was run by Miss Maria, born a Drumgoole
and married to Captain Beard, who was enamored of the deathless Muse. He made and won a bet that he could ride in a buggy
at a walk from Lebanon to Murfreesboro and never stop quoting verse nor repeat himself. He won the bet and at Estill would
sit on the front verandah reading aloud or to himself, interrupting only to call out, "Maria, Maria, the hogs are in the yard."
She would come merrily and drive them out.

He was a lawyer, a man of sensibility, agent for insurance companies which lapsed through his attentions to the deathless Muse.
He went briskly about town, savoring all sensuous temptations.
Meeting my father on the Square, he hailed him. "Bobby, I had a
fine mess of chitlings today, and none too clean." After Miss
Maria's death the two of them were in the habit of discussing the
captain's twilight courtship of Miss Curra Wendel. It did not
thrive. He couldn't figure what to do with Miss Emma, the sister
who did the heavy work of gardening, attending to orchards and
vines on their back premises, hidden by tall board fences, so that
no zephyr could taint their wrinkled virginity. When the captain's
knock on the door resounded through the house and no one
answered, he took this as a bad omen and gave up his suit.

Miss Sally, his daughter, had flashing eyes, rapid speech, and dramatic ways. On Confederate Memorial Day, with the battle flag wrapped about her, she stood within the circle of unknown but cherished dead and in quavering voice recited Father Ryan's sentimental poem on the Lost Cause. Jean Marie, her daughter, married General Douglas MacArthur.

There were many desperate lovers in Murfreesboro, whose imaginations equaled their passions. Mr. Peter Binford, a cousin of John C. Calhoun's, was a farmer and man of many interests. He had the great gift of being able to work Negro women in the field. Indeed, for a new dress he got his housekeeper to paint the house. But his passion was no distant Muse. It was Miss Katie Fowler, who lived across the street from Mama's and next to the Campbellite church. But it was in the First Presbyterian choir that she sang, and it was there that the miracle happened. It was a miracle of love. I do not say necessarily profane. There before Mr. Binford's eyes, he said, as her breast was palpitating with song, the sack of love broke about her heart, and the heart leaped two feet towards him.

The widow Fowler, being a good Presbyterian, did not believe in miracles. She forbade him the house. He told his friends he would pick every pinfeather out of old Mrs. Fowler's hide. When this rumor reached her, she set about having him put in the asylum. When the case reached court, Mr. Binford's distinguished lawyer cousin pled that any man in love was insane, and he proved this to the jury and judge's satisfaction by quoting from the poets. They decided you could not incarcerate a man for a metaphor.

He wanted my father to be his partner in a business deal. He had heard there was good money in frog legs on the Chicago market.

"How will we get them there?" my father asked.

"Hop them," he said.

There was one woman in town who baffled all her lovers. This was Miss Carmine Collier. She had an erect carriage, and I remember her best in a mustard-colored coatsuit, very handsomely cut, and it showed to advantage her figure. She wore a white leghorn hat, which I must say did much to soften and enhance features as constant as a doll's. There was a hat for more tempting occasions, one with a stiff straight brim, wide against the sun and, perched upon its top, a bird of paradise, whose plumes looked like running but diluted gold. They trembled in the wind as she walked.

She was an aging virgin, and she was a miser. She had a bird-like eye, that of a sparrow hawk, round, impenetrable, bright, and forever veiled by the distant focus of a high perch. She was a committed miser, but often courted. Amorous pleas, the abject knee, all were denied. One lover, understanding her refusal, said, "Carmine, if you will marry me, I'll put down two dollars where you put one." He only thought he understood her. She already had her love, and she guarded it well. Her routine favored her money's increase. Once she took her meals at Miss Betty Ferrell's. She took the midday meal and ate heartily, a late one so that she could go to the second run of the movie, in time to go home and drink a glass of milk and pass it before she went to bed.

One day I was playing on the hearth at Mammy's, and Miss Carmine came in to thank Mammy for the small bouquet, the bride of death holds in its hand in the coffin. The two old women had each promised the other this small service. Mrs. Ready, Miss Carmine's mother died first. She had been a merry, fat little old lady when I first saw her, dressed in black in perpetual widowhood. Her first husband, Mr. Collier, had brought her back from a steamboat trip to New Orleans. He had died, leaving his widow for consolation Miss Carmine, a big house on East Main, and money to keep it up.

But widowhood is a wearisome business, and it was noted after a while that Colonel Ready was making regular calls. The calls continued and, as time goes, had reached and passed the moment for proposal. Her brother-in-law pointed this out and not only asked his intentions but defined them for him.

The colonel made a fine figure of a man, very stiff and imposing in manner and address. He had been to Congress, and he looked so much the part of the gentleman that after the war he had been hired by the old Waldorf-Astoria to entertain its Southern guests. General John Morgan had married Colonel Ready's sister Mattie, with Jefferson Davis and the high-ranking generals in the Army of Tennessee as witnesses. He felt himself very much the Ready of Readyville. By profession a lawyer, he found that there was little need for his services those days. Land prices were depressed, and nobody had any money. Except, it seems, the widow Collier.

It suited him to be a gentleman, but he found the widow did not approve of an idle man. She set him up in the grocery business. He stood about his storehouse impatiently, like a man who has been kept waiting by his wife.

Broilers and frying-size chickens waited for purchase in small flat coops made out of what looked like dowel pins. There was a little trapdoor on top, by which you reached in and took out a chicken. You could never mistake what part of the store the coops stood in. Their odor was distinctive.

A very insistent woman wanted to buy a chicken, and the colonel gallantly tried to oblige her. He bent over from the waist and reached into the coop and brought forth by its legs a squawking bird.

"No, not that one. The little speckled pullet."

Although the colonel was red-faced from bending over, his courtesy did not fail him. He tried again, but the little speckled pullet, fearing the worst, managed to dart out of his reach. He rose up. "Madam, if you want that God-damn pullet, you'll have to catch her yourself."

Obviously the colonel was not sympathetic to the new order of things. He passed over to, we hope, a better world, leaving Mrs. Collier again a widow and leaving again Miss Carmine for solace. And now Miss Carmine was alone. She and Mammy were in Mammy's back bedroom, which had a fireplace, and there I was playing on the cold hearth, the very hearth Mammy used as an example of her disapproval of cremation. "If you put the jar of ashes on the mantel there," she said, "and not bury him in a Christian manner, the second wife is sure to knock the jar and break it on the hearth; then sweep the ashes into the fireplace." This she said to another visitor with newfangled ways. Now she turned very pointedly to Mrs. Ready's daughter. "Carmine," she said, "you are in that big house all by yourself. Now you go and buy you some hats. Go to Florida in the winter and to the springs in the summer and get you a man.

"Miss Kate," she replied, "I have thought about it. But suppose I was lying in bed with that man. Suppose he wanted the window up and I wanted it down. He would have his way, and I'd freeze to death."

"I never got cold in bed with a man," Mammy said. "I had to take a fan to bed with Bob."

Mammy died in my sophomore year at Vanderbilt. She died of pernicious anaemia. It would have another name by now. She had had a sentimental vision of this final departure. She would stand on the deck of that old Ship of Zion and wave good-bye to friends and kin. She made careful preparations for her interment. There was the shroud, slippers and stockings, and a needle and thread. Andrewena, her daughter, was often in a tight for stockings and would borrow them. So she made sure her burial clothes were intact. She took from the cedar chest fine linen sheets and towels and gave them to my mother, who was helping. My mother felt it unseemly at such a time to take them. "You'd better take them now, or you'll never get them," she said, and sure enough they were quietly put back in the chest.

But the Heavens didn't open and float that old ship to receive her. She had a slow dying and a long wait for her beloved, that younger son cast away in Texas. It was seen that he must be sent for. More and more her blood turned to water, until she could not sit up. A board was built across the counterpane, with a pillow upon it. And here she lay her head, waiting. She would not die until he came. She was no longer speaking when he arrived, but her will was strong. She raised her arms about his neck, as he bent down to receive the farewell embrace.

Only today did it occur to me that I never heard my grandfather Nelson speak of his father or his childhood on Acadia, or of the ravishment of their places on Bayou LaFourche during the Civil War; yet he must have been fourteen or fifteen when the war ended. I never even heard him mention the rice crop he made just after his marriage. I got third hand from his younger brother George that in settling up he had to pull a pistol on a surly field hand.

He was about eighteen months when his mother died. Major Nelson bought in the Cumberland Mountains above Sparta a summer place they called Bon Air. Coming home in early August, she opened a trunk and, in shaking out the clothes, caught the fever and died. So it was thought, at the time of the Yellow Fever epidemic in 1853. Nobody suspected the mosquito then. Her death in a sense orphaned the two little boys. Neither Papa nor his brother George ever knew their mother, and Major Nelson had a large family by his first wife. When he died in 1877 at the age of eighty-five, he had nine children, twenty-six grandchildren, and nineteen great-grandchildren. There was a strong family feeling, but the two little boys, without any unkindness, were made to feel their alien blood. They were half uncles to grown men and women, and certainly their inheritance was lost.

Major Nelson's son-in-law, Andrew Jackson Donelson, Jr., was the active manager and partner in their sugar business. He died in 1858, when Major Nelson was in his late sixties. But the aging man put Villa Rose and Acadia together and prospered until the Yankees swept him cleaner than the seven-year locusts: slaves, sugar, sugarcane, wagons and teams, all supplies, even fence posts and rails.

The economy never recovered, but Papa's kin continued to live high, spending the winter at the St. Charles in New Orleans, keeping servants and a carriage, when they should have practiced the severest economy. After Major Nelson died, the plantations fell to the factor, Edward J. Gay. His descendants, I believe, still own Acadia and the oil wells beneath the ground.

I now understand what I didn't for years, why Papa called himself a self-made man. That phrase was in the air, along with from shirt sleeves to shirt sleeves; but this was not what he meant. He meant that he did not rely on former prosperity and the pride of lost possessions, so prevalent in the South. Generally the child of the second wife, if she dies young, has to fend for himself, which he did. Never did he compromise on matters of principle or business. Usually in taking up lumber, where there is a doubt, you take a board and give a board. He fought over every board he thought was his. And so it was in all things, and he is bound to have learned this in Louisiana. His brother George was another matter. Once he wired Papa to send five hundred dollars to save the honor of the family. The telegraph was as public as a town crier. Papa brought him to Tennessee and formed some kind of partnership in a sawmill at Tullahoma. A lot of money was lost and Uncle George returned to Thibodaux.

Rutherford County was the Nelson seat, and Papa after he settled in Murfreesboro never left, except once to go to San Antonio after he had sold the light plant. One other time, before his oldest son Hewlett died, they went to San Francisco to look for his older half-brother William, who had disappeared in that direction. The two men from Murfreesboro got so lonesome, in that faraway place, that Papa said, "You go around the block and I will meet you." They shook hands as exiles meet unexpectedly in a foreign land.

He died some years before Mammy, while I was at Oxford. He had been out hunting doves and caught pneumonia, dying of peritonitis. Brother Smith, the Presbyterian minister, sent word that he was taking him to the Marster every evening in his prayers. Papa thanked him but sent word he would take it kindly if he brought him back in the morning.

He saw that I was in a nest of women and tried to interest me in masculine sports. I would go along to pick up the doves, and he would let me carry and sometimes shoot the rifle he brought along for squirrels. He was naturally affectionate. I remember him rubbing his whiskers against my smooth cheek, and I pulled away, as a child will. He said the women in his house nearly froze him to death. If it was so, it was because they had no adequate way to show their love and respect.

John Greer, once the houseboy, considered himself Papa's Boswell or tattler, and brought up the grandchildren on stories of his prowess and at times, his superhuman insight, such as seeing a hand through a board fence sitting down on the other side. Or, again, an entire military camp in Texas adopting his style of profanity. In front of the jail, he knocked a man down with a brickbat, sent John for his shotgun and chair and sat down, waiting the arrival of the man's kin riding in from the country. He rode over once on horseback to an enemy's lumberyard and threw his reins to a hand there. The enemy would not meet him, as John said he locked himself in, but he fired the hand who had held the horse, and Papa promptly hired him. And so the stories went, first to me, then to Polly, and then to little John Nelson, the youngest grandson.

John Greer came back from the Spanish-American War drinking heavily. The colonel, whose orderly he had been, tried to lure him to Ohio, but in those days Murfreesboro kept its own. John was extremely light in color, and I think his drinking arose from the confusion he must have felt about his blood and station. He felt as often happened that he was a member of the family, which indeed he was. I did a bad thing to him as a child. He spoke of something as ours, and I, under what training I don't know, said, "It's not yours, John, but ours." He smiled a sickly grin, but the moment passed, although I remember it to this day.

When I was away at school, he was the night watchman at the mill and lived there. I would go to the office on Sundays, where his friends, Shelton and others, sat and talked. He would bow excessively low at my entrance and with irony brush the seat I sat in. The morning's visit would begin. How big an ass I made of myself, as I pronounced large generalities from little learning, I blush to think about. The manners of the listeners were perfect, and so the visit was a real visit. At his death he wanted me to have what money he had. He had only married his wife "to keep the police from bothering him." But of course she got the few hundred dollars, although she indicated to Big John that there was more, like ignorant people who equate value with money. The puzzle of the bloods was settled when he was buried in the Nelson lot at Evergreen.

Curiously enough, it was through John that I met Sophia DeShields Lytle Harrison, my great-grandfather's last wife. I was on the wagon seat as he delivered a load of stovewood. She was then living in the house where once she had known so full and rich a life, with children and servants to look after. This day she stood before us, a woman in black, on a porch in the eastern wing of the house. We had driven up between the house and a large, brick building, the old kitchen then abandoned. The porch was in disrepair.

As John asked where to throw the wood, I looked about. I didn't know my connection with her or the house. He, with perfect manners that did not, however, disguise the business at hand nor was in any way servile, told her who I was. I don't think she spoke. She merely looked down at me, like a sibyl, wrinkled and remote. I was accustomed to smiling greetings and felt chastened, almost deprived of my humanity. Had I returned her to that moment of betrayal, or did she see somewhat a likeness to my grandfather, the one stepchild who spoke to her.

Her picture shows the merriest eye, but she seemed to me an ancient; yet she would live to be over a hundred and die in 1927, the same year her youngest son, Uncle Marion, died in the Dakotas. He was the son closest to his mother, the youngest who left home to keep from killing his stepfather. Or so it was said. I saw him once, a small, alert youngish man, slim and well dressed and with old-fashioned manners. He had brought me an alligator from Florida, which we kept in a tub in the old conservatory where John Greer fed it raw bits of meat on a straw. I used to hold its tail in my mouth for a penny or ten pins.

He went first to the University of Virginia, at a troubled time. A freedman knocked his hat off with a cane, and he shot and killed him. The judge and jury freed him after a short trial, and it was said he gave them a thousand-dollar dinner to celebrate. He left Virginia, however, and graduated from Princeton in Woodrow Wilson's class. He wandered about, getting ready one time to go to the gold strike in Alaska. He never married but did some courting, especially to a schoolteacher in Colorado. The sheriff of the county was his rival. Once they called upon the lady at the same time. There were words, for Uncle Marion picked him up and spitted him on a picket fence. I suppose he had to leave Colorado, too. At last he stopped at the ranch in one of the Dakotas.

He must have been lonely, for a Nichol cousin stopped over on business and when he tried to leave, Uncle Marion refused to let him, even drawing a gun. This is told in the family. In 1927 my father wrote him a letter, asking him to come live with us at Cornsilk, near Guntersville. A letter was returned with a newspaper clipping. He had been found dead on his ranch, his head in one place and his body in another. The stabled horses were almost starved.

I must have seen Sopilia DeShields Lytle Harrison the last time she would live in the house, but it was much later on that I got interested in it. I tried to persuade my father to buy the place, but he said the land that went with the house was the poorest on the farm. Before we talked, I had gone into the house to look. The door stood open to winds and weather. The long hall held the empty silence of a grim hospitality. In places the French block wallpaper hung in strips, showing the heavy plaster behind. It was the color of tobacco juice with threads of hog hair all twisted through it. The hair kept the plaster from cracking. At first I thought the tiny black curlicues were worms.

I climbed to the third floor, into the ballroom. It extended the length of the house, although it was narrow and the ceiling low. There were windows at the two ends which, in the gallop and swing of the dance, would not have relieved much the closeness of the air nor have done more than stir the sweet and sour odors of the heated bodies. The ceiling pressing down upon the whirling heads surely gave a sense of intimacy more compelling than touch. The floor was littered with old letters. There was a desk out of place. I read a few letters, mostly Harrison, and did not pursue this.

The halls, above and below, ran the length of the house. Dividing the lower hall was an arch with two fluted columns. Underneath the floors there were tunnels, dug no doubt during the Civil War for hiding or quick escape. Bill Patterson told me he used to crawl through them as a child, and he thought there was some entry into a room. One of them led into the potato cellar.

The stairway was at the very back, at the southern end of the hall. Down this I stepped and for a moment looked at the scenes on the papered walls. In front the light blurred itself upon the dirty fanlike panes above the entranceway. Towards this I moved, past gentlemen hunting the wild boar, past the bear at bay before leaping hounds, several lying torn and ripped by fangs and claw. There was a castle in the distance and a milder scene, a campfire near ruins, within the foreground a stag hanging from a tree and hunters eating their collops of deer. The scene changed abruptly, as if to mark a gentler habit: English men and women riding elegantly, with the fox not too distant, not a hair out of place in his brush, as unruffled as if he had just stepped over the edge of time. Save for a strip of paper hanging loose, the elegant hooves and the postured riders and the red, red fox might have galloped out of their meadows and century into the nearby gondola scene and Aphrodite's round temple.

The doors to the four rooms which opened into the hall were closed. I passed into the light of day, no ghosts following, only dust motes languidly stirring.

There had been a cabin, later turned into a loom room. The two-story weatherboarded log house built by the captain was torn down by Captain Harrison, Uncle Marion reported in anger, and used to build two cabins. What cedar was left he sold. This, the last house, had been built by the younger son, my grandfather's father, in 1836. The bricks were made on the farm, the mantels and trim brought from Philadelphia, that capital of the West long after it had lost its preeminence for the country as a whole.

As I walked out of the house, over the cedar floorboards of the porch, weathered almost white, and looked back through the small columns to the door standing ajar, I suddenly felt the ruin that had overtaken all that this dwelling had held. But in spite of this I believed the house and what it represented could be restored, or I wanted to believe it. Today the Carnation Milk Company's plant stands where the house stood. A few large trees and the office, now a tool shed, remain. Saw briers and indifferent kinds of grass cover the four-acre garden where Nancy used to sit in a canopied chair, among her roses, and direct the slaves at their work. Across the Nashville Pike, where the plot of cedar grew, a shopping center faces its parking units.

from "Remembrances for D. D."

JESSE WILLS (1899–1977)

Nashville native Jesse Ely Wills was a member of the Fugitives and a frequent contributor of poetry to their influential literary magazine. He served as associate editor of *The Fugitive* for one of its four years. In a 1922 letter to Donald Davidson, Allen Tate reckoned Wills "the finest talent in Nashville." In the same year, John Crowe Ransom wrote that Wills's poem "Eden" was "by long odds the best poem of considerable length that a Fugitive has yet perpetrated." Wills received his B.A. from Vanderbilt University in 1922, having studied under Ransom. Wills frequently read before the Old Oak Club and the Coffee House Club, two Nashville literary clubs of which he was a long-term member. He served for forty years as an officer and executive of the company his father helped found, the National Life and Accident Insurance Company, and retired in 1967 as chairman of the board. He served for many years as a trustee of Vanderbilt and his papers are housed in the Heard Library at the school. An avid gardener, Wills served as president of the American Iris Society and won a Dykes Medal from that organization for originating the "Chivalry" variety of iris. His publications include *Early and Late: Fugitive Poems and Others* (1959) and *Conversation Piece and Other Poems* (1965). His poems are included in *Fugitives: An Anthology of Verse* (1928). The following is from Wills's "Remembrances for D. D.," dedicated to Donald Davidson, from his *Nashville and Other Poems* (1973).

PART III

Nashville on bluffs within the crook of river,
A place where long ago an unknown race
Left mounds and stone box graves, so many graves.
How long ago were they, five centuries, ten?

Who were they? Were they Uchees, later named,
Who called themselves the Children of the Sun,
Living among the Creeks in separate towns.
Whatever tribe they were, why did they go,
Leaving their old fields empty for so long,
Turned back to forest? No one really knows.
Three centuries ago the Shawnees came
Out of the north to live along the river
The French called Chauvanon, now Cumberland,
We know about the trading post a Frenchman
Set up by the salt spring. We also know
Of warfare with the Chickasaw, Cherokee,
Till Shawnees who were wanderers at best
Drifted away, except for those who died
In a final ambuscade. So silence fell
Again on river, field, and forest while
Game multiplied, so even bison herds
Sought out the salt lick. The long hunters came,
And then the meeting over land and water
Of Robertson and Donelson; the Indian years
Behind the stockades, Battle of the Bluffs
That ended with the snarling leap of hounds.
All this we knew who wandered paths not far
From the great oak above a constant spring.
Don felt that past the most and in his verse
Raised up with dragon teeth from out the earth
Tall forms of men who fought and loved and died,
Whose seed grows even taller in our time.

Nashville had nurtured us. We cherished
The heritage it gave us, without thinking
Too much of years before the Civil War,
The city that was Whig, aristocratic, cultured
After the pioneers and after Jackson;
An Athens in the west before the Parthenon,

A prosperous oasis, mannered, proud.
Somehow the earthquake of the Civil War
Foreshortened gracious days preceding it;
Living above the sod of battlefields,
We skipped from Robertson to Forrest, Hood.
Nor did we dwell much on the years that followed,
Years of our parents' childhood or their youth,
While Nashville changed through times both bad and good,
The prestige then with railroads, banking, trade.
Old Nashville was in City Cemetery,
And newer Nashville increased Olivet,
The great and little with their struggles done,
Their histories reduced to names and dates.
We rimed of death but did not ponder graves.

Nashville we loved although we might deplore
The black coal smog in winter. We might say
It was not the city we once knew;
It was growing too much, we said, after the war,
Not the Civil War but Mr. Wilson's War,
So close behind us. This had taken some to France,
To Oxford. Now here we were together
At Vanderbilt, unchanged, but gathering force
To leap into new buildings and new growth.
We were students, teachers, some ex-soldiers, friends,
Most rather young, some younger, but we respected
Old wisdom in a ritual hospitality.
And some were shy and awkward, insecure,
And some were gay as grasshoppers in the sun,
Forestalling doubt with laughter, hiding this
With deferential, surface gravity at tea
With dowagers on campus. There we walked
The wellworn, wellknown paths from class to class,
Or from frat houses took the streetcar down
To Union Street where taller buildings rose.

As heirs of time, we shared the motor age;
Out the long street, West End and Harding Road,
The Essex and the Hudson hissed along;
Pierce-Arrow deemed the Cadillac parvenu.

We lived within a quiet, free of causes,
The League of Nations lost, prosperity
The slogan of the New South, President
Harding, then Coolidge. We were shamed perhaps
By the circus of the Dayton monkey trial
Where Darrow hounded Bryan to his death.
I heard a bell that tolled when Wilson died,
Tolling the change of time, a hope foregone,
So that I felt like praying in the street.
We did not comment much, but left such chances
For newspapers to drool over, turned instead
To problems of esthetics, varied verse
We, one way or another, wished to write,
To the little magazine we published as a gambit,
A venture at our pleasure, serious, yes,
But not pontifical, proclaiming theses,
Each individual with sharply different views.

Don, more than any of us, did the labor
It took to keep *The Fugitive* alert
And running briskly through its four brief years.
Time passed; we followed various stars;
Maturity's achievements grew to fame.
And as we scattered, Don alone remained
At Vanderbilt, thinking, writing, teaching
A varying tide of student generations,
Indignant often at some stupidity
Or wrong direction in the world or school,
Uncompromising, passionate, but kind.
So in his writing he held banners high
Of courtesy that came from long tradition,

Of individual virtues, courage, honor.
At feud with juggernaut, leviathan,
Tracing the history of the Tennessee,
Making his pilgrimage to a rural north,
With fond companionship he persevered
Until the desolate time where we now dwell.

He saw the city thrice surpass the size
We had deplored. He saw the Harpeth hills,
Once filled with wild flowers, fill with close-packed houses,
The smog of teeming cars replace the fog
From soft-coal chimneys, a student generation,
Most changed, some bearded like the Civil War,
Rebellious, neither military, civil,
The best against tradition, questioning all,
Groping for values that their fathers lost.
Still tall men, yes, the seven-foot student, what
A target he'd have made for arrow, tomahawk,
But now his game is only basketball.
Change, ever change, a changing neighborhood,
New hospitals, a vaster Vanderbilt
Engulfing houses, block by block. Nearby
Belmont now serves strange ministers of music,
A mountain minstrelsy, commercialized, recorded.
Should there be flames again of civil strife,
He will not see that fire on Belmont Street.

Geography of the brain must compass more
Than intellect, complexities of cortex.
It must grope out into uncharted lands
Of heart and soul, terra incognita.
He was a man complete, a complete spirit,
With ordered rule and firm defenses for
Domains of thought he loved throughout his years.

from "In the Miro District"

PETER TAYLOR (1917–1994)

Although Peter Taylor has received critical acclaim for his novels, including *A Woman of Means* (1950) and *In the Tennessee Country* (1994), he is perhaps best known in the short story form. Born to a prosperous family in Trenton, Tennessee, Taylor descended from Bob and Alf Taylor, brothers who had run against each other for the Tennessee governorship. Taylor's maternal grandfather was a close friend of Andrew Nelson Lytle's father, and Peter knew Lytle and Allen Tate from a young age. Taylor attended Vanderbilt University from 1936-1937, and continued his studies at Southwestern at Memphis from 1937–1938. His contrasting of the folkways of his natal city and of Memphis in his novel *A Summons to Memphis* won him the Pulitzer Prize in 1987. Taylor earned his A.B. in 1940 from Kenyon College, where he studied with his Nashville friend Randall Jarrell and the poet Robert Lowell under John Crowe Ransom. He married the poet Eleanor Ross in 1943. In addition to a Pulitzer, Taylor was awarded an O. Henry Award and a PEN/Faulkner Award, in addition to numerous fellowships and grants, including recognition from the Guggenheim (1950), Fulbright (1955), and Ford (1961) foundations. Taylor wrote many short stories set in and commenting on Nashville, especially the city's Belle Meade neighborhood, in his eight collections of short stories including *A Long Fourth and Other Stories* (1948), *The Widows of Thonton* (1954), and *The Collected Short Stories of Peter Taylor* (1969). Following is the titular story from his 1977 collection, *In the Miro District and Other Stories*.

It will be useful at this point to explain that before that day when I hid my girl in the wardrobe, there actually had been two other serious and quite similar face-offs between my grandfather and me, and useful that I give some account of those earlier confrontations. They both took place in the very same year as the fateful one in the front hall. And on both of those occasions Grandfather stayed on in the house afterward, just as if nothing out of the ordinary had happened. This was so despite there having been more violent interplay between us—verbal and otherwise—in those two encounters than there was destined to be in the last. The first of them was in April of that year. My parents were not out of town that time. Rather, my father was in the hospital to undergo an operation on his prostate gland. He went into the hospital on the Sunday afternoon before the Monday morning when the operation was scheduled. Possibly he and my mother regarded the operation more apprehensively than they should have. My mother managed to obtain a room next to his in the hospital. She went in with him on Sunday in order to be near him during that night. My grandfather had of course been notified of the circumstances. Mother had even made a long-distance telephone call from Nashville to Huntsboro. And since Grandfather declined still to have a telephone in his house or to let the lines to other houses go across his land, he had had to be fetched by a messenger from his farm to Central's office on the town square.

That was on Saturday afternoon, and Mother had hoped he might come to Nashville on Sunday and stay in the house—presumably to keep me company—at least until Father was safely through the operation. But the old man was offended by everything about the situation. He resented being sent for and brought to the telephone office. He resented having to hear Mother's indelicate news in the presence of Central herself (a local girl and a cousin of ours). And the worst of it was, so he said on the telephone to Mother, he didn't believe in the seriousness of the operation. Actually, when Mother and Father had previously mentioned to him the possibility of such surgery, he had insisted that no such operation "existed" and that the doctor was pulling Father's leg. I was told this afterward by my father—long afterward—who said the old man had clearly resented such an unseemly subject's being referred to in his presence by his daughter or even by his son-in-law.

Anyhow, my mother told me that Grandfather would not be coming to stay with me on Sunday. I don't know whether or not she believed it. And I cannot honestly say for sure whether or not *I* believed he wasn't coming. I know only that on that Sunday afternoon, after my parents had left for the hospital, I telephoned two of my friends, two Acklen Park boys who would be graduating with me from Wallace School that June, and invited them to come over and to bring with them whatever they might have managed to filch from their fathers' liquor closets. Actually, it was only my way of informing them of what I had in mind for that Sunday afternoon and evening, because I knew where the key to Father's closet was and knew there was more than enough bourbon whiskey there to suffice for three boys on their first real binge. Since this was an opportunity we had all been contemplating for some time, my invitation was only a matter of form.

I heard Grandfather Manley in the driveway at about half past six. In fact I had lost track of time by then. We had been gulping down our whiskey as though it were lemonade. I could hardly stand on my feet when he came into the breakfast room, where we were seated about the table. I had made a stab at getting up when I first heard his car outside. My intention was to meet him, as usual, in the front hall. But as soon as I had got halfway up I felt a little sick. I knew I would be too unsteady on my feet to effect my usual sort of welcome in the hall, which would have entailed my taking his bag to his room for him and helping him off with his topcoat. Instead, I was still seated at the table when he stepped into the breakfast-room doorway. I did manage to rise from my chair then, scraping it crazily along the linoleum floor, which, at any rate, was more than the other two boys managed. And I faced him across the gold pocket watch that he was now holding out in his open palm like a piece of incriminating evidence. Although I say I faced him across the watch, his eyes were not really on me when he spoke but on the other boys at the table. "It's more than half an hour past my suppertime." he said. "I generally eat at six." That is how I can account for the time it was. Drunk as my two friends assuredly father, visualizing them in the hospital, Father lying in the white bed and Mother sitting in a straight chair beside him. I knew that I had to go to my grandfather's room and take whatever satisfaction I could from the scolding I fancied he would surely give me.

I found him in his room, seated in his platform rocker, which like all the other furniture in the room was made of golden oak—with caning in the seat and back. He sat in it as if it were a straight chair, with one of his long, khaki-clad legs crossed stiffly over the other and one high-topped brown shoe sticking out assertively into the room. All the furniture in the room was furniture which he had brought there at my mother's urging, from his house in Hunt County. It was in marked contrast with the rest of the furniture in our house. Mother had said, however, that he would feel more comfortable and at home with his own things in the room, and that he would be more likely to take real possession of it—which, after all, was what she and Father hoped for. I suspect they thought that would be a first step toward moving him in to live with us. In the end, Mother was actually disappointed at the particular pieces he chose to bring. But there will be a time later on for me to say more about that. Anyway, there he was in his rocker, already divested of his starched collar and of the vest he always wore under his gabardine coat. His suspenders were loosened and hanging down over the arms of the chair. And he had lit his first cigarette of the evening. (He had given up his pipe at the time of his escape from the nightriders and had taken up cigarettes instead, because he said they gave more relief to his nerves. He had given up his beard and mustache then, too, because he couldn't forget how awful they had smelt to him when he had been hiding in the swamp for days on end and under stagnant water for many hours of the time.) I came into the room and stood before him, my back to the great golden-oak folding bed, which, when it was folded away against the wall, as it was now, could easily be mistaken for a large wardrobe like the one I was facing on the other side of the room, and matching it almost exactly in size, bulk, and color. I stood there in silence for several moments, waiting

me off with a slapstick anecdote or two, about shooting a man's
hat off during the raid on Memphis, outside the Gayoso Hotel,
or about meeting General Forrest on a backcountry road when,
as a boy of sixteen and riding bareback on a mule, he was on his
way to enlist in Forrest's own critter company, how General
Forrest and some other officers had forced him off the road and
into a muddy ditch and didn't even look back at him until he
yelled out after them every filthy kind of thing he could think of.
"But since I was a mite small for my age," he would say, "they
must have mistook me for some local farm boy. Only Forrest
himself ever looked back—looked back with that sickly grin of
his." And then he was sure to end that anecdote saying, "Likely
I'm the onliest man or boy who ever called Bedford Forrest a
son-of-a-bitch and lived."

That was not, of course, the kind of war story I wanted. My
father, who read Civil War history, would, in my presence, try to
draw the old man out on the subject, asking him about Forrest's
strategy or whether or not the War might have been won if Jeff
Davis had paid more attention to the "Western Theatre." And
all Grandfather Manley would say was "I don't know about any
of that. I don't know what it matters."

But that Sunday night in his room, instead of plaguing him to
talk about the War as I had always previously tended to do, I
took the opposite tack. And I think I could not have stopped
myself from going on even if I had wanted to. As I rattled on, I
felt my grandfather looking at me uncertainly, as though he were
not sure whether it was I or he that was drunk. "Tell me about
your kidnapping," I said, actually wavering on the big leather
ottoman as I spoke, and my voice rising and lowering—quite
beyond my control. "Or tell me about the earthquake in 1811
that your old daddy used to tell you about, that made the
Mississippi River run upstream and formed Reelfoot Lake, and
how you imagined when you were lost in the swamp and half
out of your head that you could see the craters and fissures from
the earthquake still there." Suddenly Grandfather lit his second
cigarette, got up from his chair, and went over and stood by a

window. I suppose it occurred to him that I was mocking him, though I couldn't have said, myself, whether or not I was. "You're all worked up," he said. "And it's not just that whiskey in you. Your mother's got you all worked up about this damnable operation of your dad's."

"Tell me what it was like," I began again. In my confused and intoxicated state, my whole system seemed determined to give it all back to him—all the scary stories I had listened to through all the years about the nightriders of Reelfoot Lake. I can hear myself clearly even now, sometimes speaking to him in a singsongy voice more like a child's voice than the ordinary man's voice I had long since acquired. "Tell me what it was like to wake up in the Walnut Log Hotel at Samburg, Tennessee. . . . Tell me what it was like to lie in your bed in that shackly, one-story, backwoods hotel and have it come over you that it was no dream, that hooded men on horseback filled the yard outside, each with a blazing pine-knot torch, that there really was at every unglazed window of your room the raw rim of a shotgun barrel."

. . .

It was hardly six weeks later that we had our second run-in. He came in to Nashville on Decoration Day, when, of course, the Confederate veterans always held their most elaborate services and celebrations out at the State Fairground. Father and Mother had gone to Memphis to visit father's sister out there over the Decoration Day weekend. They wouldn't have planned to go, so they said, except that Grandfather as usual swore he was never again going to attend a Confederate Reunion of any kind. He had been saying for years that all the reunions amounted to were occasions to promote everybody to a higher rank. He acknowledged that once upon a time he had been a party to this practice. He had been so for many years, in fact. But enough was enough. It was one thing to promote men like himself who had been private soldiers to the rank of captain and major but quite another to make them colonels and generals. They had voted him his majority back in the years before his kidnaping by the nightriders. But since the experience of that abduction by those murderous backwoodsmen, he had never attended another Confederate Reunion. For more than a dozen years now he had insisted that it would not be possible for him to pass in through the ground gates on any Decoration Day without being sure to come out with the rank of colonel. He could not countenance that. And he could not countenance that gathering of men each year to repeat and enlarge upon reminiscences of something that he was beginning to doubt had ever had any reality.

From the first moment after I had put my parents on the train for Memphis, I think I knew how that weekend was going to go. I would not have admitted it to myself and didn't admit it for many years afterward. I suspect, too, that from the time some weeks earlier when he had heard of my parents' plan to go to Memphis—that is, assuming that he would not be coming in for the Reunion—Grand-father must also have had some idea of how it might go. Looking back, it seems almost as if he and I were plotting the whole business together.

It didn't of course seem that way at the time. Naturally, I can only speculate on how it seemed for him, but he had made more than one visit to Nashville since the day he found me there drinking with my friends, and I had observed a decided change in him—in his attitude toward me, that is. On one occasion he had offered me a cigarette, which was the next thing, it seemed to me then, to offering me a drink. I knew of course that Grandfather had, at one time or another, used tobacco in most of its forms. And we all knew, as a matter of fact, that when he closed the door to his room at night he nearly always poured himself a drink—poured it into a little collapsible tumbler that, along with his bottle of sourmash, he had brought with him in his Gladstone bag. His drinking habits had never been exactly a secret, though he seldom made any direct reference to them except in certain stories he told. And whatever changes there were in his style during his very last years, his drinking habits never changed at all—not, I believe, from the time when he was a young boy in the Confederate Army until the day he died.

It is true that I often smelt liquor on his breath when he arrived at our house for a visit, but I believe that was because he made a habit of having a quick one when he stopped—along the way—to rest and to relieve himself at the roadside. Moreover, that was only like the drink he had in his room at night—for his nerves. I believe the other drinking he had done in his lifetime consisted entirely of great bouts he had sometimes had with groups of men on hunting trips, often as not in that very region around Reelfoot Lake where he had witnessed the torture and strangulation of his old comrade-in-arms and law partner and where he had later wandered for ten nights in the swampy woodland thereabout (he had regarded it as unsafe to travel by day and unsafe to knock on any cabin door, lest it be the hide-away of one of the nightriders), wandered without food and without fresh water to drink, and suffering sometimes from hal-lucinations.

I feel that I must digress again here in order to say a few things about those hallucinations he had, which must actually have been not unlike delirium tremens, and about impressions that I myself had of that country around the Lake when I visited it as a child. Actually, as a very young child—no more than three or four years old—I had been taken on a duck-hunting trip to the Lake with Father and Grandfather and a party of other men from Hunt County. I didn't go out with them, of course, when, decked out in their grass hats and grass skirts and capes—for camouflage—they took up their positions in the marshlands. I was left in the hunting lodge on the lake's edge in the care of the Negro man who had been brought along to do the cooking. I don't remember much about the days or the nights of that expe-dition. I must have passed them comfortably and happily enough. All I remember clearly is what seemed the endless and desolate periods of time I spent during the early-morning hours and the twilight hours of each day of our stay there, all alone in

the lodge with Thomas, the cook. As I sat alone on the screened
porch, which went all the way round that little batten-board
lodge (of no more than three or four rooms and a loft) and listened to Thomas's doleful singing in the kitchen, all I could see
in any direction was the dark water of the lake on one side and
of the bayou on the other, with the cypress stumps and other
broken trees rising lugubriously out of the water and the mysterious, deep woods of the bottom lands beyond on the horizon. It
seemed to me that I could see for miles. And the fact was, the
lodge being built high upon wooden pilings, it was indeed possible to see great distances across the lake, which was five miles
wide in places. During those hours on the screened porch I
would think about the tales I had heard the men tell the night
before when they were gathered around the iron stove and when
I was going off to sleep on my cot in a far corner of the room. I
suppose the men must have been having their drinks then. But I
can't say that I remember the smell of alcohol. All the smells
there in that place were strange to me, though—the smell of the
water outside, the smell of the whitewash on the vertical board-
ing on the lodge, and the smell of the musty rooms inside the
lodge which stood empty most of the year. The tales the men
told were often connected with the nightrider trouble. Others
were old tales about the New Madrid Earthquake that had
formed the Lake more than a hundred years before. Some of the
men told old folk tales about prehistoric monsters that rose up
out of the lake in the dark of the moon.

I don't recall my father's contributing to this talk. My memory
is that he sat somewhat outside the circle, looking on and listening appreciatively to the talk of those older men, most of whom
had probably never been outside the state of Tennessee, unless it
was to go a little way up into Kentucky for whiskey. But my
Grandfather Manley contributed his full share. And everyone
listened to him with close attention. He spoke with an authority
about the Lake, of course, that none of the others quite had.
When those other men told their stories about prehistoric monsters rising from the lake, one felt almost that Grandfather when

he emerged from his ten days in the swampland, according to his own account, must have looked and smelt like just such a prehistoric monster. To me the scariest of his talk was that about some of the hallucinations he had, hallucinations about the hooded men mounted on strange animals charging toward him like the horsemen of the apocalypse. But almost as frightening as his own reminiscences were the accounts he had heard or read of that earthquake that made the lake.

The earthquake had begun on December 16, 1811, and the sequence of shocks was felt as far away as Detroit and Baltimore and Charleston, South Carolina. Upriver, at New Madrid, Missouri, nearly the whole town crumbled down the bluffs and into the river. The shocks went on for many days—even for several months—and in between the shocks the earth vibrated and sometimes trembled for hours on end "like the flesh of a beef just killed." Men and women and children, during the first bad shocks, hung on to trees like squirrels. In one case a tree "infested with people" was seen to fall across a newly made ravine, and the poor wretches hung there for hours until there was a remission in the earth's undulation. Whole families were seen to disappear into round holes thirty feet wide, and the roaring of the upheaval was so loud that their screams could not be heard.

Between Memphis and St. Louis the river foamed and in some places the current was observed to have reversed and run upstream for several hours. Everywhere the quake was accompanied by a loud, hoarse roaring. And on land, where fissures and craters appeared, a black liquid was ejected sometimes to a height of fifteen feet and subsequently fell in a black shower, mixed with the sand which it had forced along with it. In other places the earth burst open, and mud, water, sandstone, and coal were thrown up the distance of thirty yards. Trees everywhere were blown up, cracking and splitting and falling by the thousands at a time. It was reported that in one place the black liquid oozed out of the ground to the height of the belly of a horse. Grandfather had heard or read somewhere that John James Audubon had been caught in some of the later, less violent shocks and that his horse died of fright with him sitting it. Numbers of people died, of course, on the river as well as on the land, and many of those who survived were never afterward regarded as possessing their right senses.

Among the hallucinations that my grandfather had while wandering in the low ground after his escape was that that earthquake of a hundred years before—almost to the day of the month—had recurred or commenced again, or that he was living in that earlier time when the whole earth seemed to be convulsed and its surface appeared as it must have in primordial times. And he imagined that he was there on that frontier in company with the ragged little bands of Frenchmen and Spaniards and newly arrived American settlers, all of whose settlements had vanished into the earth, all of them in flight, like so many Adams and Eves, before the wrath of their Maker.

My father told me more than one time—again, long after I was grown—that it was only after Grandfather Manley had had a few drinks and was off somewhere with a group of men that he would describe the times of wandering in the swamps and describe his hallucinations about the earthquake. And I myself heard him speak of those hallucinations, when I was at the lodge with them and was supposed to be asleep in my cot, heard him speak of them as though they were real events he had experienced and heard him say that his visions of the earthquake were like a glimpse into the eternal chaos we live in, a glimpse no man should be permitted, and that after that, all of his war experiences seemed small and insignificant matters—as nothing. And it was after that, of course, that he could never bring himself to go back to those reunions and take part in those reminiscences with the other old soldiers of events so much magnified by them each year or take part in their magnification of their own roles by advancing themselves in rank each year.

Grandfather could only confide those feelings of his to other men. He would only confide them when he had a little whiskey in him. And what is important, too, is that he only drank alone or in the company of other men. He abhorred what my father

and mother had come to speak of in the 1920s as social drinking. Drinking liquor was an evil and was a sign of weakness, he
would have said, and just because one indulged in it oneself was
no reason to pretend to the world that there was virtue in it.
That to him was hypocrisy. Drinking behind closed doors or in
a secluded hunting lodge, though one denounced it in public as
an evil practice signified respect for the public thing, which was
more important than one's private character. It signified genuine
humility.

And so it was, I must suppose, that he in some degree approved
of the kind of drinking bout he had caught me in. And his
approval, I suppose, spoiled the whole effect for me. It put me in
the position, as I understand it now, of pretending to be like the
man I felt myself altogether unlike and alien to.

And so it was that the circumstances he found me in were
quite different on that inevitable Decoration Day visit of his. My
parents were no sooner aboard the train for Memphis, that
Friday night, than I had fetched a certain acquaintance of mine
named Jeff Patterson—he was older than I and had finished his
second year at Vanderbilt—and together we had picked up two
girls we knew who lived on Eighth Avenue, near the Reservoir.
We went dancing at a place out on Nine Mile Hill. We were
joined there by two other couples of our acquaintance, and later
the eight of us came back to Acklen Park. (I must say that I was
much more experienced with girls by that age than I was with
liquor.) We had had other similar evenings at the house of the
parents of the two other boys who joined us that night, but until
then I had never been so bold as to use my parents' house for
such purposes. The girls we had with us were not the kind of
girls such a boy as I was would spend any time with nowadays.
That is why this part of the story may be difficult for people of a
later generation to understand. With one's real girl, in those
days, a girl who attended Ward Belmont school and who was
enrolled in Miss Amy Lowe's dancing classes, one might neck in
the back seat of a car. The girl might often respond too warmly
and want to throw caution to the wind. But it was one's own

manliness that made one overcome one's impulse to possess her and, most of all, overcome her impulse to let herself be possessed before taking the marriage vow. I am speaking of decent boys and girls of course and I acknowledge that even among decent or "nice" young people of that day there were exceptions to the rule. One knew of too many seven-month babies to have any doubt of that. Still, from the time one was fourteen or fifteen in Nashville, one had to know girls of various sorts and one had to have a place to take girls of the "other sort." No one of my generation would have been shocked by the events of that evening. The four couples went to bed—and finally slept—in the four bedrooms on the second floor of my parents' house in Acklen Park. As I have indicated, I had never before brought such a party to our house, and I gave no thought to how I would clean up the place afterward or how I would conceal what had gone on there.

It was only a few minutes past seven the next morning when I heard Grandfather's car outside in the driveway. I was at once electrified and paralyzed by the sound. Lying there in my own bed with that girl beside me, and with the other couples still asleep in the other rooms, I had a vision of our big, two-story brick house as it appeared from the outside that May morning, saw the details of the stone columns at the four corners of the house, the heavy green window blinds and the keystones above the windows, even the acanthus leaves in the capitals of the columns on the front porch. I saw it all through my grandfather's sharp little eyes as he turned into the gravel driveway, and saw through his eyes not only my parents' car, which I had carelessly left out of the garage, but the cars also of the two other boys who had joined us, all three cars sitting out there in the driveway on Sunday morning, as if to announce to him that some kind of party—and even *what* kind of party, probably—was going on inside.

He didn't step into his room to set down his Gladstone bag. I heard him drop it on the floor in the front hall and then I heard his quick footstep on the long stairway. Then I heard him opening the doors to all the bedrooms. (We *had* had the decency to close ourselves off in separate rooms.) He opened my door last, by design I suppose. I was lying on my stomach and I didn't even lift my head to look at him. But I knew exactly how he would appear there in the doorway, still wearing his long coat and his summer straw hat. That was the last thought or the last vision I indulged in before I felt the first blow of his walking stick across my buttocks. At last he had struck me! That was what I thought to myself. At last we might begin to understand one another and make known our real feelings, each about the other. By the time I felt the second blow from his stick I had realized that between the two blows he delivered me he had struck one on the buttocks of the girl beside me. Already I had begun to understand that his striking me didn't have quite the kind of significance I had imagined. By the time he had struck the girl a second time she had begun screaming. I came up on my elbows and managed to clamp my hand over her mouth to keep the neighbors from hearing her. He left us then. And over his shoulder as he went striding from the room he said, "I want you to get these bitches out of this house and to do so in one hell of a hurry!" He went back into the hallway, and then when I had scrambled out of bed I saw him, to my baffling chagrin and unaccountable sense of humiliation, hurrying into the other rooms, first one and then another, and delivering blows to the occupants of those other beds. Some of the others, I suppose, had heard him crack the door to their rooms earlier and had crawled out of bed before he got there. But I heard him and saw him wielding his stick against Jeff Patterson's backsides and against the little bottom of the girl beside him. Finally—still wearing his hat and his gabardine coat, mind you—he passed through the hall again and toward the head of the stair. I was standing in the doorway to my room by then, but still clad only in my underwear shorts. As he went down the stairsteps he glanced back at me and spoke again: "You get those bitches out of your mother's house and you do it in one hell of a hurry."

Even before I was able to pull on my clothes, all four of the girls were fully dressed and scurrying down the stairs, followed immediately by the three boys. I came to the head of the stairs and stood there somewhat bemused, looking down. The girls had gone off into the front rooms downstairs in search of certain of their possessions. I heard them calling to each other desperately. "I left my lipstick right here on this table!" And, "Oh God, where's my purse?" And, "Where in the world are my pumps?" I realized then that one of them had gone down the stairs barefoot, and simultaneously I saw Grandfather Manley moving by the foot of the stairs and toward the living room.

I descended slowly, listening to the voices in the front room. First there had come a little shriek from one of the girls when Grandfather entered. Then I heard his voice reassuring them. By the time I reached the living-room doorway he was assisting them in their search, whereas the three boys only stood by, watching. It was he himself who found that little purse. Already the four girls seemed completely at ease. He spoke to them gently and without contempt or even condescension. The girl who had been my date left with the others, without either of us raising the question of whether or not I might see her home. As they went out through the wide front door the four girls called out, "Goodbye!" in cheerful little voices. I opened my mouth to respond, but before I could make a sound I beard Grandfather answering, "Goodbye, girls." And it came over me that it had been to him, not me, they were calling goodbye. When he and I were alone in the hall, he said, "And now I reckon you realize what we've got to do. We've got to do something about those sheets."

It is a fact that he and I spent a good part of that day doing certain clean-up jobs and employing the electric iron here and there. I can't say it drew us together though, or made any sort of bond between us. Perhaps that's what he imagined the result would be. But I never imagined so for a moment. I knew that one day there was something he would have to know about me that he couldn't forgive. Though he and I were of the same blood, we had parted company, so to speak, before I was born even, and there was some divisive thing between us that could never be overcome. Perhaps I felt that day that it was my parents, somehow, who would forever be a wall between us, and that once any people turned away from what he was, as they had done, then that—whatever it was he was—was lost to them and to their children and their children's children forever. But I cannot say definitely that I felt anything so certain or grand that day. I cannot say for sure what I felt except that when he spoke with such composure and assurance to those girls in my parents' living room, I felt that there was nothing in the world he didn't know and hadn't been through.

As he and I worked away at cleaning up the bedrooms that morning, I asked myself if his knowing so well how to speak to those girls and if the genuine sympathy and even tenderness that he clearly felt toward them meant perhaps that his insistence upon living alone in that old house over in Hunt County suggested there were girls or women in his life still. Whatever else his behavior that day meant, it meant that the more bad things I did and the worse they were, then the better he would think he understood me and the more alike he would think we were. But I knew there was yet something I could do that would show him how different we were and that until I had made him grasp that, I would not begin to discover what, since I wasn't and couldn't be like him, I *was* like. Or if I, merely as a result of being born when I was and where I was, at the very tail end of something, I was like nothing else at all, only incomparably without a character of my own.

In July, Mother and Father went up to Beersheba Springs, on the Cumberland Plateau, for a few days' relief from the hot weather. Beersheba was an old-fashioned watering place, the resort in past times of Episcopal bishops, Louisiana planters, and the gentry of Middle Tennessee. By the 1920s only a select few from the Nashville Basin kept cottages there and held sway at the old hotel. It was the kind of summer spot my parents felt most comfortable in. It had never had the dash of Tate Springs or the homey atmosphere of Monteagle, but it was older than either of those places and had had since its beginning gambling tables, horses, and dancing. Behind the porticoed hotel on the bluff's edge the old slave quarters were still standing, as was also the two-story brick garconnière, reached by a covered walkway from the hotel. There was an old graveyard overgrown with box and red cedar, enclosed by a rock wall and containing old gravestones leaning at precarious angles but still bearing good Tennessee-Virginia names like Burwell and Armistead. Farther along the bluff and farther back on the plateau were substantial cottages and summer houses, a good number of them built of squared chestnut logs and flanked by handsome limestone end-chimneys. The ancient and unreconstructed atmosphere of the place had its attraction even for Grandfather Manley, and my parents had persuaded him to accompany them on their holiday there.

He drove in to Nashville and then, still in his own car, followed Mother and Father in their car to Beersheba Springs, which was seventy or eighty miles southeast of Nashville, on the edge of the Plateau and just above what used to be known as the Highland Rim. It seemed a long way away. There was no question in my mind of the old man's turning up in Nashville this time. I looked forward with pleasure to a few days of absolute freedom—from my parents, from my grandfather, and even from the servants, who were always given a holiday whenever my parents were out of town. I was in such relaxed good spirits when Father and Mother and Grandfather Manley had departed that I went up to my room—though it was not yet noon—and took a nap on my bed. I had no plans made for this period of freedom except to see even more than usual of a Ward Belmont girl with whom I had been having dates during most of that winter and spring and whom my parents, as an indication of their approval of my courting a girl of her particular family, had had to dinner at our house several times and even on one occasion when my grandfather was there. She was acknowledged by my family and by everyone else to be my girl, and by no one more expressly than by the two of us—by the girl herself, that is, and by myself.

I was awakened from my nap just before noon that day, by the ringing of the telephone in the upstairs hall. And it so happened that the person calling was none other than she whom I would have most wished to hear from. It was not usual for such a girl to telephone any boy, not even her acknowledged favorite. I have to say that as soon as I heard her voice I experienced one of those moments I used often to have in my youth, of seeming to know how everything was going to go. I can't blame myself for how things did go during the next twenty-four hours and can't blame the girl, either. Since this is not the story of our romance, it will suffice to say that though our romance did not endure for long after that time, these events were not necessarily the cause for its failure. The girl herself has prospered in life quite as much as I have. And no doubt she sometimes speaks of me nowadays, wherever in the world she is living, as "a boy I went with in Nashville," without ever actually mentioning my name. At any rate, when she telephoned that day she said she was *very much* upset about something and wanted *very much* to see me at once. She apologized for calling. She would not have been so brash, she said, except that since I told her of my parents' plans she knew I would probably be at home alone. The circumstance about which she was upset was that since her parents, too, were out of town, her two older sisters were planning "an awful kind of party" that she could not possibly have any part in. She wanted me to help her decide what she must do.

My parents had taken our family car to Beersheba, and so it was that she and I had to meet on foot, halfway between Acklen Park and her home, which was two or three miles away, out in the Belle Meade section. And it ended, of course, after several hours of earnest talk about love and life—exchanged over milk-shakes in a place called Candy Land and on the benches in the Japanese Garden in Centennial Park—ended, that is, by our coming to my house and telephoning her sisters that she had gone to spend the night with a classmate from Ward Belmont. The inevitability of its working out so is beyond question in my mind. At least, in retrospect it is. Certainly both of us had known for many days beforehand that both sets of parents would be out of town; and certainly the very passionate kind of necking which we had been indulging in that summer, in the darkness of my father's car and in the darkness of her father's back terrace, had become almost intolerable to us. But we could honestly say to ourselves that we had made no plans for that weekend. We were able to tell ourselves afterward that it was just something that happened. And I was able to tell myself for many years afterward—I cannot deny it categorically even today—that I would not have consented to our coming to my house if I had thought there were the remotest possibility of Grandfather Manley's turning up there.

And yet, though I can tell myself so, there will always be a certain lingering doubt in my mind. And even after it was clear to both of us that we would sleep together that night, her sense of propriety was still such that she refused to go up to the second floor of my house. Even when I led her into Grandfather Manley's room, she did not realize or did not acknowledge to herself that it was a bedroom we were in. I suppose she had never before seen anything quite like the furniture there. "What a darling room!" she exclaimed when I had put on the floor lamp beside the golden-oak rocker. And when I pulled down the great folding bed, even in the dim lamplight I could see that she blushed. Simultaneously almost, I caught a glimpse of myself in the mirror or the oak bureau and I cannot deny that I thought with certain glee in that moment of my grandfather or deny that I felt a certain premonition of events.

My first thought when I heard his car outside the next afternoon was, We are in *his* room! We are in *his* bed! I imagined that that was what was going to disturb him most. The fact was we had been in and out of his bed I don't know how many times by then. We had not only made love there in a literal sense, and were so engaged when he arrived, but we had during various intervals delighted each other there in the bed with card games and even checkers and Parcheesi, with enormous quantities of snacks which the cook had left for me in the refrigerator, and finally with reading aloud to each other from volumes of poetry and fiction which I fetched from my room upstairs. If there had been any sense of wrongdoing in our heads the previous after-noon, regarding such preoccupations as would be ours during those two days, it had long since been dispelled by the time that old man my grandfather arrived—dispelled for both of us, and not just that time but probably for all future time. (As for myself I know that I never again in all the years since have had any taste for taking my pleasure with such females as those Eighth Avenue-Reservoir girls—in the casual, impersonal way that one does with such females of any class or age.)

When I told her there beside me that it was the tires of my grandfather's car she and I had heard skidding in the gravel and that it was now his quick, light step on the porch steps that I rec-ognized, she seized me by the wrist and whispered, "Even if he knows I'm here, I don't want him to see me, and I don't want to see him. You have to hide me! Quickly!" By the time we had pushed up the folding bed, there was already the sound of his key in the front door. There was nothing for it, if she were to be hidden, but to hide her in the wardrobe.

"Over there," I said, "If you're sure you want to. But it's his room. He's apt to find you."

"Don't you let him," she commanded.

"You put on your clothes," was all I could say. I was pulling on my own trousers. And now she was running on tiptoe toward the wardrobe, with nothing on at all, carrying all her clothing and a pillow and blanket from the bed, all in a bundle clutched before her. She opened the wardrobe door, tossed everything in before her, and then hopped in on top of it. I followed her over there, buttoning my trousers and trying to get into my shirt. As I took a last step forward to close the door on her, I realized that, except for her and the bundle of clothing she was crouched on, the wardrobe was entirely empty. There were no possessions of Grandfather's in it. I thought to myself, Perhaps he never opens the wardrobe, even. And as I closed the door I saw to my delight that my brave girl, huddled there inside the wardrobe, wasn't by any means shedding tears but was smiling up at me. And I think I knew then for the first time in my life how wonderful it is to be in love and how little anything else in the world matters. And I found myself smiling back at her with hardly an awareness of the fact that she hadn't a piece of clothing on her body. And I actually delayed closing the door long enough to put the palm of my hand to my mouth and throw her a kiss.

Then, having observed the emptiness of the wardrobe, I glanced over at the oak bureau and wondered if it weren't entirely empty, too. I was inspired by that thought to quickly gather up my books, along with a bread wrapper and a jam jar, a kitchen knife, a couple of plates and glasses, and also my own shoes and socks, and to stuff them all inside a drawer or the bureau. On opening the heavy top drawer I found I was not mistaken. The drawer was empty and with no sign of its ever having been used by Grandfather—perhaps not since the day when the furniture had first been brought from Hunt County and Mother had put down the white paper in it for lining.

Already I had heard Grandfather Manley calling my name out in the front hall. It was something I think he had never done before when arriving at the house. His choosing to do so had given me the extra time I had needed. When I closed the big bureau drawer I looked at myself in the wide mirror above it, and I was almost unrecognizable even to myself. I was sweating profusely. My hair was uncombed. I had not shaved in two days. My trousers and shirt were all wrinkles. But I heard my grandfather calling me a second time and knew I had to go out there.

When I stepped, barefoot, into his view I could tell from his expression that he saw me just as I had seen myself and that I was barely recognizable to him. He was standing at the foot of the stairs, from which point he had been calling my name. No doubt my face showed him how astonished I was to have him call out to me on coming into the house—at the informality and open friendliness of it. No doubt for a minute or so he supposed that accounted wholly for my obvious consternation. He actually smiled at me. It was rather a sickly grin, though, like General Forrest's, the smile of a man who isn't given to smiling. And yet there was an undeniable warmth in his smile and in the total expression on his face. "I couldn't abide another day of Beersheba Springs," he said. "The swells over there are too rich for my blood. I thought I would just slip by here on my way home and see what kind of mischief you might be up to."

Clearly what he said was intended to amuse me. And just as clearly he meant that he preferred whatever low life he might find me engaged in to the high life led by my parents' friends at Beersheba. Presently, though, he could deceive himself no longer about my extraordinary appearance and my nervous manner's indication that something was wrong.

"What's the matter, son?" he said.

"Nothing's the matter," I said belligerently.

The very friendliness of his demeanor somehow made me resent more bitterly than ever before his turning up at so inconvenient a moment. This was my real life he had come in on and was interfering with. Moreover, he had intruded this time with real and unconcealed feelings of his own. I could not permit him, at that hour of my life, to make me the object of his paternal affection. I was a grown man now and was in love with a girl who was about to be disgraced in his eyes. How could there be anything between him and me? His life, whether or not it was in any way his fault, had kept him from knowing what love of our sort was. He might know everything else in the world, including every other noble feeling which I could never be able to experience. He might be morally correct about everything else in the world, but he was not morally correct about love between a man and a woman. This was what I felt there in the hall that afternoon. I was aware of how little I had to base my judgment on. It was based mostly on the nothing that had ever been said about women in all the stories he had told me. In all the stories about the nightriders, for instance, there was no incident about his reunion with his wife, my grandmother, afterward. And I never heard him speak of her by her first name. Even now I wonder how we ever know about such men and their attitude toward women. In our part of the world we were all brought up on tales of the mysterious ways of Thomas Jefferson, whose mother and

wife were scarcely mentioned in his writings, and Andrew
Jackson and Sam Houston, whose reticence on the subject of
women is beyond the comprehension of most men nowadays.
Did they have too much respect for women? Were they perhaps,
for all their courage in other domains, afraid of women or afraid
of their own compelling feelings about women? I didn't think all
of this, of course, as I faced Grandfather Manley there in the
hall, but I believe I felt it. It seemed to me that his generation and
my own were a thousand years apart.

"What's the matter, son?" he said.

"Nothing's the matter," I said.

There was nothing more for either of us to say. He began to
move toward me and in the direction of his room. "Why don't
you wait a minute," I said, "before you go into your room?"

His little eyes widened, and after a moment he said, "It ain't
my room, y'know. I only stay in it."

"Yes," I said, "but I've been reading in there. Let me go clear
up my books and things." I had no idea but to delay him. I said,
"Maybe you should go out to the kitchen and get something to
eat."

But he walked right past me, still wearing his hat and coat, of
course, and still carrying his little Gladstone bag. When he had
passed into his room and I had followed him in there, he said, "I
see no books and things."

"No," I said, "I hid them in the bureau drawer. I didn't know
whether you would like my being in here."

He looked at me skeptically. I went over and opened the
drawer and took out my books and my shoes and socks. Then I
closed the drawer, leaving everything else in it. But he came and
opened the drawer again. And he saw the plates and other
things. "What else are you hiding?" he asked. No doubt he had
heard the knives and the plates rattling about when I closed the
drawer. Then he turned and walked over to the wardrobe. I ran
ahead of him and placed myself against the door. "You got one
of those bitches of yours hidden in there, I reckon," he said.

"No, sir," I said, trying to look him straight in the eye.

"Then what is it?" he said. And he began blinking his eyes, not because I was staring into them but because he was thinking. "Are you going to tell me, or am I going to find out for myself?" Suddenly I said, "It's my girl in there." We were both silent for a time, staring into each other's eyes. "And you've no right to open the door on her," I finally said. "Because she's not dressed."

"You're lying," he came back at me immediately. "I don't believe you for a minute." He left me and went to the folding bed and pulled it down. He set his bag on the bed and he poked at the jumble of sheets with his cane. Then he stood there, looking back at me for several moments. He still had not removed his straw hat and had not unbuttoned his coat. Finally he began moving across the room toward me. He stood right before me, looking me in the eye again. Then, with almost no effort, he pushed me aside and opened the wardrobe door. She still hadn't managed to get into her clothes but she was hugging the pillow and had the blanket half pulled over her shoulder. I think he may have recognized her from the one time he had met her at dinner. Or maybe, I thought to myself, he was just such an old expert that he could tell what kind of girl she was from one glance at her. Anyway, he turned on me a look cold and fierce and so articulate that I imagined I could hear the words his look expressed: "So this is how bad you really are?" Then he went directly over to the bed, took up his bag and his cane, left the room, and left the house without speaking to me again.

When I had heard the front door close I took the leather ottoman across the room and sat on it, holding hands with that brave and quiet girl who, with the door wide open now, remained crouching inside the wardrobe. When finally we heard him drive out of the driveway we smiled at each other and kissed. And I thought to myself again that his generation and ours were a thousand years apart, or ten thousand.

I thought of course that when Grandfather Manley left Acklen Park he would continue on his way to Hunt County. But that was not the case. Or probably he did go to Hunt County, after all, and then turned around and went back to Beersheba Springs from there. Because he arrived at Beersheba at about eleven o'clock that night, and it would be difficult to explain how he was dressed as he was unless he had made a trip home and changed into the clothes he arrived in. He left Acklen Park about four in the afternoon, and from that time through the remaining ten years of his life he was never again seen wearing the old gabardine coat or either of his broad-brimmed hats. When he arrived at Beersheba, Mother and Father were sitting on the front gallery of the hotel with a group of friends. They were no doubt rocking away in the big rockers that furnished the porch, talking about the bridge hands they had held that evening, and enjoying the view of the moonlit valley below Cumberland Mountain.

When they saw him drive up, the car was unmistakable of course. But the man who emerged from it was not unmistakable. Major Basil Manley was dressed in a black serge suit, and in the starched collar of his white shirt he wore a black shoestring tie. I can describe his attire in such detail because from that day I never saw him in any other. That is, except on Decoration Day in those later years, when he invariably appeared in Confederate uniform. And in which uniform, at his own request, he was finally buried, not at Huntsboro and not in the family graveyard, but at Mount Olivet Cemetery, at Nashville. My father's account of his arrival on the hotel porch is memorable to me because it is the source of a great discovery which I felt I had made. My parents didn't recognize him for a certainty until he had passed along the shadowy brick walkway between the hovering boxwoods and stepped up on the porch. And then, significantly, both of them went to him and kissed him on the cheek, first my mother and then my father. And all the while, as my father described it, Major Manley stood there, ramrod straight, his cheeks wet with tears, like an old general accepting total defeat with total fortitude. And what I understood for certain when I heard about that ceremony of theirs was that it had, after all, been their battle all along, his and theirs, not his and mine. I, after all, had only been the pawn of that gentle-seeming couple who were his daughter and son-in-law and who were my parents. It is almost unbelievable the changes that took place in Grandfather from that day. He grew his beard again, which was completely white now, of course. It hid his lean jaw and weak chin, making him very handsome, and was itself very beautiful in its silky whiteness against his black suit and black shoestring tie. The following year—the very next May—he began attending the Confederate Reunions again. And of course he was promptly promoted to the rank of colonel. Yet he did hold out against ever wearing the insignia of that rank, until he was in his coffin and it was put on him by other hands. So far as I knew he never allowed anyone—not even the other veterans—to address him other than as Major Manley. And in the fall after he had first appeared in his new role at Beersheba Springs, he began coming in to Nashville more often than ever. I was not at home that fall, since that was my first year away at college, but when I would go home for a weekend and find him there or find that he had been there, I would observe some new object in his room, an old picture of my grandmother as a girl, bareshouldered and with dark curls about her face, the picture in its original oval frame. Other family pictures soon appeared, too. And there was a handsome washbasin and pitcher, and there were some of his favorite books, like Ramsay's *Annals of Tennessee* and lawbooks that had belonged to his father, my great-grandfather. And then, very soon, he began to bring in small pieces of furniture that were unlike the golden-oak pieces already there.

When my mother had first urged Grandfather Manley to come live with us, it was just after my grandmother died and before we had moved into the big house in Acklen Park. He had said frankly then that he thought he would find it too cramped in our little house on Division Street. But when they bought the new house, they had done so with an eye to providing accommodations that would be agreeable to an old man who might before many years not like to climb stairs and who, at any rate, was known to be fond of his privacy. They consulted with a number of their friends who had the responsibility for aging parents. It was a bond they were now going to share with those friends or a bond which they aspired to, anyway. In those days in Nashville, having a Confederate veteran around the place was comparable to having a peacock on the lawn or, if not that, at least comparable to having one's children in the right schools. It was something anybody liked to have. It didn't matter, I suppose, what rank the veteran was, since he was certain to be promoted as the years passed. The pressure on Major Manley to move in with his daughter and son-in-law was gentle always, but it was constant and it was enduring. One of the most compelling reasons given him was that they wanted him to get to know his only grandson and that they wanted the grandson to have the benefit of growing up in the house with him. Well, when the new house was bought and he was shown that room on the first floor which was to be reserved perpetually for him whenever he might choose to come and occupy it, and when he was urged to furnish it with whatever pieces he might wish to bring in from Hunt County, he no doubt felt he could not absolutely reject the invitation. And he no doubt had unrealistic dreams about some kind of rapport that might develop between him and the son of this daughter and son-in-law of his. I don't remember the day it happened of course, but it must have come as a considerable shock and disappointment to Mother when a truck hired in Huntsboro arrived, bearing not the rosewood half-canopied bed from her mother's room at home, or the cannonball four-poster from the guest room there, but the fold-away golden oak piece that came instead, and the other golden-oak pieces that arrived instead of the walnut and mahogany pieces she had had in mind. Yet no complaint was made to the old man. (His daughter and son-in-law were much too gentle for that.) The golden oak had come out of the downstairs "office" in the old farmhouse which he had furnished when he first got married and moved in with his own parents. No doubt he thought it most appropriate for any downstairs bedroom, even in Acklen Park. The main object was to get him to occupy the room. And, after his fashion, this of course was how he had occupied it through the years.

But by Christmas of the year he and I had our confrontations he had, piece by piece, moved all new furnishings into the room and had disposed of all the golden oak. The last piece he exchanged was the folding bed for the walnut cannonball bed. When I came home at Christmas, there was the big four-poster filling the room, its mattress so high above the floor (in order to accommodate the trundle bed) that a set of walnut bed steps was required for Grandfather to climb into or out of it. And before spring came the next year Grandfather had closed his house in Hunt County and taken up permanent residence in Acklen Park. He lived there for the rest of his life, participating in my parents' lively social activities, talking freely about his Civil War experiences, even telling the ladies how he courted my grandmother during that time, and how sometimes he would slip away from his encampment, make a dash for her father's farm, and spy on her from the edge of a wood without ever letting her know he had been in the neighborhood.

Such anecdotes delighted the Nashville ladies and the Nashville gentlemen, too. But often he would talk seriously and at length about the War itself—to the great and special delectation of both my parents—describing for a room full of people the kind of lightning warfare that Forrest carried on, going on late into the evening sometimes, describing every little crossroads skirmish from Between The Rivers to Shiloh, pausing now and then for a little parenthetical explanation, for the ladies, of such matters as the difference between tactics and strategy. Sometimes he would display remarkable knowledge of the grand strategy of the really great battles of the War, of Shiloh and Vicksburg, of Stone River, Franklin, and Chickamauga, and of other battles that he had no part in. When he had a sufficiently worthy audience he would even speculate about whether or not the War in the West might have been won if Bragg had been removed from his command or whether the whole War mightn't have been won if President Davis had not viewed it so narrowly from the Richmond point of view. Or he would raise the question of what might have happened if Lee had been allowed to go to the Mountains.

I heard my parents' accounts of all such talk of his. But I heard some of it myself too. The fall after I had graduated from Wallace School, I went away to the University of the South at Sewanee. My father had gone to Vanderbilt because he had been a Methodist, and Vanderbilt was the great Methodist university in those days. But he and Mother, under the influence of one of his aunts, had become Episcopalian before I was born even. And so there was never any idea but that I should go to Sewanee. I liked being at Sewanee and liked being away from Nashville for the first time in my life. The University of course was full of boys from the various states of the Deep South. I very soon made friends there with boys from Mississippi and Louisiana and South Carolina. And since Nashville was so close by, I used to bring some of them home with me on weekends or on short holidays. They of course had never seen Grandfather Manley the way he had been before. And they couldn't imagine his being different from the way he was then. He would gather us around him sometimes in the evening and talk to us about the War Between the States. The boys loved to listen to him. They really adored him and made over him and clamored for him to tell certain stories over and over again. I enjoyed it, too, of course. He seemed quite as strange and interesting an old character to me as he did to them. And sometimes when I would ask him a question, just the way the others did, he would answer me with the same politeness he showed them, and at those times I would have the uneasy feeling that he wasn't quite certain whether it was I or one of the others who was his grandson, whether I was not perhaps merely one of the boys visiting, with the others from Sewanee.

from *The Storyteller's Nashville*

TOM T. HALL (1936–   )

Tom T. Hall was born a preacher's son in Olive Hill, Kentucky
and rose to the heights of country music fame. At age sixteen,
Hall worked as an announcer for a traveling promoter who
showed movies on a screen mounted on the roof of his car. As
an added attraction, Tom Hall and the Kentucky Travelers
played before the movies were shown. After work as a disc
jockey and a songwriter, Hall had a multimillion-selling hit with
"Harper Valley PTA," recorded by Jeanie C. Riley in 1968. A
plaque erected in Olive Hill by townspeople declared that Hall
has "used his God-given talents to become one of America's bal-
ladeers, telling in music form the story of the common folk and
the daily happenings which color their lives." His number one
Top 40 Country songs include "A Week in a County Jail"
(1969), "(Old Dogs, Children and) Watermelon Wine" (1972),
and "Faster Horses (The Cowboy and The Poet)" (1976). In
addition to many short stories, Hall has published the semi-
autobiographical *The Storyteller's Nashville* (1979), as well as
The Laughing Man of Woodmont Coves (1982), *The Acts of
Life* (1986), *Spring Hill, Tennessee: A Novel* (1990), and *What
a Book!: A Novel* (1996). Hall was honored in 1990 with a
chair in creative writing at Middle Tennessee State University
established in his name. The following excerpt is from his 1979
book which Molly Ivins praised in the *New York Times Book
Review* for having "none of the saccharine piety that often mars
country music."

The next morning—January 2, 1964—was *cold*. I dressed to go
outside to look for a coffee machine and a newspaper rack. The
wind took my breath away. There was no coffee machine, no
newspaper rack, and no one in the office. Panic rippled my
stomach as I realized I must be *blocks* from a cup of coffee. I
retreated to my room, sat on the bed, and lit a cigarette. Boy,

was I scared. What the hell was I doing in Nashville with a god-damned guitar and forty-six dollars? But I am, after all, a philosopher, and it wasn't long before I was pretending I knew exactly what I was doing; and that this was a perfectly decent and sane way to make a living; and I had nine members of my immediate family to call on if I needed help, etc., etc., etc. So! Let's get some coffee and be about our business.

The rose-colored Cadillac started. Making myself as small as possible, I drove three blocks to a sign that commanded, "EAT," and went in. I was beginning to be embarrassed about this damned car. Why, people will think I am already rich and famous and . . .

"Move your hands!" somebody said. I jumped.

"I'm sorry," I said. The waitress had caught me staring at the "Opry" ashtrays. She wanted to wipe off the table.

"How much are those ashtrays?" I asked.

"Ninety-eight cents."

"No."

"No what?" She glared.

"No, I don't want one," I replied.

"I thought you meant 'No, they ain't ninety-eight cents,'" she said. "But they's ninety-eight cents all right."

I attempted to redeem myself in the eyes of this little bitch and replied, "I'm sure they are, ma'am, but I just want a cup of coffee, please."

"It's sitting right there in front of you."

And it was.

"Thank you," I whispered.

Boy! I must be crazy. My first day in Nashville and my mind wasn't working worth a shit. So I decided to save this whole deal by shutting up. I heard once that people think you're smart if you shut up . . . so, I shut up.

But I couldn't shut up. I have never been able to shut up. I have this horrible compulsion to make everything right again. Even knowing that being silent would be better, I charge onward trying to fix everything again. My nine-for-ten failure record does nothing to deter me.

"How far is it to Nashville?" I broke the silence again. She paused in the middle of scraping the grease off the grill.

"This *is* Nashville."

"Yeah," I said, "but I mean the middle of town."

"Well, they's a train station in the middle of town. You want to go to a train station?"

"No. Music Row."

"You a musician?"

"No. I'm a songwriter."

"Well, the middle of town is a train station, like I said. Music Row is up on the hill along in there where Decca is. I was out there once and seen Warner Mack make a record. His cousin used to come in here and I asked him whatever happened to the song he was recording that night. He said, 'They didn't push it.' They sometimes push 'em and they sometimes don't. See, you just got to understand show business."

I digested this bit of information a moment, then got up and walked over to the window. It was all steamed up from the heat.

"You better not mark on that window," she said. "It dries up and you can still see the marks. I'm the one's got to wash 'em."

My thoughts turned to the day's problem. I was going to have to go into town and face the guys who had brought me down to Nashville. I had already written several songs that sold records and did well on the radio "play" charts. This was all in my favor, but I was drunk the night my publisher told me to come to Nashville. He was drinking too. So I was not really sure, when I left my job at radio station WELU in Roanoke, if I would have a job when I reached Nashville. There remained the distinct possibility that E. Jimmy Key (my publisher) would say, "Look, boy, you misunderstood me. I meant you could come down here *someday*, not *any day* and especially not *to-day*."

It was with this phantom exchange still lurking in the pit of my stomach that I picked up the telephone and waited for the operator, who was the skinny guy at the desk with my eight dollars.

"Yeah?" he says.

"Two-four-two-three-seven-six-one."

"Key Talent, Newkeys Music! Good morning!"

"Marie? This is Tom Hall."

"Tom! How are you?"

"Where am I? is a better question. I'm in Nashville!"

"Jim said he thought you were coming in yesterday."

"Yeah, well, I got in late, and I was a little tired, so I checked in a motel and got some rest."

"Are you coming in?"

"Yeah, I'll be down in a little bit when I get dressed."

"We're looking forward to seeing you."

"Thank you, ma'am. See you after a while."

"Bye!"

"Bye!"

Well! They really were expecting me. I was happy to know the offer still stood and that my forty-six dollars was not the only thing between me and a sinkful of dishes.

My career begins! Those were my thoughts as the rose-colored Cadillac and I were easing along Sixteenth Avenue South on Music Row. Also easing along Sixteenth Avenue South, on foot, were the owners of the publishing house that I hoped to be working for, Newkeys Music: E. Jimmy Key, Dave Dudley, and Jimmy C. Newman. A great deal of my future walked with these men down Music Row this cold morning, but we started off inauspiciously enough.

"You gentlemen want a ride?"

"Well! Hello there, Thomas!" Key grinned openly. He called me Thomas because of the letter I wrote him once telling him to put my Christian name on all my contracts. I was always pretty uptight about legalities.

"Where you guys headed?"

"Over to Mercury to pitch some songs for Dave," Key replied. "He's cutting tonight, and we want to get some tunes on the session. Why don't you go by the office and have some coffee. We'll be back in a few minutes."

"O.K."

Marie Ratliff, the mainstay of the office, was sitting in the front part of the tiny area housing Key Talent and Newkeys Music. The building was called the Eight-Twelve, as the address was 812 Sixteenth Avenue South. Unfortunately, I had caught Marie in the midst of an emergency operation on some piece of office equipment. I watched in amused silence for a moment or two, privately not giving the patient much hope for recovery, before she noticed me with a start.

"Welcome to world-famous Music City!" she blurted. "Did you have a nice trip?" And we exchanged pleasantries until Jimmy, Jim, and Dave returned from their meeting to talk about my deal.

That deal: I could turn in my songs as I finished them. During that time I would get a fifty-dollar-per-week "draw." A draw is an advance against the royalties a songwriter hopes to earn. And since a songwriter receives royalties only every six months—when the publishers do their bookkeeping—the draw is essential for providing square meals between accountings.

With that settled, the meeting was over, and I was on my own—supported by the promise of fifty dollars a week from Newkeys Music. Jesus, with that kind of money I had to get busy and figure out a way to spend it. You can't let money like that just pile up, you know.

And, of course, I already had the spending part planned. First an apartment, then—as thousands of us did in those days—a night on the town.

Around the corner from Newkeys, on South Street, I found an eight-dollar-per-week, one-room affair which passed as an apartment. Ah, music lovers, just picture it: a room where I kept all of my stuff in the middle; a room with a bed that was supposed to fold up into a couch but didn't; two straight-backed chairs, so loosely joined that I found it soothing to sway back and forth in one of them as I picked my guitar; and a stove, sink, and refrigerator—all in a row along the wall. Finally, who could forget the floor of patchwork consisting of six layers of different-colored linoleum?

I pulled back the Venetian blind from the lone window over the couch-bed and drew a picture of a rabbit, then wrote my name.

Somehow I didn't think anyone would mind.

And this wasn't the first time I had found myself in such a room. Before coming to Nashville, I had worked and lived in a lot of such places . . . mobile homes, one-room apartments, army barracks, the backs of automobiles. This was just another dirty, dangerous, depressing, food-odored apartment. The landlord did not require that I like it. He only required rent in advance and that I leave him alone to entertain himself with his "secret" observations.

I guess he was disappointed when I placed a picture of Connie Francis over the hole in the bathroom wall.

Now to my first night on the town.

There was only one place I intended to go that night—the Nine-O-One Club. It was a bar like no other, and the watering hole for more country talent than any other in the world. It has been in business for at least twenty years, under various names . . . but the decor is the same. A ceiling papered with record-album jackets. The walls, with eight-by-ten glossies of country-music stars and "would-be's." And never let it be said that there's not room for new talent, for the Nine-O-One had a restroom free for people to write—in pencil or pen—poetry on the walls. Or the more frustrated ones could carve it into the woodwork. And just to make sure that opportunities were provided for the up-and-coming, the room was painted every five years. Into this heaven walked Tom (without the "T.") Hall, wearing my jacket (previously described), my army uniform, a crew cut, and my black army boots shined with a damp tissue. As I reached the bar, Merle Haggard was singing "Strangers" from the jukebox.

The bar area was a shotgun arrangement. There was a line of bar stools to my right and some booths next to a pool table in the rear. You could walk in the front door and then walk right through the place like an alley before exiting out the back door, Several people walked that straight line that night: each coming in, walking slowly through the place, and then right on out the back door. How many nights would I repeat that walk—when broke, depressed and lonely . . . ? It was not every night that I could afford a beer at the Nine-O-One.

But tonight was my first, and I had money.

The waitress found me looking up at the album covers on the ceiling. "Beer, fella?"

"Bud."

"That'll be thirty-five."

I put a dollar on the counter and watched her stack the change in a neat little pyramid. I decided to make conversation.

"You need some new album covers."

"The well-known album cover." She nodded.

"Huh?"

"Are you in the army or somethin'?"

"No. I was."

"Thought you were from Fort Campbell." She congratulated her intuition.

"I'm from Kentucky."

"Ain't that where Fort Campbell is?" My mind was still pre-occupied with her phrase "well-known album cover."

"You're right about that," I consented. But I was to learn that "well-known" was the catch phrase for everything in the music business at that time: the "well-known" beer bottle, the "well-known" hangover, the "well-known" asshole, etc.

Then it struck me. I was going to have to learn an entirely new language in this town! Adjusting to my new career was not going to be as easy as I had thought. Thus the phrase that had originated from a John D. Loudermilk song, "Life Can Have Meaning"—your "well-known" hit—was simply the first of many adjustments for the new songwriter in town.

Three beers went by as I sat staring at the waitress: black shoes, black hose, black tights, short-short black skirt, black blouse, and a silver necklace with a pendant that looked like a zodiac sign . . . though I didn't necessarily stare in that order.

Then a little guy walked in with a guitar.

"Gaaawddammmn! It's colder'n a witch's tit out 'tare." He

laid the guitar, without case, flat-backed on one stool and sat down on the other.

"Sharon," he said to the waitress, "could I leave this well-known, hit-writin' guitar here for a few days and drink beer on it till I get paid for that demo session?"

Sharon held out both hands in front of her as though fending off a thrown beer bottle and almost screamed, "Eddie, Eddie, Eddie . . . Jim would raise hell for that. This ain't no pawnshop, and I ain't no bookkeeper. And just how many did you have Friday night, anyway?"

"I paid Jim for that last night—ask him!"

"How in hell can I keep all that straight? Why don't you just drink when you got the money and sober up the rest of the time?"

"Well, don't make a goddamned federal case out of it. I pay my bills."

Boy, did I feel great right along in there. Here I was in Nashville, half drunk, and people were talking about demo sessions and waving guitars around as if they were weapons— which they are.

"I'll buy him a beer, Sharon!"

"Allllriiiight! See there? The world is full of folks that appreciate real talent. My name's Eddie . . ." (I never listen for last names.)

"I'm Tom Hall."

Ole Eddie and me became friends right off. Or at least until I found out he was determined to drink his way through my forty dollars.

In a few minutes the waitress—I was calling her Sharon by now—yelled into nowhere, "Webb, you-all ready for a drink in there?"

Following the direction of her glance, I saw a little room off to the left with a curtain drawn across the door. Just then an arm drew the curtain back . . . and I saw—can it be?—my first star!

There was Webb Pierce, talking to a fellow who needed a hair-cut and shampoo pretty bad. (The popular style of the day was a razor cut, producing shaped hair that required hair spray to lock it into place—giving the impression that everyone was wearing a black leather hat.)

"We just need a little water and some ice in here," Webb responded.

Granted, the place was only supposed to be selling beer, but the big stars could sneak a flask into the side room and order set-ups. Usually, they left a big tip for Sharon . . . or they would get drunk and give Jim a shotgun or something special.

And you can be sure by now I was having a big time . . . sure as hell. After a few more minutes, assured by the fact that I knew everybody, I said, "Let me see that guitar there a minute."

"You in the music business?" Eddie inquired.

"I wrote 'D.J. for a Day' for Jimmy Newman." And Eddie was impressed.

"No shit? Hey man, that's pretty good!"

"Thank you! I write for Newkeys."

"Sing sump'n!" Eddie begged.

If you have ever been in Nashville, in a bar, at nine in the evening, and asked someone to sing something, I can guarantee you have never been refused. I strummed a few clever chords on the guitar and offhandedly parodied Merle Haggard's record of "Strangers."

"From now on all of my strange is gonna be friendly," I sang in my best Haggard imitation.

"Hey—that's funny, man," Eddie laughed. "Hey, Webb! Did you hear that? Sing it again, Tom!"

"From now on all of my strange is gonna be friendly."

Webb Pierce looked up from his conversation, not getting the joke.

"Carl Smith has the hit on that record, son. That other boy sings too much like Lefty." Without blinking, Webb looked at me through the smoke for a minute, then said in a surprisingly high, nasal voice, "Close this damned curtain, Sharon. This is a business meetin' in here."

However, the rebuff didn't affect me then. Eddie and I had become big buddies. I was buying the beer, and he had informally become a press agent for me. When anyone came through the door, Eddie would say, "This is Tom Hall. He wrote 'D.J. for a Day.' Listen to this!"

And I would sing, "From now on all my strange is gonna be friendly." Ole Eddie would laugh and buy the guy a beer on my tab.

Boy did it grow tiresome. The first night. And I would spend a thousand nights just like this one.

Then, just as I was ready to leave, Eddie asked me if I wanted to have a *real* party. Probably out of nothing more than exhausted, first-night blues, I agreed, and he handed me what he called an "old yeller" otherwise known as an upper. Now, I had never taken a pill before. And I was to later hear Roger Miller say that, when he took pills, he got so nervous he could thread a sewing machine while it was running. In a very short time the pill took effect, and my mind begged, "Lead me to a sewing machine!"

Well, Eddie did. He took me to someone's apartment, and we sang songs to seven or eight other people who, in turn or at the same time, sang us songs until ten the next morning. By noon of what had now become the next day, I was writing songs like crazy and looking for Sharon. My mind was made up. This was the girl who would share my life. I would move her into my apartment, and we'd seek fame and fortune together.

Somehow, Eddie and whoever had driven us out there arrived at my apartment door. Eddie saluted and spun right back to the car. As it pulled away, he shouted back at me, "I am going to the well-known bed."

So what's the motivation behind a man who packs into such a dingy apartment and spends all of his forty-six dollars on the first night in Nashville?

In a word, those first hours in town were symbols of an inner, all-consuming desire—a desire that devoured all of us roaming the streets of Music City: the well-known HIT.

Good God, it's been said a million times: a hit will cure anything . . . a broken arm, the clap, cancer, or any other damned malady known to man or beast. Shit, man, you give me a hit and I'll ride that sum-bitch right into hell and back. You give me one hit record, and I wouldn't give a damn if the sun ever came up again. You give me a hit, and I'll tell Music Row to piss up a stump. You give me a hit, and I'll buy you a damned old yeller as big as a manhole cover. You give me a hit record, and I'll run for Congress. You give me a hit, and I'll kiss your ass on the Grand Ole Opry stage on Saturday night and get Minnie Pearl to hold your britches.

It was all-consuming

But it was frightening, too.

Though on the surface I never cared, I wanted a hit like everybody else . . . and it was just a lot of fun being there . . . trying.

Jimmy Newman, several years later, explained that success is like a bird. If you hold it too tight, you'll kill it. If you don't hold it tight enough, it'll fly away.

I guess I believed that then, because I didn't try too hard. I was just there, just doing what came next and waiting for someone to find me.

The amazing thing about being such a glorious fool was . . . they did!

"Triptych 2"

MADISON SMARTT BELL (1957–   )

Madison Smartt Bell was born in Nashville and was raised on his family's farm in Williamson County, Tennessee. He was Phi Beta Kappa at Princeton and earned an M.A. at Hollins College. Critic Andy Solomon describes Bell as a regional writer, that region being "the foggy border that buffers purgatory from hell in the sootiest creases of contemporary society." Indeed, Bell's fifth novel, *Soldier's Joy* (1989), was his first using the South as his fictional landscape, rather than his usual setting, the gritty underworld of a violent, drug-addled New York. His episodic 1993 novel *Save Me, Joe Louis* is a manic tale of a petty grifter returning from New York to his family farm outside of Nashville. He provided photographs for a 1992 edition of Andrew Nelson Lytle's *A Wake for the Living*. Bell has published two short story collections, including *Zero db* (1987) and *Barking Man and Other Stories* (1990), as well as a 1985 history of Vanderbilt University's Owen Graduate School of Management. Bell presently teaches as part of the English faculty at Goucher College in Baltimore. The following short story was first published in *The Crescent Review* in 1984.

I

The tree line at the top of the ridge was stirred by wind so that the light snow fell off the branches and scattered down the ragged slope. The snow parted in grains before the wind and settled in the low places. Not enough had fallen to coat the long gulley that ran down the hillside and the gulley lay bare, a reddish slash in the pale skein of snow. No snow stuck to the old disc-harrow or to the pump at the bottom of the gulley and these dark forms were outlined sharply, like the dark trees against the sky. Their iron was so cold it would burn skin at the touch. The iron latch of the gate near the foot of the hill was cold too, so that no one wanted to put his bare hand to it. The wind swept down around the grey board house and carried the smoke from the chimney down to the ground. The men working in the yard all ducked their heads away from it. The wind blew across Lisa's face, disturbing her pale hair and bringing water into her eyes. In a moment it was calm again.

Lisa was well wrapped against any kind of cold, with her corduroy coat down to her knees and her jeans stuffed into red rubber boots. She sat cross-legged on top of a washtub by the table where some women were cleaning chitlins. The sharp smell didn't bother her; it was alien and exciting. She was five years old and without prejudice. Her hair and skin were white enough to make her an albino, but her eyes were ordinary grey. The hog-killing animated her and she couldn't sit still for long.

Jack Lee and Luther were working over the hog in the long scalding trough. The steam from the water mingled with the smoke of the fire under it, and there was thin vapor coming from the mouths of the two men, who were holding the carcass half out of the water with a length of iron chain. They turned the hog over with the chain to scald it evenly and pulled large clumps of bristles off with their hands. Hair and patches of scum floated on the surface of the cloudy water. When the bristles began to come away easily they raised the hog out of the water and rolled its body onto a bare board platform that was against one side of the trough. Then they scraped and shaved the hair away with big knives, occasionally rinsing the skin with hot water.

The hog's eyes were clenched shut and his jaws were locked together. Lisa scratched a white line along his flank with a scraping disc. It amused her to see the hair coming off in the wide places, but when they had to work closely around the joints and the head the job became difficult and boring. Lisa set her scraper down on the platform and ran off to the shed where the women were trimming scraps for sausage.

Amelia Tyler and Elizabeth were chopping the meat under the shelter. Their black hands moved rapidly across the planks, slicing some of the fat away from the lean meat so the sausage wouldn't turn out too greasy. From time to time they wiped their hands on the fronts of their aprons, and the aprons were blotched brown. Amelia had on a thick coat with the stuffing coming out in places, and her hair was pulled back from her forehead under a bandanna. There was a dent in the front of her head that a small hen's egg could have fit into and she had once told Lisa that something bad had been growing in there and they had cut it out in the hospital. They had talked about it all one evening when Amelia was Lisa's babysitter.

Amelia pushed some of the extra fat over to Lisa and gave her a knife to cut it with. Lisa sliced the strips of fat into small square chunks, and Amelia said for her to take it out and put it in the crackling pot. There was a big iron kettle in a frame over a fire outside and Lisa dropped the little squares of fat into it to boil and make the cracklings. Some of them were already done and she dipped one from the surface of the water. It was crisp and golden but it had very little taste at all, and she didn't really want to eat another one.

Over near the scalding trough there was a thick pole lashed into the forks of two trees and four of the seven hogs were hanging from it waiting to be cleaned. The hogs were suspended from pointed sticks which were thrust over the pole and through the tendons of their hind legs, so that the hogs hung head down. Their heads aimed blindly at the frozen ground, and the slashes in their throats were bloodless now and white. They had been scalded and scraped and their bare skin was blue and grey, the color of a bruise. All seven of them belonged to Mrs. Denmark, who was Lisa's mother, but two of them would go to Amelia and Ben Tyler to help pay for all the work they did. They would take the heads and chitlins of all seven hogs too, because white people didn't eat those things.

Ben Tyler was up on the road where the cars were, with Luther. They were sharing bootleg whiskey from a flat unmarked bottle. Looking up there, Lisa could only see their feet under Luther's truck and their hands passing the bottle, through the windows of the cab. Ben was short and stooping and very dark. His face looked almost Chinese and he had a little beard around his mouth and chin. He was still strong, although he was starting to like to talk about how old he was getting. Amelia or Mrs. Denmark would be angry at him most times for drinking but hog killing was a big party for everybody. He told Lisa once that there was nothing like a drink for a cough and then he told her not to tell her mama. She knew that what he said was true because her mother would give her a spoon of whisky with sugar in it if she was coughing and sick.

Robert and Jack Lee were blocking out a hog that had already been gutted. Jack cut off the head with a chopping axe, and then used the axe to separate the backbone out from the ribs. The spine came out in one piece, with the stiff little tail still at the end of it. The men began to section up the sides of meat with their knives.

Ben Tyler came down from the parked cars and went over to where the hogs were hanging. He had a foot tub with him, which he set under the nose of one of the hogs. From the back pocket of his overalls he took a long butcher knife, and he threw down the cigarette that was in his mouth, Lisa was watching attentively, standing near the scalding trough.

Ben stood up straight and pushed the round hat he always wore to the back of his head. He put the point of the knife in between the hog's hind legs and pulled it straight down, almost to the big cut on the throat. Then he laid the knife on the scuffed snow beside the tub and parted the opening he had made. A great knot of blue entrails began to roll out of the hog's chest. Ben guided the tangled guts into the tub with his veiny hands. When they were all detached he took out the liver and began to slosh water into the cavity.

Lisa was backing up, watching Ben closely, and without knowing it she touched her thighs to the rim of the scalding trough. When she tried to take the next step she flipped over the edge and into the water. She was so heavily dressed that very little water got to her skin, but it wasn't easy for her to get out. She hadn't opened her mouth, but Ben and Amelia both came running at the sound of the splash.

Ben grabbed her hands and pulled her scrambling over the lip of the trough. Amelia began to yell at him before she stopped running.

"Why you can't keep an eye on her? Miz Denmark gone skin us alive over this."

"Reckon I better care her back down to her mama's house."

"I'm gone take her right inside here before she freeze to death." Amelia led Lisa to the cutting table and rubbed some fat on her hands and face. The child didn't seem to be badly burned. Amelia picked her up and carried her over the broken steps of the porch and into the house.

There was no light in the room they entered except for a red glow from an opening in the large cylindrical woodstove which heated the house. The windows were blinded and the room was dark and close. They walked across vague lumps of cloth and invisible clutter; nothing could be seen clearly. Amelia took Lisa's outer clothes off and hung them by the stove to dry. She put Lisa down on a sofa and covered her with some blankets.

Lisa lay quietly and looked at the orange eye of the stove. It was hot in the room and there was a heavy smell of wood smoke and human musk. She imagined being swallowed by an animal. The patch of light shimmered and expanded in her eyes, and Lisa went to sleep.

She woke up again in her bed at home without knowing surely how she had come there. There was moonlight out the window and her mother was sitting at the edge of the bed.

"Mama," she said, "I know how come Benjamin's so black. It's cause he works so hard in the dirt and he put his arms up in the pig's belly."

Mrs. Denmark touched her forehead and felt that it was cool.

"Don't say that" she said. "It's not polite to Ben, and it isn't true."

Lisa closed her mouth and turned her eyes to the window. She could see the beginning of the road that ran from her house to the hill where the hog-killing had been. Now she remembered being carried out of the house in the twilight, when the stars were starting to show. Out in the yard there were dark stains and footprints in the snow, which had been melted by the people's walking and had frozen again. The heads of seven hogs rested on the railing of the porch, all the hair scraped from the dull skin except for the toughest bristles. Their eyes were narrowed or entirely closed, and their jaws were shut in jagged smiles. In the vague December light each face seemed to possess some secret.

II

Ben Tyler felt like some piece of scorching wood, walking under the August sun, thinking how the heat might drive him out of his mind. From old habit he wore old clothes that covered everything but his hands and face, and now his body could not breathe. The air was still and heavy and it took effort to penetrate it. He had to keep moving though, to get on with the extra work the drought made for him to do.

All along the barn lot the dirt had hardened and cracked into small octagons and trapezoids. Ben ground powder with his feet, walking on the packed earth. Near an old bathtub which was used as a watering trough a sweaty horse stood, moving only to twitch flies away. Ben passed the tub on his way up the little grade to the barn, and turned the faucet on to refill it. It had not rained for weeks. The pasture was yellowing in the dry heat and the grass seed he had planted on the lawn for Mrs. Denmark had had no chance to sprout.

Mrs. Denmark said it was more important to save the garden than to try to grow grass, so that was how Ben would spend the afternoon. There were sprinklers and hoses in the barn and he would carry them down to the garden to try to keep the ground there moist. Water spilled directly on the plants would boil and scald the leaves, but it would be some help to keep the earth around them from hardening. When he pulled the barn door open it dragged roughly across the small stones fixed in the ground. He needed to raise the hinges.

It was no cooler in the hall of the barn, though the darkness there was a relief to the eyes. Ben's thick shoes sank deeply and coated themselves in the dust of the dirt floor, a much finer powder than the dust outside. He walked up a pair of wooden steps and opened the door to the room where the saddles were kept. The same grit covered the saddles and the shelves that ran along the walls. Ben knelt down and felt in the corners below the lowest shelf for the hose-pipes that had been stored there. He pulled out a length of hose and flexed it in his hands to see if the drought and heat had cracked it. The particles that his motion raised glowed in the flat shafts of sunlight which came through the cracks between the boards of the wall.

He tested all the pieces of pipe he could find and tied them into coils with bits of baling twine. There were two sprinklers under the shelf that he thought were not broken and he took these out also. His tongue felt rough and swollen, too large for his mouth, and he began to think of how thirsty he was. The dim space of the barn smelled of musty straw and dried horse manure. He wished there would be a breeze.

When he came outside again he saw Lisa walking down the steps from the door of her mother's white house. She walked in the dense shade under the big trees of the yard, watching her feet on the brick path and swinging her hands. The dress she wore was pale blue and hung straight to her calves, unbelted. Looking at her across the bare lot, Ben thought that she seemed to be moving in an improbably cool globe, although he knew it was as hot in the yard as anywhere else.

With the coils of hose slung over his shoulder he walked back to the horse trough and sat down on one of the large pocked stones beside the faucet. He reached for the cup that he kept there, filled it from the tap and drank. When he was halfway down the second cupful he looked back toward the house. Lisa had come to the end of the walk and mounted the low brick wall that ran to the gate of the barn lot. She walked along the top of the wall and climbed the square brick post that met the wire fence enclosing the lot. She stood poised on top of the post, her hands out a little from her sides, and stared away over the drying pasture and wooded hill in the direction of Ben's own house. The hem of her dress and the ends of her hair seemed to flutter slightly, though there was no wind to move them. Ben thought that when he had finished his water he would go over and talk to her a little, before he went to the garden.

In the Tyler house it was dark and sweltering; the windows were small and didn't admit much light or air. Amelia had dressed as lightly as possible in a cotton print skirt, but she felt like her huge body was burning from inside. There were four rooms in the house and each was small and low-ceilinged, so that she always felt cramped. The doors between them were almost too narrow for her to pass through.

The front room with the woodstove seemed unnatural in hot weather, for it was meant to hold heat and keep the air out. There were several layers of wallpaper on the walls, too torn and dirty to be decorative. The paper insulation fixed the heat in the room, as did the ragged stuffed furniture. The room was grey with the dirty light that came through the windows. Amelia walked to the door, pushing aside some litter with her feet, newspapers, part of a child's tea set, and a headless doll. She swung the door open, hoping to start some air moving through the house, and stopped to rest a moment, looking down the concrete steps to the gravel road a few yards away.

The toys belonged to Amelia's granddaughter, Jenny's child. Jenny couldn't get along with the man she was married to so she was staying at home for a while. She had never been able to get along well in life and she hadn't married Prester until the baby was almost born. Now she said he was a no-count and she wouldn't stay at his house anymore. She kept the baby, who was four now, but she didn't seem to understand how to take care of her. So Amelia had to watch over the girl whenever she was here, but today she was with Prester's old mother.

From the time she was a baby Jenny never seemed to have good sense, and she didn't have any head for school. She would often stand and stare blankly like she couldn't hear whatever you were saying to her, but it was not until she grew up to the age of sixteen that she began to have the sickness that makes people holler and fall down. When Mrs. Denmark got to know about the falling down she said for Jenny to be taken to the hospital of Central State. There a doctor told Amelia that Jenny would never be smart, which everyone had already known, and it was also discovered that she had become pregnant. They gave names to the things that were wrong with her but Amelia couldn't remember them after they got home, any more than she had remembered the name of the thing that had been growing in her brain that other time. Jenny was given a medicine for the falling sickness, but it often seemed that either she did not take it or it did not work.

When Son, so called because he was named for his daddy, came on leave from the Army, he tried to bring Jenny into the arms of the Lord. For days she had turned her head away when he talked, but when he got her to go to a meeting she became as excited about it as she ever was about anything. Soon she became more devoted than Son had ever been, and she began to go to the meetings where people cry out and speak in unknown tongues, not like the church the Tylers had always belonged to.

It was then, just before Son went back to the Army camp, that Jenny had gone to Prester and got him to marry her. All the family was cheered by this act, and they made the best celebration for her they could. But later it appeared that her life had not really been changed.

Amelia was in the kitchen now, shaking pepper into the pot of pork backbone she was boiling on the electric stove. She felt so hot and bad that it was tiresome to do the smallest things. Some days she couldn't understand what she was working for anymore, when it seemed to take all her efforts just to stay in one place.

Out of all her children only Son had not been a disappointment to everybody. He had gone in that program in the Army where they give you school for nothing. He had a safe job in the Service and now he was an officer. Everyone could tell he had a serious mind.

But the other boy, Henry, had never been able to find a straight path for himself. For short stretches he would work and seem to live right, but it always turned out that he would break loose and spend all his money on wickedness. Because of that he never had any job that amounted to much and in the end no one around wanted to hire him anymore. Finally he got angry with them all and declared he would go to New York or Chicago, where he said there was a better life. No one in the family believed he had the money for such a trip and it was not until he had been gone a few days that they began to notice the small things of value that were missing. They never heard from him and he didn't write to them even for money.

Now she couldn't even talk to Benjamin anymore about all the problems. In her heart she still felt that he was a good man but she could never understand how the bad seed had come into the family. She remembered how he was when they both were young, quick and funny and so strong for his size that everyone was amazed by it. These days his mind was no longer clear and he would always think of drinking whisky and it would be up to her to stop him.

In the bedroom at the front of the house Jenny was still asleep, and she had not undressed yet from coming in the night before. She would often sleep until late in the afternoon, and she never cared to do anything useful. Amelia thought of waking her up, but it seemed there was no reason to. She couldn't think of any direction she herself should move in. She was tired, so tired, and looked forward only to the day when everything would be explained to her. Wiping big drops of sweat from her forehead, she took a step back from the heat of the stove.

Secretly, without at first declaring itself, the malignancy in Amelia's brain had returned and grown to a painful size. As she moved it broke apart and swirled forcefully all through her head. The picture that the room made in her eye diminished to the size of a postage stamp and then disappeared completely, as she fell across the top of the stove. Her elbow struck the boiling pot, which bounced from the wall to the floor, spilling the meat and the water. The crook of her arm rested on the glowing coil of the stove, and after she had lain there for a while the arm began to char.

In the room by the road Jenny turned over on her back and swung her feet to the floor. She put her head into her hands and rubbed at her eyes for a minute or two. Her mouth was sticky and stale, and she rose and moved toward the kitchen to look for something to drink. She walked a little unsteadily, bumping against the door as she left the room.

There was a little sick smell of burning that met her from the kitchen before she entered. When she stepped into the room her eyes grew round and white, and her mouth opened itself and hung waiting. For a moment she stood breathing deeply, and then her hands rose and waved twice in front of her face.

"Oh little Jesus," she said. "Send the demons out of my body." On the last word she threw herself at the floor and rolled there, flailing her arms and legs. Moaning came from her mouth and her spine moved in long violent jerks. A wild sweep of her leg upset a wooden chair, which fell across the door that opened to the back yard. The convulsions of her trunk became stronger and her body thrashed like a snake after it has been hit and before it dies. Her limbs and head were tossed at random by the motion that came from the center of her body, and foam appeared at the edges of her chewing mouth. With each jerk her head slammed soundly against the floor. Gradually the jerks became less frequent, and Jenny lay slackly on her side, knees drawn up toward her chest.

Out in the yard a starling skipped toward the open door in zigzags, picking at the dirt. He hopped onto the edge of the fallen chair and turned his scruffy head sideways to the room. Jenny twitched and raised her head, and the starling flapped sloppily into the air. Jenny clasped the edge a shelf and raised herself to her feet. She stood and stared at the spilled pot and the massive body humped on the stove. Then she turned and ran out the door, catching her loose shoe on the chair. She rushed into the clumps of buckbushes and cedars at the edge of the yard, following the straightest way to the Denmark house. Her mouth flew open and she began to cry out, not in grunts as she had before, but in high pure screams. As she moved into the thicket her clothes caught on thorned vines, and she began to tear at the front of her garments with her hands, not slowing her pace.

Lisa stayed standing when Benjamin came over to the post; she moved lightly from foot to foot. She would turn her head to look at him and then look away, back to the hill and the trees. Ben's voice rolled out smoothly, explaining how the heat sapped all the life from him, how the weather didn't give a man a chance, how he was feeling his age. All of this Lisa had heard before, too often to be interested, but she loved to hear the sound of his speaking. She shifted her feet and swung her head in rhythm to the talk. An object detached itself from the trees at the edge of the pasture, and Lisa's head stopped moving. Her eyes sharpened and began to track the object on its path down the hill.

Ben was facing away from the hillside, so he couldn't see the running figure. Lisa kept watching and saw that it was a person, that the person was waving its arms and stumbling as it rushed toward the gate between the field and the lot. As it fumbled with the gate latch Lisa recognized it as a woman. The woman thrust the gate open and ran through, leaving the gate swinging. Her feet, sockless in heavy unlaced boots, beat a cloud of dust from the cracked ground. A twig of bramble hung from the skirt of her dark dress, which was torn in front to disclose white underwear and heaving black skin. Her eyes rolled and her mouth flopped exhaustedly, and it was not until Benjamin turned to look at her that she began to scream again.

Ben turned to follow Lisa's glance and saw her coming through the gate. He stood quietly, looking toward Jenny's pumping legs as she came on, crying, "Mama done dead, mama dead," over and over, with other sounds that were not words. Lisa looked down at him from the post and he seemed to bend and shrink smaller in her eyes. Then she felt her mother's hands on her shoulders, turning her back to the house, and heard her voice telling her to go back, to go up to her room and wait, to take a nap. Almost frightened now, Lisa hurried away along the wall, looking back over her shoulder to where Mrs. Denmark was speaking, first to Ben who was shriveling so small, then to shrieking Jenny, trying to extract some form of sense from this mad situation. The scene contracted under the burning sun, as Lisa moved through the green shade into the cool shadows of the house.

III

One hog stood half hidden by a drooping branch of a cedar tree, halfway up the little rising from the shed where they all were fed. He was white with many black blotches, and was covered with wet brown mud, which the rainy winter kept stirred up in the hog lot. The hog and his four brothers of the litter had churned the mud constantly with their small heavy feet, so that around the shed it was worked into a soft gripping paste, several inches deep. But up the rising and back in the lot the ground was firmer, though slick, and there were rocks and roots to stiffen it. The mud on the prickly back of the hog beneath the tree was streaked by the cold morning drizzle.

Inside the feed room Benjamin was sitting on a sack of shelled corn, stopping to breathe a while, for he often felt bad in the mornings now. He took a little drink from the secret bottle that he had left under the empty sacks. The room had a small window and with the door shut it was so dark he could see nothing but shadows. The bottle glinted a little in the dim light and clanked when he set it down. After he had replaced it in the hiding place he could hear disturbed mice moving, under the sacks. He kept several bottles now, hidden in the outbuildings, and believed that no one knew about them. He had told Lisa to wait for him outside the gate, so she wouldn't see him take his drink.

He heard her voice, clear in the foggy air, saying, "Look, Benjamin, the hogs are out." He got up slowly to peer out of the high window, and there was the hog, wrinkling his long snout. Ben picked up a coffee can from the floor and scooped it half full of corn. He opened the door and went out into the lot, rattling the corn to attract the hogs back to the shed. The hog by the cedar tree stiffened and then bolted, and Ben could see the backs of all five of them through the trees as they ran grunting into the brush. Somehow he must have forgotten to latch the door tight the night before, and Jack Lee and Luther were coming to kill this morning. He knew Mrs. Denmark was going to bite his head off when she found out about this.

Lisa leaned all the way back, supporting herself with a hand on the wire gate, and looked up at the sky. There was nothing to see but the mist drifting and a cover of dull-colored cloud. Light rain fell on her face, and she lowered her head and pulled up the hood of her raincoat. Then she turned around and leaned her back against the gate. She could now see Luther's old battered truck coming unevenly across the rough ground, past the cow barn and toward the hog lot.

The truck pulled up beside the lot fence and Luther got out and let down the tailgate, so that later they could load the hogs and haul them away for cleaning and blocking. Lisa could see that both men had white stubble on their faces, and she smelled liquor when they came near. Each carried a light rifle. Ben had come around to the gate to meet them, bringing his own gun.

Ben scratched the back of his neck while he explained that the hogs had got loose, and Luther answered him, mumbling. Luther and Jack Lee came through the gate and the three of them walked up toward the thicket, with Lisa following at a little distance. The hogs had stopped under some low bushes and they had all turned their heads back to the sheds. They tensed as the men came near them but they kept watching and did not run. When the three men raised their rifles a couple of hogs grunted and the group began to swing away. There was a ragged sound of gunfire and squealing as the hogs scattered through the thorn bushes. One burst out into the clearing and ran to the creek bank behind the shed, where it collapsed, floundering. Ben pursued it, almost falling in the mud which clung to his feet as he tried to run, and as he drew near he pulled the butcher knife from his pocket. When he reached the twitching body he dropped onto his knees, shoved the knife hard into the side of the hog's throat, and made a quick slash all across it. The hog kicked and twisted, and a great rush of fresh blood came out and ran into the creek water. Ben stood up and began to walk back toward the others. Lisa, who had been standing apart, trailed behind him, watching everything sharply.

All of the men were laughing and shouting, excited and out of breath. They came together and leaned on their rifle barrels, trying to get their wind back. Only two hogs had been killed by the shots, and they weren't sure how many might have been hit. They didn't rest long before they spread out into the thicket, holding their guns at their hips. Lisa tried to follow them but she was quickly outdistanced. She slowed to a walk and wandered down near the fence at the far end of the lot.

On a high rocky place there was a hog waiting, partly concealed by grey shoots of thorns. Its nostrils were widened and its long flanks moved heavily with its breath. Lisa was near enough to hear the sound of the breathing from the place where she stood. As she watched the hog there were a couple quick cracks and she saw two round red holes appear in the hog's dirty hide. She heard a man yelling and the hog squealed and ran at her, scattering rocks on its path down the slope. When it came near her it sheered away and plunged into the creek bed, heading toward the fence. Lisa turned to follow the hog with her eyes and saw it wriggle through a broken water-gate and disappear into the woods. She ran along the creek to the fence and scrambled over, then followed the hog among the trees.

The hog had run far ahead of her and she had no idea where it could have gone. She looked on the wet ground for tracks, but there were no clear prints, because of the fallen leaves. With her head lowered she moved on into the woods, looking for tracks or traces of blood. These woods were strange to her and they were not on her mother's land, so she knew she should stay near the sound of the creek to be sure of finding her way back again. The noise of running and shooting died away behind her as she went farther into the forest.

Walking, she began to forget about the killing and the hog she was looking for. Around her, everything was pleasantly calm. Brown sparrows were hopping on the ground and fluttering in the trees. Above the tree tops the sky had cleared of rain clouds, though it was still the color of damp limestone. All along the sky looked flat and even, and Lisa thought she saw a buzzard turning through a gap in the branches. It had not become much lighter.

The creek bent across Lisa's path and as she started to cross it she saw that for several feet the stream was heavily stained with blood. For a moment she thought of the hog she was looking for, but then she remembered the one that had fallen in the water earlier. She was surprised, because she wouldn't have expected all the blood to hang together so far down the creek. She began to follow the red patch as it slipped and wound along the stream.

Lisa was fascinated by the quality of the moving blood, how it seemed to be so much more solid than the water. It floated in many small strands which wove themselves in a complicated matrix, and each strand looked as solid as a piece of fiber. Yet when Lisa put her hand into the water the strands divided around it and became insubstantial. She wondered what blood looked like when it was inside a body, and this thought absorbed her so deeply that she would never have noticed the hog if it had not fallen very near the creek.

It lay dully on its side with its hind feet at the edge of the water. Lisa could see no wounds on it, and she thought they must be on the side against the ground. Its body had not stiffened yet, but the eyes were glazing over. Lisa was glad to have found it, and proud that she knew what needed to be done. Then she realized that she had no knife.

Benjamin climbed over the hog lot fence near the place where Lisa had done so and hurried into the woods. He couldn't clear his mind of the picture of Mrs. Denmark's angry face. It had been bad enough when she saw how the hogs had escaped, but when she learned that Lisa was missing she had become almost too furious to speak.

Luther had told Ben that he thought he had seen the girl going over the fence, and so Ben had a chance to be the first to find her. He felt sure that the child would have the sense to stay near the creek, for she had lived around the woods all her life. He moved as fast as he could along the bank, afraid to call her name because there might be no answer. His fear was about to break out in a shout when he came around a turn in the stream and saw her.

She was sitting on the ribs of the warm dead hog, with her hands holding each other in her lap. She wasn't looking in his direction, but away through the trees. At once he saw that she was unhurt and no terrible harm had been done, and his head throbbed with the relief. The thrill of safety made him feel young again, and he ran up to touch her as she turned to look at him. He lifted her under the shoulders and stared into her face, and her eyes were clear and empty as the sky.

from *All Is Well*

JULIUS LESTER (1939–   )

> Julius Lester spent most of his youth in the Midwest and South.
> He received a B.A. in English from Fisk University in 1960.
> Lester, once a professional musician with two recording credits,
> has performed with Pete Seeger, Phil Ochs, and Judy Collins,
> and has worked as a radio announcer in New York City. He is
> the author of numerous children's books, a volume of poetry,
> and two novels. He won the Newbery Honor Medal for his *To
> Be a Slave* (1969). His *Long Journey Home* was a National
> Book Award finalist in 1993. His most recent novel, *And All
> Our Wounds Forgiven* (1994), is about the civil rights move-
> ment. His books have been translated into eight languages.
> Lester has taught since the early 1970s in the Afro-American
> Studies and in the Judaic Studies program at the University of
> Massachusetts at Amherst. The following excerpt is from Lester's
> 1976 memoir *All Is Well*. Nashville also figures in Lester's second
> memoir, *Lovesong: Becoming a Jew* (1988), the National Jewish
> Book Award-winning account of his conversion from Methodism
> to Judaism at age forty. Lester's first visit to a synagogue was to a
> Jewish congregation on Nashville's West End Avenue in the fall of
> 1956. In this excerpt from *All is Well*, "the question" to which
> Lester refers in the section about his arrival at Fisk University is
> the existence of God.

We moved south in the summer of 1953. My father had been
appointed to the Board of Evangelism of the Methodist Church,
whose offices were in Nashville, Tennessee. "The Lord works in
mysterious ways," he said, when I complained about moving to
the country of NO COLORED ALLOWED. "He might have a
purpose for you in the South." I was unconvinced.

We moved into a white neighborhood (I was mowing the lawn
one autumn Saturday morning and heard a girl's voice greet me.
I looked up and saw a white girl wearing sunglasses and holding

a poodle on a leash. Because of the glasses, I assumed she was blind, for she wouldn't have spoken to me otherwise. I'd never heard of poodles being used for seeing-eye dogs, however, but what did I know about white people. I continued mowing the grass. She spoke again. I became a little annoyed with the blind white girl who was going to get me lynched, if I wasn't careful. I continued mowing. Finally, as if she knew what I was thinking, she said something which indicated that she was aware of, and unimpressed with my racial identity. Though terrified of talking to a white girl in full view of the white neighbors, I had to. If she had enough courage (or innocence) to speak to me, I could not do less. We had not talked long, however, before her grandmother called her home. I was more than a little relieved and as I watched her cross the street, I knew she would not be back. A few minutes later, however, she returned, muttering imprecations against her grandmother. During the brief month or two we knew each other, there was never a time she came to see me that her grandmother didn't frantically call her home. There was never a time when she didn't return.

It was important that in my first relationship with a white person, that person risked herself for me. She acted contrary to everything I'd been taught about white people, and because she did, I had to disregard my teaching. Thereafter, I willed myself to trust whites, not wanting to accept or believe that they would not respond in kind. Many didn't, but they were unable to uproot the seed of faith that fourteen-year-old girl helped me plant.

Though I trusted her, the centuries-old fears to which I was heir would not be stilled. We played basketball in my backyard, and though she did not hesitate to push, grab, and hold me to make me miss a shot or lose the ball, I was afraid to guard her closely. What if I tried to steal the ball from her, and accidentally touched those pubescent breasts or alabaster thighs glaring at me from beneath her shorts and she yelled, "Rape!" I'd read too many stories in the black press about black boys and men who'd been lynched for nothing more than looking at white women.

to each other. (Cloudy day. April, 1966. The hill country of Mississippi, off the main road, off the state highway onto a gravel road winding its way up and down, back into the hills with mouse-gray sky of scudding clouds overhead with their adumbrations of rain. No houses to be seen, only the wooded hills. Four Corners, the old man had said, and anybody can tell you. Bob Fletcher, an old friend from college and, that spring, a photographer for the Student Non-Violent Coordinating Committee [SNCC], and I were looking for an old guitar player, one who might remember the songs everyone else had forgotten. Fifteen, twenty miles from the main road until, finally, Four Corners. It was an intersection of gravel roads with a store and filling station on one corner and a store on another. Bob pulled the truck up to the store and we went inside. Three women standing there. The one I saw first was young, with deep sad eyes, and beautiful like the sound of early morning rain falling on spring leaves. I dared not speak to her. Her eyes said too much about Four Corners, the crossroads of nowhere, with its store and glass cases, the interminable days of a bag of potato chips, a piece of bubble gum, a can of string beans and a pound of bacon. I looked to the second woman, who was in her thirties, but already the lines in her forehead testified to the crime of Four Corners. Her mouth was tight, the breasts sagged beneath the print dress, the hair was pulled tight around the head, and she held a baby in her left arm. I turned away to look at the large woman at the back of the store. The progression was complete. The double chin, the rimless glasses, the large bosom, the expression of open hostility. I didn't know if they were related by blood, but they had been mothered by the South, by a con-stant struggle to stop the hunger, by the leaves falling from the trees. I opened my mouth to speak to the older woman, know-ing that no one would come with a lynching rope if I addressed her, but she turned away, deliberately. I didn't know what to do, wanting and not daring to look at the youngest one, for I would not keep my eyes at the floor where they were supposed to be when a black man spoke to a white woman. I would have to look at her, knowing that my eyes would tell her of her beauty and my desire to be a part of it. "May I help you?" I turned and she was moving toward me, smiling, but the eyes retained their sadness, eyes that had either seen too much and turned away, or had seen nothing and knew they never would. I told her who we were looking for and my eyes stroked her face. "Oh, he lives right down the road a piece," she said, pointing. "Go 'til you come to a house with a dog-run. You know what I mean? A porch in the middle of it." I nodded. "You can't miss it. It's on the right-hand side of the road and there's a lot of junk in the yard." I thanked her, smiling, as unafraid as she. I started for the door, but she was beside me, talking. Of what I don't remember, but her voice did not stop in its desperation to find words, any words. I wanted to buy a soda, a few slices of cheese and some crackers and sit with her on the porch. I wanted to take her with me and I knew, I was certain, she would come. But we left her standing in the doorway and when we got into the truck, I asked Bob, "I didn't imagine anything, did I?" If he'd said, "What are you talking about?", I would've known that I had, but he only shook his head, unable to say more than "Uh-uh," quietly, with awe. He had seen it, she and I loving each other and if it had not been Four Corners, I would have taken her to me and washed the sadness from her eyes, dried the tears from her soul, and swum in the life of that body. But she and I were helpless, because one day some white man felt guilty about his lust for a black woman and went and lynched a black man, because . . . He created fantasies about that black man and his fantasies said a black man had a bigger one and could use it better and if you weren't careful he'd be after your wife and sister and daughter and that's all niggers think about anyway because that's all he thought about and they came with ropes and guns and kerosene and knives and they tied the black man with chains across a log, or to a tree, poured the kerosene and set him afire. Sometimes they hung him from the limb of a tree and afterward took his body to his house and threw it on the porch and laughed when the wife, mother, children came to the door to see what that noise on the porch was. Always, though, they used their knives. Because.)

My quasi-sexual adventure in Art Lane Alley was brief. One day the black janitor at the television station called me over and said that the white people at the station didn't like to see me sitting there talking to "that white girl." I told him I didn't care what the white people said. He said he didn't either, but he didn't want to see me get in trouble. The next day I looked at my friend on television and wondered if she would ever know why she would not see me again.

Like a boxer in the early rounds of a fight, I had begun feeling out the white world, testing the limits, irritating white clerks in stores by refusing to address them as "sir" or "ma'am," knowing that blacks have been lynched for something as small as that.

But I had to assert myself and refuse to accept the white-imposed proscriptions on my being. My parents were afraid for me, yet admiring. I was afraid, too, but to accept the fear was to legitimatize the white world's claims to my body and soul. I would not do that.

. . .

The proper place for someone with such a question is college, which I entered the fall of 1956. Fisk University in Nashville gave me a place and resources for four years to answer it and the other questions which logically followed, once I said No. My college life centered on the International Student Center, where foreign films were shown every weekend, lectures, play readings, art exhibits, and poetry readings given throughout the school year. The vitality of the ISC came, however, from its habitués, the campus intellectuals, who made the Center their private club.

Though intimidated by the lofty conversations about Sartre, Camus, Baldwin, Kierkegaard, and others whose writings dominated the college intellectual's life in the latter fifties, I brought my questions about God into this arena. The campus intellectuals, a little disdainful of this freshman who dared speak in their midst, dismissed me with the pronouncement that it was impossible to know if God existed, and until it could be proven or disproven, they reserved opinion. I thought that to be an evasion of the question and intellectually dishonest. How could one base his life on the impossibility of knowing? Then, John Brown, a stocky, brilliant history major who usually had only the most brusque remarks for me, said one day, brusquely, "You might find Sartre interesting, Lester." After asking him to spell it, I rushed to the library, and what Shelley had conceived, Sartre midwifed.

Sartre argued that the actual fact of God's existence or nonexistence was unimportant when compared to his function in people's lives. A belief in God bestowed *a priori* meaning on life, which he summarized as "Essence precedes existence." Sartre denied this. People exist, and the task of life was to give that existence meaning, i.e., "Existence precedes essence." Because there was no *a priori* meaning, people were "condemned to be free." Most, however, were unwilling to accept the responsibility of innate freedom and, thus, created God to relieve them of the horror of that freedom.

I had never read anything so convincing and was ecstatic at the prospect of assuming responsibility for my life, even if it meant, as Sartre said, accepting the consequences of my acts before I acted. This seemed more honest than acting good because a point would be recorded for me in the Good Deeds column of God's moral ledger, as a Sunday school teacher had once told me.

I became an atheist, not so much to deny God's existence (who can base their life on a teleological denial?), but to wholly affirm my own. When I announced my atheism proudly to the ISC claque, however, they were shocked. I had assumed that they would understand and when they didn't, I understood that I took God so seriously that I would deny His existence. They scarcely regarded Him seriously at all, allowing Him neither existence nor nonexistence. Thereafter I knew that intellectuals were merely athletes, using words and ideas instead of balls to play their games. (Mother was taking a casserole from the oven when I told her. "I've been thinking, Mother, and I don't believe in God anymore." She always controlled her emotions carefully, and my words did not cause her facial expression to change, or slow her motion in taking the hot dish from the oven and placing it on top of the stove. She closed the oven door and, reaching in the nearest cabinet to take down the dinner plates, said evenly, "Well, you're no son of mine," and walked past me to set the table.)

December 27, 1956

(Journal) Read Huxley's *Ape and Essence*.

Daddy gave me a sermon today which went something like this: "There are times when reason is no good. Now I want you to stop all this mess about not believing in God. Who do you think you are to set yourself up as not believing. You read some fool book and let that tear down all you've been taught. Well, you're going to church whether you want to or not. That's all there is to it. All I get comes from God and therefore all you get comes from God. If you aren't going to believe, you won't get what God gives me."

In other words, he was saying, "Believe or get out." His approach isn't quite right. He still doesn't think I'm serious. He figures this ultimatum will work. I could live a lie or I could leave. If it comes to that point, I shall do the latter.

Brave and fearless words worthy of an adolescent rebel, but leaving would mean having to go to work, an undertaking for which I was singularly unqualified. But no threat of my father's would have made me recant, and perhaps he remembered the Sunday morning many years before when I, five or six at the time, refused to go to church. Five separate times he spanked me and five separate times I cried and reiterated my refusal, until both our wills broke simultaneously, and just as he was about to relent (so I learned years later), I walked out the door to church, without saying a word. Perhaps he knew that this time I would not be broken and nothing more was said, except that he expected me to continue going to church. Shelley would have refused, but my atheism was not in emulation of Shelley's, nor was I rebelling against my father. I was groping for my life, and it was unimportant whether I attended church, as long as I could follow this incipient stirring of my inner life.

. . .

Books were my guru, but I needed people to listen to me, to respond and empathize with my struggles. In the English department, where I took my major, I was fortunate to have three teachers whose influence on my life was to be permanent. Bernard Spivack, chairman of the department and a Shakespearean scholar, gave me a permanent love of the beauty and magic of language; Charlotte, his wife, was an artist in the classroom, but I learned equally as much on those Thursday mornings when I sat in her office, where she tolerated me for two or three hours as I grappled with Plato, Spinoza, and always, Sartre. It was she who introduced me to Gide, Camus, Chinese poetry, Graham Greene, and Georges Simenon, who became, and remains, my model for a writer of fiction.

Charlotte Spivack believed in and encouraged my initial efforts to write, but it was the poet, Robert Hayden, who told me bluntly that I was a writer, and that was at the core of my problems. He was a surrogate father, who knew that writing was not only learning the craft of using words, but even more, a psychological condition. A writer was a different kind of person, and it was that person in me he recognized and instructed. To be a writer, one must not only "face chaos," but set up residence within it.

However, I also needed a female contemporary whose hand I could hold during the labor pains of giving birth to myself. But being shy to the point of catatonia, I had accepted that I would never have a girl friend, unless she took the initiative. (One had, at camp the summer before my freshman year. She tired of my lack of aggressiveness and one day kissed me, thrusting her tongue into my mouth and forever changing my life. Ah, Gwen!) Whenever I fantasized about taking a girl on a date, the screen went blank as I arrived on her front porch. What would we do? According to street corner discussions, you took a girl out to "get in them panties." Exactly how this was accomplished was never said, not to mention the more monumental problem of finding some place secret enough to do it, assuming one knew how. If by some act of Divine Intervention (which could not occur since I was an atheist), I "got in her panties," I still had a problem. I wasn't particularly interested in being there. Michele hated boys, for she overheard the vulgar way they talked about girls; I could not regard another girl in a way Michele did not want to be regarded. Moreover, I really didn't want to make love: I wanted to talk. ("Do you think a man on a raft in the middle of the ocean would have a concept of time?" was one of my favorite conversational openers, good for at least a half-hour of silence.) Oddly, though, the girls I knew expected a boy to try to kiss them, and sometimes, more. I didn't understand why they would want to get near that ugly thing boys were so proud of, and Michele swore that no boy would ever stick it in her.

Another part of me, however, ached to feel that flesh which swelled behind the starched white blouses and straight skirts. I masturbated two, three times a day, hating whatever it was that seized and shook my body like a tree in high winds. I particularly hated that thing drooping from the end of my torso like a fat worm, pulsating to an aching hardness as if it lived wholly independently of me. I wanted to cut it off and throw it to a passing dog. I envied Michele, whose organ was invisible to her, hidden, though I was never exactly sure where, unable to embarrass her as mine did me, protruding against my pants with such rigidity that sometimes it felt like a third leg.

Michele prevented me from treating girls as sexual objects, but my own sexual feelings persisted. Not knowing how to accept them as a natural part of myself, and, because of Michele, being unable to wholly admit that I had them, I came to hate girls. My earliest short stories were about young artists so distracted from their work by a world seething with feminine pulchritude that they became murderers of women. The only escape from the dilemma was to find a girl with whom I could talk. Then, if we developed a physical relationship, there would be no shame.

I wanted a female me, a Michele who lived outside me. The fall of my sophomore year, someone said, "That's interesting," when I posed Chuang Tzu's butterfly riddle, and I knew that I had found her. I met Sylvia in the only place my first love should have begun, the library. She was a gentle, soft-spoken, light-skinned girl with narrow, almost Oriental eyes. An art major from New York City, she was a graduate of the elite High School of Music and Art, and we met at the moment when each of us was obsessed with learning who we were and what we were going to do with our lives. "I don't know any of the answers," she wrote me once, "but that won't stop me from trying to find answers that will be true ones. God! This swiftly tilting planet—this green and blue ocean of hope and despair. Of truth? and men. Of truth and life. What am I to do with it? What are we to do with it? Is there only a different answer for each of us—or is there one answer for us all? Is life always a searching and never a finding?"

I had never known one such as her, who cared passionately, who never told me, as other girls had, "You take things too seriously." She was as serious about her life as I was about mine and most amazing, she was as awed by me as I by her. It was the perfect "marriage"; we were two souls in search of our selves and how much less frightening to make that search together. By being together, we affirmed each other and were no longer alone.

She was more than the female me, for her experiences had included concerts at Carnegie Hall, the Metropolitan Museum of Art, folk music, the drawings of Paul Klee, the watercolors of Dufy and the sculptures of Rodin. I envied and idolized her, for she seemed to think, see, and feel more deeply than I. "The birds

look like black pepper flung against the sky," she said one afternoon as we walked across campus, and how I wished I could
open my mouth and speak a poem. She talked more often in
images than concepts, and I did not understand her. She showed
me her strange drawings of naked, black trees, or of Giacometti-
like figures leaping and jumping between asteroids and planets,
and I was frightened. She lived someplace I had never been.

Every Saturday afternoon we sat in the ISC and listened to the
Metropolitan Opera broadcasts, and one Saturday I borrowed
my father's portable radio and we walked to Centennial Park and
sat on the steps of the replica of the Parthenon there, to listen to
Tristan and Isolde. We'd been there about an hour when the park
policeman told us to move. I knew that blacks were not allowed
in the park, but pretending ignorance, I asked him why. "You just
can't," he said, flustered. "Don't make trouble. Just leave." I
refused, badgering him until he became angry, and then, in our
great love, we laughed and walked away to the strains of Wagner.

She called me "Jay" and told me that my eyes were beautiful
and that I had the hands of an artist. I wanted to believe her,
because no one had ever said that anything of me was beautiful.
I told her that I was going to be a writer, composer, painter, and
she did not laugh. She tried to convince me of God's existence,
but loved me when I remained skeptical. We pored through art
books together and she taught me the humor of Dufy, the passion of Van Gogh, the truth of Rembrandt, and I was overjoyed
the day I "discovered" de Chirico and had something to give to
her. We clung to each other desperately, fearful of being returned
to the desert of our prior loneliness.

And we touched each other, clumsily, and without consum-
mation, but it did not matter. To know myself beneath her hands
was to feel myself as a person of beauty, an experience thereto-
fore unimagined. Her breasts were the first I touched and I held
them in my hands as if I were a pilgrim to Chartres receiving
communion wafers. We found a secret place in the library where
we undressed each other and knew ourselves in each other's

mouths and tongues, and though I longed to lie wholly within her, we were afraid to risk the child we did not want.

We were going to be married. I would move to New York, get a job and we would make love to Chopin nocturnes, have many children and live happily ever after—painting, writing, composing, dancing, sculpting, and drawing. Between us there was scarcely an aspect of the arts we had not studied and we laughed with anticipatory joy at the world's amazement on experiencing our creations.

But the following year, she did not return. She didn't like Fisk, and, also, she wanted to be away from me, feeling that she was being absorbed by me and increasingly unable to exist unto her self. I didn't understand. We wrote constantly for the next two years, still planning to be married until it was evident that she wouldn't marry me until I told her how I was going to earn a living. By this time I was living on North Beach in San Francisco at the tail end of the Beat Generation, subsisting on rice, jasmine tea, and an occasional handout of a sandwich from a Catholic priest with a wart on his chin at the church on Washington Square. It was a perfect life, and I couldn't understand why she didn't want to share it. Finally she wrote and told me that I was "immature" and was obviously never going "to grow up." That last letter begged me to return or destroy her letters, and the sketchpads of her drawings. I couldn't. Without them I feared the passage of time would make me believe that I had dreamed her. (The winter of 1963 I accidentally saw her in, of all places, the library on Manhattan's West Twenty-third Street. It had been five years since we'd seen each other and I was surprised at how nervous we were. It was evident that time had let us remain what we had been, but I was married now and I didn't want to know if she was, too. Afterward I hated myself for running from the library in fear, for not hugging her and telling her that I still had her letters and drawings, the books of mine in which she had scribbled poems and her French book. She had believed in me, had helped me paint the colors on my dreams, and mine were, I had begun to believe, going to come true. But she did not look as if hers were, for the shining intensity I'd known in her eyes had changed to the fright of one being hunted and beginning to gasp for breath. Two years later I saw her again at the same place and this time she ran from me as if she'd seen a specter.

It was the Sunday of July Fourth weekend, 1972. Joanne and I were walking through Washington Square Park in Greenwich Village when I saw Olivia, a classmate from Fisk who was the only person I knew who'd known Sylvia in New York. After exchanging pleasantries and gossip, I asked Olivia what I'd wanted to ask before saying hello to her. "How's Sylvia?"

She looked at me strangely. "You don't know?"

I hoped she was not going to tell me what I already knew from the tone of her voice. "Know what?" I asked, hoping my smile would shield me.

"Sylvia walked into the ocean at Rockaway Beach."

I asked her when.

"Oh, let me see. It was, must have been around 1963 or 1964."

I thought back to the last time I'd seen her. "Must've been after that, because I ran into her the spring of 1965."

Olivia shook her head. "You have to be mistaken. She was dead then."

I asked her if Sylvia had married. She had not.

I came home and that evening, read her letters for the first time in thirteen years. I had forgotten just how much we loved each other. "If I don't love you, where is my home?" I'd forgotten just how completely we were all the other had had at one time, and how desperate our need was for each other. "Just ask the sun and the summer breeze and the moist black earth. They'll tell you. I love you." It was there, in her rapid scrawl, on practically every page, and for the first time, I noticed how often she'd written of one day letting waves cover her. I was too angry at her to cry, for she left me with an emptiness which would never be filled. It was her place and as long as I knew she was somewhere in the world, that place hummed a quiet song. As long as I could walk the streets of New York knowing that one day I would see her, it was all right not to see her. But she had irrevocably deprived me of herself and I wanted to swim into the ocean after her. On that day, I wonder if she knew how much of me she was drowning, also. But I didn't know until she'd done it.)

from *A Turn in the South*

V. S. NAIPAUL (1932–)

Sir Vidiadhar Surajpradas Naipaul was born in Chaguanas, a
small town in the central sugar cane belt of Trinidad. He was
educated in private schools in Trinidad before matriculating
from University College, Oxford. Except for a brief stint in the
cataloguing department of the National Portrait Gallery in
London, Naipaul has supported himself exclusively through his
writing, a long list of publications including novels, short stories, history, travel journalism, cultural criticism, and reviews.
His first attempts at travel writing included his impressions of
the continuing British, French, and Dutch influences in the
post-colonial West Indies in *The Middle Passage* (1962) and of
what he perceived as religious excesses among Indian Hindus in
An Area of Darkness (1964) and among Middle and Far East
Muslims in *Among the Believers* (1981). His forthrightness of
opinion about culture practices he considered backward and
highlighting, for example, such habitudes as public defecation
and belief in karma in some sectors of Indian society, earned him
alternately harsh criticism and curt dismissal in the areas he portrayed. He turned his unblinking critical eye to the former slave
states of the American South in *A Turn in the South* (1989) and
visited Nashville, Atlanta, Charleston, Tallahassee, Tuskegee,
and Chapel Hill. Again his direct, even satiric observations made
him few friends in the area he visited. Following is an excerpt
from *A Turn in the South*.

The magazine in my hotel room, mixing its metaphors, said that
Nashville was "the buckle of the Bible Belt." Churches took up
twelve pages of the Yellow Pages directory. *The Tennessean* had a
"religion news" editor, and there was a weekly page of "religion
news," with many advertisements for churches (especially Church
of Christ churches), some with a photograph of the stylish-looking
pastor or preacher. Most of the Protestants in Nashville belonged

to the fundamentalist frontier faiths; the predominant denomination was the Southern Baptist.

The classier churches, the Presbyterian and the Episcopalian, looked at this Baptist predominance from a certain social distance, without rancor or competitiveness.

Dr. Tom Ward, the Episcopalian pastor of Christ Church, said that the Southern Baptists who sometimes came to his church found it too quiet: "'Y'all don't preach.' The Baptist ethos is the preached word. Which is the ethos of the Christian church in the South. Preaching meaning the emotional speech rather than the learned essay of the Church of England—preaching the word and counting the number of saved souls. But I have to say this. To say, 'I'm a Southern Baptist,' is another way of saying, 'I'm a Southerner.' What I mean is that that is the ethos, religiously. What is buried in their psyches is the fear of hellfire and damnation. My father was read out of the United Methodist Church in Meridian, Mississippi, in 1931—when he was seventeen—because he went to a dance. That's the Methodist Church. A lot of the Ku Klux Klan literature is Christian. Revivalism—why? To rekindle the spirit. What spirit? One bad step; many bad steps; and you have the Ku Klux Klan."

The Presbyterian pastor of Westminster, K. C. Ptomey, agreed that the Southern Baptist identity was in part the Southern identity. "That's very accurate. You see, a Southern Baptist distinguishes himself from an American Baptist. American Baptists are much more open-minded; they are not so rigid. I would add about the Southern Baptists: it has to do with sharing biblical literalism; it has to do with morality. For example, to be a Southern Baptist is to be a teetotaler. Morality, dancing, drinking—it encompasses the whole of life."

I asked him about the revivalism.

"The revivalist mind-set is 'to get back to God.' You often hear the words used."

"'Back'?"

"'Lost' is the word they use. And what they mean by that is 'damned.' And therefore they need to be revived."

The second-largest denomination in Nashville was the Church of Christ. It was also fundamentalist, and also originally a frontier faith. It had started (K. C. Ptomey told me) as a breakaway from the Presbyterians; and in some ways it aimed at a greater purity than the Baptists.

"They have developed into a sect or denomination that believes they are the only true Christian denomination. The Baptists wouldn't say that. But the Church of Christ people would say, 'You are not a Christian. You have to be in the Church of Christ, because it is the only true church.'"

There were more Church of Christ churches in Nashville than in any other city. Reverend James Vandiver, who was of the church, told me why.

"The mid-South is at a pivotal point. It is so near the place of American origins. People came here from the seaboard, and they migrated from here to Texas, Oklahoma, and the prairies—and in all these places you will find the numerical strength of the Church of Christ. From a cultural and socioeconomic point of view, the people in this area have common value systems and basically an agrarian economy. And basically people of that niche tend to be a bit more religious."

Reverend Vandiver gave me much of his time. He was happy to talk about his church and anxious to help with my inquiry. I found him absolutely fair. I wanted to meet someone from the church who had developed doubts about it. He promised to arrange that, and he did. Later he even put me in touch with someone who had left the church.

He was the pastor of the Harpeth Hills Church of Christ, a good way to the south of downtown Nashville. When he was giving me directions on the telephone he referred to his church as a "facility." When I came to a certain boulevard or ring road I would turn left; a hundred yards on I would see "the facility." I liked the word. I had first heard it used in a comparable way in Grenada in 1983, at the time of the American invasion: at a morning briefing the military press officer had referred to the temporary barbed-wire compound for prisoners as a "facility."

The Church of Christ facility at Harpeth Hills was of clean red brick: a prosperous church of a prosperous community. Reverend Vandiver was perhaps in his forties, sturdily built, with glasses. He asked me to call him James or Jim.

"That informality suits me and suits our theology. We try in every way possible to erase the distinction between clergy and laity."

Music was playing in the office.

Jim said, "A soft-music station. I had it on while I was doing some work this afternoon. The younger generation would call it elevator music." He smiled.

He was in shirtsleeves, but he was wearing a tie. He sat on a three-seater settee against the paneled wall. Above him was a painting of an arbor; to one side of the settee was a ficus tree. One whole wall was of bookshelves.

Jim said: "Let me explain the Church of Christ in the simplest way historically. We are seeking to do two things in religion. One is to accept the Bible as our sole rule of faith and practice. We believe in the inerrancy of the Scriptures." The other thing the church was trying to do was to go back to the very earliest Christian faith. "Within three centuries of Christianity's foundation Romanism was predominant, until Luther, Calvin, and the great reformers, the people who said, 'Let's give the Bible to the common man, and reform the Roman church. Let's lay aside the abuses, the corruption that's developed.'

"There's always a thread that looks back to the Scriptures and says, 'Let's duplicate.' In the early 1800s here, with the westward expansion, there arose these frontiersmen—as well as people of the seaboard—and I think the frontier spirit had a lot to do with it. These people represented a broad mainstream of Protestantism—especially the Methodists, the Baptists. The Church of Christ represented an abandoning of Protestantism, and did not represent a return to Rome, but to the very beginning of the faith, all the way back to Pentecost, the first Biblical dating of the Christian culture.

"That was the frontier spirit. 'We're on the frontier now. Let's lay aside differences. Let's be brothers in Christ.' I'm not trying to be coy, but I think the church of which I'm a member was established in A.D. 30. I'm just saying that the restoration movement here is a historical tracking of that movement on American soil."

"When was that?"

"Early to mid-1800s. That was the period we refer to as the American restoration."

"What was the need, you think?"

"Every great religious renewal has been sparked by a return to the Scriptures."

"You are so close to the Baptists. And yet you are so opposed to them."

"We are close to the Baptists in many things. Bible, Trinity, a church, evangelism, personal conversion to Christ. But we are different in other things. We sing without music. We observe the Lord's Supper weekly. We teach that baptism is *essential* to salvation. The Baptists teach baptism only as a requirement for admission to the church. And we're autonomous; every church is independent."

But, important as the church was in Nashville, it was in decline. The church that had suited the needs of frontiersmen was less suited to city-dwellers. Jim was aware of the difficulties; he was clearsighted and frank.

"We are in a time of great change, and that's a real challenge for us. Change? From agrarian to business and industry, from rural to urban, from blue-collar to white-collar, from lower to middle and upper class."

In *The Tennessean* I had read an item by the "religion news editor" that six Nashville Church of Christ churches were thinking of a merger, "to overcome high overhead . . . flagging membership and to rekindle enthusiasm for fellowship and missions." The six churches had a total membership of twelve hundred: six small churches, of an earlier, more rural time.

Henry came into Jim's office. That had been the arrangement: that Jim and I would talk alone for a while, and that Henry would then join us. Henry was twenty-six. He was of middle size, with well-brushed-back hair, white jeans, and a short-sleeved blue Polo shirt. He had been a student all his life, and though his doctoral studies were in an inconclusive, suspended state, he still had academic ambitions. He had just been to Uganda on behalf of the church, prospecting that country for mission work. At the moment, for money, he was working as a carpenter, just breaking even on his $8.00 an hour.

I asked what he thought about the church's chances in Uganda.

He said, "Very good. But the situation could be evolving into a situation ripe for another coup." (And yet, within a few minutes, he was to make me understand that his ideas about Africa and mission work were not so straightforward.)

In southeastern Uganda he had seen terrible things. He had seen hundreds of people tied up and sitting in circles. That had made an impression on him, but he didn't appear to know what to do with the knowledge and experience.

I wanted to know about the development of his faith—this young man in jeans and a Polo shirt. Had he had some kind of spiritual illumination? Had he made a confession of faith? I had been told that it was necessary.

He said, "There is a loophole. An irony. My parents were both pillars of the faith. There was a strong bonding between father, mother, and child. But—what this is to say—I knew what the necessary steps were to salvation in Christ. As early as five or six, I knew what those steps were. That's not uncommon at all."

"It's like part of your identity."

"Sure. I followed those steps of faith at the age of eight. I was baptized, fully covered in water, at the age of eight. But, going back to your question about spiritual experience, the answer is, candidly, no. In retrospect, I question whether those actions at the age of eight mean anything." He broke off and said, "I'm in a whirlwind at the moment. I've experienced a split with my family."

I was surprised. Jim had promised to arrange a meeting with someone with doubts, but I had been expecting to meet that person on another day.

Jim said, "As a mentor, let me say first of all I think Henry is typical of a person who grows up in a religious setting in which he makes a profession of faith."

Henry said, "As a doctoral student I have come to question the objectivity—the rational processes—which the Church of Christ—"

I had noticed at the beginning how he qualified his words. Now he appeared to be having trouble completing a train of thought: many new things were breaking into the original idea.

He said, "I feel compelled to throw this. My African experience has reinforced a suspicion I've had that there might be something amiss—what I want to say—a Westerner's thought processes or thought form—I believe I can broaden this, and include not only the Church of Christ but other conservative Protestant churches as well—our misuse of reason—the Western mind—the conservative evangelicals—"

I noticed that he was wearing an Yves Saint Laurent belt.

Jim said, "I see you headed to the reduction of a lot of concepts."

"I got to Africa and I was repulsed by what the missionaries had done. Instead of teaching the Africans first-century Christianity, they had taught them a Western, white-man's Christianity. Of all things—many of the young African ministers did not see themselves as carrying out their ministry in the most proper way without, for example, wearing a sports coat and tie, something that's totally un-African."

That appeared to make a whole: the ideas of the Church of Christ fusing with a rejection of colonial mimicry.

And Henry went on along that line. "Christianity was born out of an Eastern framework—"

A thought, unexpressed, came to me: an Eastern religion for the Wild West? Had the early Church of Christ really been presented to its followers like that? Or was the Easterness of the religion a more recent idea?

"—and we need to know when to separate the true essence of Christianity from Western cultural baggage."

That made a whole, but then Henry said, "My parents' mentality is very exclusivistic, in terms of who is going to get to heaven. It's as basic as saying who are really—with a capital 'R'—Christians. The real tension began when I went to the university. They were not happy at all about that. I've been questioning parts of the body of church knowledge. And the idea seems to be that, if I don't have the same set of beliefs as my parents, I am rejecting the right belief." Abruptly he said, "I feel so desensitized to what's going on."

He said that with relief, as though glad to give up the juggling with so many new and unrelated ideas.

Jim said, "That's typical of questioning people of conservative churches."

I said, "Somebody told me that I should study the Southern churches well. Because in fifteen years it's all going to change."

Jim said, "I agree."

Henry said, "I agree." He added, "The whole package of Christianity is bothering me. The point is, Jim, that is what is going on in my mind intellectually. But emotionally I have a very strong attachment to this *fellowship*."

An experience of Africa, the shock of a tribal civil war, a new vision of missionary effort, leading to a wider questioning: what had once been the complete, satisfying faith of a complete, clear, enclosed world no longer answered. And he was "in a whirlwind."

"Sources of Country Music"

ALAN CHEUSE (1940–   )

New Jersey-born Alan Cheuse's three wives have all been Southerners, a fact which Cheuse has said accounts for his feeling that the South is his "step-landscape." After teaching at Bennington College for a decade, he moved to Knoxville, Tennessee, where his second wife taught English and American literature at the University of Tennessee. Before his current teaching position at George Mason University in Fairfax, Virginia, he taught comparative literature at the University of the South in Sewanee, Tennessee. He is the author of ten volumes of fiction and nonfiction, among them the novels *The Grandmother's Club* (1986) and *The Light Possessed* (1990), and the short story collections *Candace* (1980) and *Lost and Old Rivers* (1998). As a book commentator, Cheuse is a regular contributor to National Public Radio's *All Things Considered* and is host of the Center for the Book- and NPR-produced short fiction magazine *The Sound of Writing*. His articles on Tennessee subjects, including James Agee and Robert Penn Warren, have appeared in the *Boston Globe Sunday Magazine* and Cheuse has written on the *Hee-Haw* television show for *TV Guide*. The following short story, "Sources of Country Music," is from his 1990 *The Tennessee Waltz and Other Stories*. The title derives from the 1974 Thomas Hart Benton mural of the same name commissioned by the Country Music Foundation for the Country Music Hall of Fame and Museum. Benton was the grandnephew and namesake of the man who once dueled Andrew Jackson on the Public Square in Nashville.

Take the Music City tour. That's what Brenda's up and doing, risen up out of that steamy bed where Billy is snoring like something out of a Florida gator farm, showering, dressing in her best jeans and jean jacket—the one with the wagon wheels and cac-

tus embroidered by her Gran—and leaving the room in the
Shoney's Motor Inn without, as far as she could tell, Billy stirring more than once.

George Jones is singing on the loudspeaker in the hallway
that's leading her toward the lobby. His voice makes Brenda give
a shrill little laugh, because it's one of Billy's favorites, and she's
smiling to herself, full-mouth, as she walks into the lobby, thinking about how glad she is she's here, and married, and she's only
just a little bit nervous about taking the tour by herself. She
couldn't feel all that awkward about going alone, not after
growing up by herself in Gran's house after her folks died in that
crash, not after all the nights she and girlfriends have spent
going out to bars (one or two times even as far away together as
Birmingham). If she could hear her boot heels clacking on the
floor, that would give her confidence, walking like a cowgirl. But
there's only carpeting here.

And a rat-nosed old man behind the desk.

"Taking the tour?" he asks, brushing the shoulder of his red
blazer as he looks up from his newspaper.

"Good morning. How'd you guess?" Brenda delivers her
medium-priced smile.

"It's the time," the man replies, gesturing with a puffy hand
toward the thick glass door to the street where the light of a
March morning seems pale compared to sunshine down in
Selma. "Here she is," he says, his hand still in the air—it's as if
he's about to cue in an invisible band—as a dark van with a guitar and Stetson painted on the side and

BLACK JACK TOURS
MUSIC CITY
USA

beneath them pulls up outside the door.

"That's me," Brenda says, still heavy with the thoughts of
absent Billy. But in a moment she's out the door, allowing a
bearded, pot-bellied fellow in faded blue workshirt and jeans to

slide open the side of the van. He nods his silent confirmation. Once she's up into the vehicle, hitching onto the seat next to a woman with weather-worried skin and a man with thinning hair, she can hear the driver calling in a deep pleasant voice through the glass door to the clerk behind the desk, "Have a Nice Day," and she's determined to have a good time.

"Howdy," the woman says with a smile, "we're the Ravens and we're on our way from Florida to Iowa."

"Own a farm," the man says, staring out at the traffic. It's a Saturday, so there doesn't seem to be much of it, and when their bearded guide and driver climbs up behind the wheel and steers them toward the roadway, there's no wait before roaring off on their tour.

"NOW FOLKS," his voice flares up out of a loudspeaker in the roof of the van, "Now Folks," he modulates the voice but it's still loud and metallic though he's sitting only just in the seat in front of them, "I'd like to welcome you to Nashville and say thanks for choosing Black Jack Tours." He clears his throat, and Brenda thinks again of Billy, his eyelids all buttery with fatigue, as he sank down beneath the covers when they came in from their night of celebrating.

"Pretending we're a crowd," says the farm woman, Mrs. Raven.

"His voice reminds me of my husband's," Brenda says.

Mrs. Raven nods. "You lose him? I'm sorry."

"Oh, no, no," Brenda is quick to answer. "We just got in real late and he was too tired to get out of bed."

"We lost a boy," Mrs. Raven says.

"Oh, I'm sorry," Brenda says.

"Ten years ago," Mrs. Raven says, bumping her husband on the shoulder.

"Ten years?" says Mr. Raven, still staring straight ahead.

"Farm machine," Mrs. Raven says.

"I'm sorry," Brenda says. "My own folks got killed in a car accident when I was a little girl myself. I got raised by my Gran, my Mama's mama. My Gran, she's the one embroidered this jacket I'm wearing."

The farm woman scrutinizes the stitching, and then says, "She's awful pretty with her needle."

"Thank you," Brenda says, settling into her place on the seat.

The speaker has been crackling static all this while, but now the driver-guide bursts out again.

". . . WE'VE GOT A STIMULATING three hours for you here, folks, right here in Music City and its environs. . . ."

"I didn't know it was going to be all that long," she says with a sigh. Her picture of Billy hulking there under the covers keeps fading in and fading out, in and out, like the tour guide's voice over that microphone. But darn it, she says to herself, making her fists into little balls of knuckle.

"FOLKS, OUR FIRST STOP in this panoramic visit to our capital of country music, is the birthplace of the Grand Ole Opry and a national landmark, the Ryman Auditorium. . . ."

He double-parks the van, he's out of his seat, out the door, and around the side of the van, sliding open the panel and offering to help Brenda down onto the roadway.

"Thank you," she says, refusing his hand, thinking how quick he is despite that big beer belly. The sun bursts out from behind a layer of cloud and Brenda squints her way into the arched entrance of the large brick building. Inside the low-ceilinged auditorium smells of must and wood. The floors creak. A few other tourists stand at the souvenir booth at the rear of the hall. Brenda and the Ravens pause on the stage, peek into the dressing rooms. Brenda imagines the farm couple with their little boy, sitting in front of the radio out on that Iowa farm, Saturday nights listening to the Opry. The floor gives a good series of creaks for emphasis. She remembers watching TV, TV, TV, with her Gran, the woman embroidering pillows, bedspreads, later her jean jacket, clutching the lapels to ward off a little chill.

"So small," says Mr. Raven as they return to the van, the first remark he's made, really, since the tour began. Brenda's thinking about the hall, small, and then she kicks herself in her mind for not stopping at the souvenir booth.

"NOW FOLKS CAN YOU TELL ME—" They're rolling along now through the middle of the city and it reminds her of the school tour she once took in Birmingham and how everybody kept hoping to see the governor—here's the Tennessee State Capitol right alongside them—him cruising along the sidewalk perhaps in his wheelchair, and Billy was there messing around in the back of the bus with his buddies, the same boys enlisted with him and went to the DMZ. And now he's working, Brenda goes on to herself, as though she's taking inventory in the medical laboratory where she works, he's at the military school, security, and we've got the car almost paid for, and the ladies' man has settled down—we're married.

"—WHAT INDUSTRY is Nashville's largest? What industry, folks?"

Mr. Raven sits suddenly forward and says, "Music!"

"SORRY," the driver blasts out over the speaker, "but as much as we'd like to think it's true, sadly it's not. It's *in*surance, the *in*surance industry, folks, and after *in*surance believe it or not, the publishing industry. That's right, Nashville, music capital of our United States, is a book town, a print town, with Bibles and sheet music taking the lead over records as the city's most famous product. . . ."

"You live and learn," Mr. Raven says slouching back in his seat.

"Indeed you do," says his wife in reply.

Brenda is studying the traffic, the buildings squat and marble beneath the broad and cloudy sky.

" . . . PASSING THE CITY JAIL!" the driver is saying, "WHERE A FAMOUS country singer had a heart attack and died. Can you tell me who that was?"

"We don't know," Brenda says without even giving the Ravens a chance to speak for themselves.

"TEX RITTER," the driver intones, catching Brenda's eye in the rearview mirror. "Tex Ritter died in the Nashville jailhouse." But this turns out to be a joke, since he goes on to explain that Ritter had arrived at police headquarters to inquire about a nephew who had been arrested because of some delinquent parking tickets and, while there, the singer felt his heart give out. He died.

Brenda's not sure how much time has gone by, but they're picking up momentum now, crossing the bridge over the Cumberland River—she doesn't know this, the Ravens don't, the driver tells them—passing through poor neighborhoods, and pretty soon the houses of people pretty rich. There's Earl Scruggs's house, their guide tells them; there's Earl himself, fetching the Saturday A.M. mail from his postbox. Hey, Earl! Let's all wave! They wave. He's waving back! Earl Scruggs, ladies and gentlemen, the immortal picker himself! And then there's Barbara Mandrell's church, the Willie Nelson and Family Music Store, they're heading northeast toward Old Hickory Lake, he tells them, toward . . .

HELLO DARLIN

It's Twitty City! Conway's enclave, with his famous song, and greeting in raised bricks in the wall along the highway. They don't slow down; they'll come back, the driver explains, and the next thing Brenda knows they're up the road aways, turning right onto a dirt road bumping them along toward the lake.

"THAT TRAILER THERE FOLKS is where the Cash family caretaker lives."

"They got a caretaker," Brenda hears herself saying, her chest filling up with breath to be breathed.

"AND HERE'S the spot where, one night, a car full of members of the Man in Black's family—"

"The Man in Black," the farmer says. "Oh, I can tell what's coming." Brenda bluffs out all that air.

"—and another car full of fans of his, like yourselves, was passing by . . ."

Mrs. Raven lays a hand on Brenda's arm. "Don't you think about it now, honey. Or if you have to, think it's a song."

"How'd you know I was?"

"*I* was. Why wouldn't *you* be?"

They're talking, feeling deep inside themselves, and when they look up the driver has them turning around in front of the fence that surrounds the house they've come to gawk at, a series of large connected boxlike buildings made of redwood, set down at the edge of the lake.

"It's as big as my whole apartment complex down in Selma," Brenda says.

"That's where you and Granma is living?"

"Me and my husband," Brenda says, staring out beyond the gate.

"Oh, and I forgot that. I'm sorry, darling."

"That's all right," Brenda says. "It's all so new I could forget sometimes myself. Why you know—" They've turned completely around and the redwood house with its guardian fence is drifting behind them. Woods quickly block the view, and they're bumping up that rocky road back to the highway.

"What's that, darling?" The farm woman's voice sounds awfully familiar to Brenda just for that minute—her husband is looking away, away out the window toward the receding woods, the disappearing house and lake.

"Nothing," Brenda says. "Sometimes I don't even know what's on my mind. Here it is, half the tour is almost over, and it seems like no time at all."

"NOW," breaks in their tour guide, "NOW HERE WE ARE," and it seems again but a moment, "ABOUT to make that stop I promised you, at TWITTY CITY, folks. Conway's own little kingdom."

They approach that wall again, and turn into the wide drive just before it, parking in the paved area in front of the high-gated, brick-enclosed compound. A gift shop and small amphitheater stand outside the walls.

"You know what I like," the plain-faced farmer is saying as they step out of the van. "I like the way it's all one big family."

"It is a little like coming to your rich uncle's house," Brenda says to both farmers and to neither. He's got such sad, half-lidded eyes she can't bear to meet them—she's showing something even more painful than him. "Though I never had a rich uncle with a big house like that to come to." She stops on the way to the entrance to the shop and peers through the wide bars of the compound gate. There's a large white building with pillars, like something out of old Selma, and beyond that a row of bright brick condominiums, something like—though twice as solid looking—like the Wind Tree where she and Billy moved in a few days before.

"He built those condos for his children," a voice says in her ear. It's the guide. She doesn't recognize his voice at first, naked as it is without the microphone.

"I hoped I could build one for mine sometime," Brenda says, glancing at him and then back through the gate.

"You've got children?" The guide can't hide his disappointment, an emotion Brenda didn't think she'd produce when she quickly decided to make her own situation clear.

"Not yet, I just got married two days ago," she says, and throws him a warm, though quick, smile.

The guide sighs a sigh like static over his loudspeaker in the van, and says, "Going to come inside? They got a lot of things to choose for souvenirs. You'll want to take something home to your husband."

"I'd planned on it, thank you," Brenda says, twisting around on the boot heel there in front of the gate. "He's back waiting for me at the motel. I know he's going to be so sorry he missed the tour."

"*I* would," the guide says right back to her, his meaning clear and bold.

Brenda normally doesn't get huffy. Normally she wouldn't even blink at a remark like his. But just two days married, two days! And he knows it! You'd think that he would try to curb his behavior. All this she's thinking as she glares at him, and then follows the farm couple as quickly as she can in her boots to the entrance of the store. She's holding a red satin jacket just like Conway's in her hand, fortunately the right size, when there's a commotion on the other side of the racks of cowboy shirts and jackets, by the door near the record albums, and she wanders in that direction. The Ravens have already headed out the door. Brenda drops the jacket on the counter and, with an appeal with upraised hand to the woman at the register, goes outside herself. She sees her tour companions in front of the gate to the compound. Only a few yards on the other side, standing next to a long dark automobile, talking to the driver, is a man of medium height with the thick-browned face of a diesel driver, a Nashville Sounds baseball cap on his head, a satin jacket—telling point—slung over one shoulder, and blue running shoes.

"Conway? It's Conway!" Brenda gives a schoolgirl's little jump up and down in her boots.

"So be it," says Mrs. Raven.

"Conway!" Brenda calls out, pressing close to the bars.

"Conway," the farmer says, quietly, as though in prayer.

The man in the baseball cap and satin jacket turns, breaks into a grin, and waves.

"*Hello, darlin'*," they hear him say in a gravelly baritone. Then he's climbing into the back seat of the long black car and is gone.

"Conway Twitty, folks," the tour guide says behind them, as though he's still holding his microphone in front of his lips.

Brenda turns, feeling her forehead crinkling, the kind of thing that gives you lines after years and years of frowning.

"Did you *arrange* that?" she asks.

"I'd like to say I have the power," the guide says, "but it's just our lucky day." He smiles at Brenda, showing tobacco-stained teeth. "So what'd you get your husband for a souvenir?"

"Why, I nearly forgot!" Brenda doesn't care about showing alarm in front of him, though so little has passed between them. Boys like this. It's what she married to get away from! "Darn it all!" she says, and runs hip-hip-hop in those back into the store. By the time she comes out again, package in hand, the farm couple has climbed back into the van. So has the driver. They're waiting for her, the engine running. She climbs in. The vehicle pulls out of the parking lot and heads hack toward the highway, back toward town, and she's sitting quietly, remembering Conway—his voice, his face. He seems more real to her, even in memory, than her recollection of the sleeping Billy back at the motel, and she doesn't like that.

"IT'S NEARLY TIME, FOLKS," the driver says in their ears, and Brenda doesn't even flinch at the noise level, though as with electric music she knows her ears will be ringing later on. "ONE MORE STOP ON THE TOUR, on this particular route, because we do have others, Nashville by Night, Opryland, which includes an evening at the Opry itself. . . ."

"We've got tickets for tonight," Brenda says to the farm wife.

"Why so do we," the woman responds. "Don't we, Mel?"

The farmer has been staring out the window—familiar sights, now that they're heading back the way they've come, the Willie Nelson and Family store, the subdivision where they saw the greatest living picker of them all, the bridge over the Cumberland. There must be other sights to see but this is the route they have taken.

"Do we?" he says.

"Which show?" Brenda is feeling something, thinking.

"First," the woman says.

"Oh," Brenda says. "We got the second. Billy likes the late show, usually. But maybe we could arrange to meet in-between. Be nice if you could meet Billy."

"That'd be real nice," the farm wife says, "if we can arrange it. Don't you say so, Mel?"

That farmer—he appears to be lost in the sights again, and his wife has to jiggle his shoulder to get him to respond.

"Thinking about spring planting, are you?" his wife teases.

"Thinking about our boy," he replies.

"THE FINAL STOP on our little tour this morning, folks, the Country Music Hall of Fame and Museum . . ." the guide, doing his job, breaks in.

"That's right by our motel!" Brenda says, glad to have something to say.

"You're a lucky girl," the farm wife says. "The two of you."

"I know," Brenda says, reading into the woman's words everything that's there. "Really."

Now here's the museum, just across the road from their motel—a great location. It's warmer in the parking lot here than out at Twitty City. Spring is coming on even this far north, and she feels warm *in*side after they pay their admission and pass into the exhibition—because there's Elvis's white Eldorado, and when Mrs. Raven comes up next to her and pushes the button on the little fence between them and the car and roof goes back and they can see the gold records inlaid in the ceiling, and the bar and the TV, too, she hears the woman take in a deep breath.

"Father," says the farm wife, "it would have been worth coming all the way *just* for this."

"I suppose," the farmer says, reminding Brenda of her own tight-lipped Billy.

She edges along to the next exhibit, and, standing there in front of the place on the wall where they put Patsy Cline's own cigarette lighter, the one they found at the site where she died in that airplane crash, Brenda can sense real heat coming on, inside and out, and she strips off her jacket, folding it over her arm. That crash! the flames! the fiery end! She gives a shiver—how can you feel so cold thinking about things so hot?—and moves along to watch some videos of the old-time performers, stopping in time to tap her toes, rock back and forth on her heels to some old-timer she never heard of singing "The Orange Blossom Special." She smiles at his yodeling, then slows down to listen to the Carter Family wail slow and deep and broad-noted, "Amazing Grace." She looks around for the farm couple, wants to say, "That's the in-laws of the Man in Black." She knows that much. But they're nowhere in sight. So she keeps on moving. Now she steps into a room full of photographs of the living greats:

Crystal, with her long rug of hair flying up and all around her, the picture catching her in mid-leap toward some high note Brenda can imagine clearly in her mind—Crystal, now there's a nice sounding name for a little baby girl—and there's Kenny, white-haired, bearded, distinguished at an early age, and Merle, a face of experience, eyes full of confidence. It's all like a family album, and she wants to say that to the farm couple, but they're still nowhere in sight. She wants to say how she knows these people, though she doesn't know them, all these real, familiar faces.

But as she's looking around, what catches her eye from across the room but the powerful shapes and colors of a painting. Clacking her way across the parquet floor, she gets close enough to read the plaque alongside the canvas. "Sources of Country Music," the sign tells her, a painting commissioned by Tex Ritter from his friend, artist Thomas Hart Benton.

It's the finest work of art Brenda's ever seen! The banjo picker on the side, the women with their unfurled skirts before them, the steamboat churning down the river, the railroad train racing on the shore, its dark smoke steaming behind it like a flag—and on the right-hand side the cowboy twanging his guitar, the fiddlers, more women dancing, clap your hands and stomp your feet, the land coming up in spring.

"Billy?"

No answer from the other side of the motel room door, no sound of TV, nothing. She spins around, clutching the package to her chest, to see the Mustang parked just where they had left it last night. On the other side of the parking lot lies the restaurant, and she starts walking toward it. Once she arrives she feels unsure, looks around smelling the meat, eggs, the lightest touch of grease, coffee in the air, cigarettes, all with the chatter of the lunch crowd in the background. Everyone here looks like the Ravens. But none of them's them.

"How y'all today?" the hostess greets her. "One?"

Brenda gives her only the smallest glimpse of her usually friendly smile and says, "I'm looking for my . . ."

What stops her? She sees a tall waitress with her back to her, her left hand crossed over her waist and cupping her right elbow while her right hand is placed flat against the right side of her face. She's got long braids, and one dangles loosely to the right of her neck, the other straight down. Brenda can't see her eyes, but her posture says that she might be smiling. A cloud of smoke billows up around her, and Brenda pushes forward through the room.

"Gol," Billy says, looking up at her, "I woke up so hungry I coulda ate a car. Hey, you have a good tour? Sit you down here and tell me about it." The waitress slides away as if on greased shoes.

"It was real nice," Brenda says, following the other woman's departure toward the salad bar, "but I want you to come up and see something now."

"See what?"

"I just want you to come across the street and see something."

Billy narrows his dark puffy eyes and picks up his cigarette, cowboylike is how Brenda thinks of it, cowboylike and almost mean. There's a flicker in his eyes, too, that she can't explain and doesn't want to try, except that she sparks another look herself off in that same direction, and she catches a glimpse of that waitress holding still like some forest animal at the edge of a clearing before dashing off to the other end of the room.

"I want you to see something, Billy," she repeats herself.

"Car?" he says. "Some car I'd like?"

"You could see a car, that's part of it. But not the whole thing."

"Well, I'll come look at a car," he says, reluctantly rising from his chair. He makes a big show about leaving a tip, something unusual for him, and there's something new about his mouth, too, something that she can't describe, or maybe it's just something she never noticed before.

"Now what is it, honey?"

They're walking across the parking lot, boots clacking together. Brenda's still holding her package; Billy's lighted another cigarette.

"Something in the Country Music Museum," she says, looking up. "I was just there on the tour." The clouds have parted—

a long trail of birds returning north gives her something to concentrate on.

"What y'all see?" he asks, taking her elbow and squeezing, coming back to her, as if out of deep sleep.

"Lots of things," she says. "It was real interesting. I met some real nice people, and we saw Johnny Cash's house. And, Billy, we met Conway. Oh," she says, hugging her package, "here—here I was carrying this. But I was looking for you." She hands it over.

He stops in the middle of the roadway and takes the jacket out of the paper sack.

"Well," he says. "Well, well. Well. Well. Thanks. Well, here," he says, handing it back. "You carry it now, hey?"

Brenda shivers again, a little chill around her heart part of the chest, but she takes it from him, stuffing it back into the sack.

"Now here?" he says, stepping up to the entrance of the museum. It's clear from the way he's working his head that he hasn't counted on going into a building like this as part of his morning.

"We got to pay," Brenda says. "But I got it." And she takes some money from her little leather bag and hands it over to the woman sitting in the booth in the middle of the entrance hall.

"They got Elvis's car here?" Billy says, looking up at a sign.

"They got all that," Brenda says. "They got Patsy Cline's cigarette lighter, you know, the one they found where her plane crashed? And lots of things, but I want you to see something first."

She takes him by the hand and leads him to the room with the photographs and the painting. Now look at this, she says to him with her eyes. And guides him forward to the wall, maybe four feet back from it,

"Uh-huh," he says.

"Now look at it," she says.

"I'm looking." He looks over at her.

"Well?" she says.

"Well what?" he says, looking back at her.

"Well, doesn't that just get you?" she says.

"That picture? Not me," Billy says. "It'll take a lot more than that to get me."

from *The Devil's Dream*

LEE SMITH (1 9 4 4 –   )

Lee Smith was born in the coal-mining region of Gundy,
Virginia. She studied creative writing with Louis D. Rubin Jr. at
Hollins College and drafted her first novel, *The Last Day the
Dogbushes Bloomed* (1968), while there. Smith set her third
novel, *Fancy Strut* (1973), in Alabama where she lived with her
first husband, poet James Seay. When Seay accepted a job in
Nashville in 1971, Smith followed and taught seventh grade at
the Harpeth Hall School there until 1973. Smith again followed
her husband when he joined the creative writing faculty at the
University of North Carolina at Chapel Hill and spent the years
that followed teaching at Duke University and at the University
of North Carolina at Chapel Hill. The seven years between that
novel and *Black Mountain Breakdown* (1980) were spent working in the short story form and two of her stories won O. Henry
Awards. Her *Oral History* (1983) combines the Appalachian
setting familiar to Smith's writing with an experimental form
combining ersatz oral histories and first-person narratives to
form a multi-perspective novel spanning locales, narrators, and
generations within a single family. Her novels *Family Linen*
(1985) and *Fair and Tender Ladies* (1988) were well received
by the reading public and critics alike. Smith returned to the
sprawling multiple-perspective of *Oral History* in *The Devil's
Dream*, a novel she dedicates to "all the real country artists."
The first and last chapters of this 1992 novel are the story of
the reunion at Opryland of the musical Bailey family. Chapters
in between chronicle more than a century of the family's history.
Smith feels an affinity between the history of her natal
Appalachia and the country music industry. The spirits and souls
of both, she has said, have been commodified and commercialized. Smith joined the English faculty of North Carolina State
University and lives with her husband, journalist Hal Crowther,
in Chapel Hill.

I'm not going to tell the next part of this story in too much detail, because this here is where my story gets to be just like everybody else's. There's a whole lot of knocking on doors up and down 17th Avenue, a lot of following up leads that go noplace, a lot of living on one meal a day at Linebaugh's, a lot of people that run out on you. There's a lot of nursing beers at the Exit/In, hoping you'll meet somebody important. And then there's always a producer who listens to your demo and takes you out to dinner and tells you how much he can do for you and then takes you out on his houseboat at Percy Priest Lake for the weekend and tells you some more about what he can do for you, and gives you a margarita.

I know all about that.

I've been out to Percy Priest Lake.

Any woman who makes it in this business has been out there, no matter how sweet and down-home and pure as the driven snow she comes off sounding in an interview ten years later. She's been out there, too. She's had that margarita. She's had several. But finally she's figured out that this don't help much. Nothing is going to happen overnight, in spite of what you read. Finally it's all a combination of good luck and good timing, not talent, not looks.

This town is full of pretty girls that can sing their hearts out, it's full of country boys with a great song written down in pencil on a sheet of notebook paper folded up real little in their back pocket. Most of those pretty girls will go back to singing in their own hometowns eventually, and then they'll get married. They'll sing in church. Most of those boys will go back home, too, and get a job doing something else, and sing on the weekends for a while with some old boys they went to high school with, and then they'll quit, too. They'll think about Nashville some over the years, about the time they spent here, they'll make it out in their minds to be better than it was.

Because it was not fun, mostly. It was hard, hard.

The first thing you do, of course, is call up whoever you know, but when I tried to call Rose Annie I got a recording that said, This number is no longer in service at this time. I was sure it was the right number—I had written ahead to Rose Annie and she'd written back on the nicest notepaper with a color picture of their home on the front. So I kept trying from a pay phone, and getting that recording.

I was staying then in a room at the Parthenon Tourist downtown, right across from the park. When I went out to get some supper, I passed a rack of newspapers and saw immediately why I couldn't get Rose Annie on the phone. "BLACKJACK JOHNNY SHOT BY WIFE" pretty much said it all. I bought a couple of newspapers and a couple of beers and some nabs and went back to my room and read all about it. It was just tragic for Rose Annie, to have left Buddy Rush for *him* and have it turn out this way. I was sure he'd deserved shooting, since she'd shot him. I never thought otherwise. As I was reading, it occurred to me that Johnny Raines had been just waiting for that bullet his whole life long. I can't tell you exactly what I mean by that, but I know it is so. There's some men that are born to be killed, Johnny Raines was one and Wayne Ricketts was another, and every minute they're alive is borrowed time. Right then, in that dark back room at the Parthenon Tourist, I started writing my song "Borrowed Time."

The next day I went back out to the pay phone and called Mamma.

"Mamma?" I said. "This is Katie."

"Katie who?" she asked.

"Your *daughter* Katie," I said.

"I used to have a daughter," Mamma said, "but she went to Hell."

"Now Mamma," I started to say, but she had hung up on me. I stood there in that phone booth looking at the Parthenon in the park across the street. You know it is an exact replica of the real one in Italy. It's real pretty, with perfect proportions, as this hippie fiddler would tell me later, who went to Harvard. He said the Parthenon was Art.

Right then I wasn't studying on Art. I missed my girls, and the money I'd saved up was going fast. I kept trying to get ahold of

Dawn Chapel, but it was hard to get the call through, and then when I finally did get her on the phone, we had the strangest conversation.

At first she was real nice.

"You know I just *loved* that song you sent me," she said when she finally remembered who I was. "I still get requests for it all the time. I'm going to put it on my new album, *The Best of Dawn Chapel.*"

"Wow! Great!" I said. "I can't tell you how honored I am, Miss Chapel."

"*Dawn.*" she said. Then she asked me if I'd been writing any more tunes. At this point in the conversation, she was still being real nice.

"Why, yes ma'am, as a matter of fact I have," I said.

"*Dawn,*" she said. "Call me *Dawn.*"

This is the point where, if I had played my cards right, I might have gotten someplace, at least I might have gotten her to listen to some more tapes. But I was still upset about Rose Annie, and more desperate than I realized. So I said, "As a matter of fact I have just recently moved to Nashville, and I'm trying to get somebody to listen to me sing. Do you have any ideas, Miss Chapel? Who is your agent, anyway?"

A silence as definite as a black blanket fell over the line.

I cleared my throat and went on, "I cut a record with Mamma Rainette and the Raindrops in 1952," I said, "and then I did 'New Eyes' for Four Star, and it did pretty good. Maybe you heard that one? I could bring it by," I said, "if you'd like to hear it."

Dawn Chapel's voice got funny and faraway, like I was a Jehovah's Witness that had come to her door, or somebody selling burial insurance. "That sounds nice," she said. "Call my agent, honey, why don't you?" And then she hung up without ever telling me who her agent was, and I stood there looking at the Parthenon.

No matter how big I get, I will always remember this moment. I will always try to be nice to the kids coming up in this business and treat them decent, not like Dawn Chapel did me. It's a great feeling to help another artist who's really struggling as a newcomer. And I know what it means to a new artist for someone else to just speak up for them a little bit.

So I will always be grateful to those people that finally did help me, especially Jim Reeves and Chet Atkins, and Tom Barksdale, who signed me with MCA and produced my first album, *Call Me Back When You've Got Time*, which featured "New Eyes" of course, but also the tune that turned out to be a surprise hit, "You Made My Day Last Night," which went on to be nominated by the Country Music Association for Single of the Year. So I bought the house on Harding Place and brought Rhonda and Don and the kids up here from Shreveport at last. They just loved Nashville from the start, all of them, taking to it like a duck to water! Tommy had his first drum set by then, so he could take lessons with the best. Rhonda ran into Patsy Cline in the grocery store at Green Hills the day after they got up here, and almost died she was so excited! Rhonda took over running the house and Don took over some of my business for me, as it was getting to where I just couldn't keep up with everything.

They were all right there when I got invited to sing "You Made My Day Last Night" on the Grand Ole Opry. This is a night I will never forget, April 10, 1964.

I can't even begin to tell you how much it meant to me because of all the nights in my life I had listened to those Grand Ole Opry broadcasts on the radio, dreaming of someday being there myself and meeting some of the greats, like Ernest Tubb, who turned out to be the *first person* I happened to run into backstage. I couldn't believe it!

"We're mighty proud to have you on here tonight, darling," he said. He seemed real warm and did not appear to notice my outfit one way or the other, which was good.

I was worried to death about my outfit.

The truth is that during the period "You Made My Day Last Night" was climbing the charts, Tom Barksdale stuck onto me like a leech. He told me where to go, what to do, who to talk to.

I gave in to him on everything, including image. So not only did my first album have a real smooth, contemporary sound, but I myself was no longer the same girl I'd been in my appearances with Wayne Ricketts. Tom Barksdale had me wearing my hair long and straight now, "California hair" he called it. I had on white cowgirl boots and the littlest white fringed skirt you ever saw. I didn't know what folks on the Opry would think of my outfit, but since that's what I was wearing on the album cover, it had become my trademark at the time. Tom said we were aiming for a bigger audience now, and that I'd be cutting my next album in L.A.

Tom said Nashville was dead and L.A. was where it was happening. He was switching all his operations to L.A.

Tom was *not* backstage with me at the Opry that night, though—I put my foot down. Tom Barksdale had long blond hair and wore things like turtleneck sweaters, and while I knew I was real lucky to have him produce my album and all, I just didn't want to let him come backstage at the Opry with me.

The Opry was for *me* in a way that I knew Tom would never understand, as he was a northerner from Michigan who had gone to the Berklee College of Music. "A technical genius," people were calling him.

Maybe so.

But I preferred to stand by myself at the right side of the stage, where I could see everything that was happening, and if anybody minded my outfit, they sure didn't show it. They were nice as pie, making me feel like it really *was* one big happy family, as it had always seemed to me, and for that night anyway, I was part of it. Lucile White asked me where I was from, and I got to hear Roy Acuff sing "Great Speckled Bird" and work his yo-yo! He's great with the yo-yo! Skeeter Davis was on that night, and the Wilburn Brothers. And Jim and Jesse, who I have always been crazy about, were making a guest appearance, too.

Standing back there waiting for my turn, I got real nervous for the first time in years. I wanted a drink so bad! Of course, I had tossed back a stiff one across the alley in Tootsie's Orchid

Lounge before I went in the Ryman. That's what you do. You go in Tootsie's first. Because of course you can't have a drink at the Opry, those people are real straight-laced. The only thing you can get backstage is a Coke from a machine, or coffee and orange Kool-Aid, which they've got laid out on a table.

There was something like a *church* about the Opry in those days when it was still at the Ryman Auditorium—why, shoot, the Ryman used to be a church, come to think of it. It's got those pews, and the balcony, and stained glass in the windows. There's something solemn about the crowd, too—even now, over at the new Opry House—something worshipful, which has to do with how far the fans have driven to be there, and how long they've been listening to their favorites, which is *years*, in most cases. For you know, the country music fan is like no other, they'll follow you for years, through good times and bad, and never tire of hearing your old tunes one more time. They are the biggest-hearted, most devoted folks in the world, and they are the ones that have made the business what it is today. It is not the stars. It's the fans.

Standing backstage at the Ryman was when I really realized this, watching them get up and slip forward as their favorites came on, walking one at a time right up to the footlights to take their own photos to carry back home. It's exactly like people going up for Communion in a big Catholic church, if you ask me, the fans moving forward in a steady stream to pause and snap, pause and snap, and then move on, back to their seats, back to Ohio and Maryland and West Virginia and all the places they came from, where they will get these pictures developed and put them in frames where they can point to them and say, "I was there. I was right there." It was just wild when "Pretty Miss Norma Jean" and Porter came on, you never saw so many flash bulbs! It was like fireworks on the Fourth of July. Norma Jean must have been seeing spots before her eyes. You sure couldn't tell it from her performance, though. On her way offstage, she passed real close to me, and reached out and squeezed my hand. She was pretty as could be. "Good luck, honey!" she said. And

I'll confess, I was starstruck! I felt like I was a kid again, instead of a grown woman with my own kids in the audience. I felt ridiculous in my outfit.

I could look out and see my own girls right up front and Tommy who looked so much like Wayne Ricketts it spooked me, like he was a ghost sitting up big as life in the Ryman Auditorium, waiting for me to come on.

There was a Martha White commercial ("Martha White self-rising flour! The one all-purpose flour! Martha White self-rising flour has got Hot Rize!"), and then I heard them call my name.

As I walked forward with my guitar, I just couldn't believe it—the fans were streaming forward for *me* this time, the cameras were flashing for me. For *me*! So some of these were *my* fans. Mine! I couldn't hardly quit grinning long enough to sing my song. After it was all over with, everybody gathered around backstage to congratulate me and say how fine I did, and I left that stage feeling like I was walking on air.

But when I finally made it back to the dressing room—they have these big dressing rooms—to get my purse and my coat, there was Lucile White, taking off her wig. She looked awful without her wig. And she was not even all that old, fifty-five I would guess. But she looked like she had been rode hard and put up wet, as Virgie used to say.

Lucile White was once the most beautiful woman in Nashville— this is how everybody described her, as the most beautiful woman in Nashville. She still looked great onstage. She had the prettiest smile, which she smiled at me right then, in spite of getting caught with her wig and her blouse off, smoking a cigarette. The great stars are real friendly.

"You did so good," she said. "It's exciting, isn't it?"

Now Lucile White had been a child star, so she had been a member of the Opry practically since she was born, but she could tell what I was feeling.

"Yes," I said. "Yes, it is. It's been a long time coming," I said. "I got here in kind of a roundabout way." I was thinking about all the hard times I had had in Shreveport with Wayne Ricketts while Lucile White was an established star.

"Sweetie, let me tell you something," she said, leaning over so that I could see how folded and crepey the skin around her neck was. "There ain't no free ride. And a body can get tired. Real tired." Then she smiled her famous smile, and a twinkle came into her eyes. "You know, it ain't hard to figure out who to fuck to get *on* the Opry," she said. "The hard thing is figuring out who to fuck to get *off*." Then she just about died laughing, so I couldn't tell if she was serious or not. But I sat down and smoked a cigarette with her, and she put some bourbon in my Coke from a little silver flask she carried in her purse.

So this was another peak moment for me, sitting in the deserted Opry dressing room with Lucile White after the show, putting our feet up and talking girl talk.

Lucile White was always real nice to me after that, and gave me a lot of breaks. I opened for her several times, and sang on her *Forever* album. When she died of an overdose five years after I met her, I couldn't hardly get over it. She always acted like she was having a ball. But then it came back to me what she'd said in the dressing room that night, "There ain't no free ride."

The official cause of her death was heart failure.

"The Termite Inspector"

JAY MCINERNEY (1955-   )

Hartford, Connecticut-born Jay McInerney attended Williams College and Syracuse University. After his well-received 1984 debut with *Bright Lights, Big City*, a minimalist tale of the excesses of a drugged-out New York fact checker, the popular press termed him and his stylistic contemporaries (Bret East Ellis, Tama Janowitz, and David Leavitt among them) the "Literary Brat Pack." He followed his early success with more tales of the New York club and Wall Street sets, *Story of My Life* (1988) and *Brightness Falls* (1992). *The Last of the Savages: A Novel*, a tale of a life-long friendship between a well-bred, self-destructive Tennessean and a blue-collar New Englander striving for respectability, was published in 1996. His latest work is *Model Behavior: A Novel and Seven Stories*, published in 1998. He married jewelry designer Helen Bransford in 1991. The couple and their twins divide their time between New York and Bransford's hometown of Nashville. McInerney contributes a wine column to *House & Garden* magazine. The following story first appeared in *Harper's Bazaar* in 1993.

"Fine," she says, as we drive up to the house. "Have it your way."

"I will," I snap. And I mean it.

Who knows what we're fighting about. Not really anything specific; more an endemic situation, like one of those underground coal fires that smolder away inconspicuously for months and years. Normally, we get along.

We're dragging home from the bank, where we've been hacking through the paperwork to refinance the mortgage. Turning into the driveway, I see a red-haired kid sitting on our front steps. "What the fuck," I say, looking across at my wife. She shrugs in her no-fault manner.

The kid stands up as I rattle to a stop in front of the house, and I see that he's older than I thought. In fact, he looks like a cross between a child and an old man, elfin and ageless in the manner of certain redheads, his thin orange hair poorly concealing his scalp, which barely comes up to my chest as I approach. On closer inspection his head appears too big for his body. He focuses on the loose flagstones, which he probes with the toe of his boot.

"Beg pardon, I'm here for the termites, sir," he says, still without looking at me. His accent is thick and slow as sorghum.

"Here for what?" I ask.

"You remember," my wife says, coming up beside me. "We need the certificate from the exterminator to get the new mortgage."

"Yes, ma'am," he says.

"Inspect away," I tell him, walking past him up the front steps. My wife is in charge of this kind of shit—part of the articles of marital division of labor.

"If you'll excuse me, sir," he drawls after me, apparently imagining he needs to deal with the man of the house. "I took the liberty of inspecting the outside of the premises while I was waiting."

I pause at the door. He's still looking down; I can just barely see his pale blue eyes which are the same color as the veins beneath his pale, translucent skin.

"I hate to be the bearer of bad tidings, but there's signs of termite activity around the foundation."

"Christ," I say. He winces. One of those very Christian, good country people, no doubt, fresh to the city from the hills and hollows that surround us.

"If you can spare a moment I'll show you, sir."

"Karen, can you please deal with this?" I plead. "I've got to make some calls."

I retreat to my office, deciding after a brief internal debate to leave the door ajar. Shutting the door will be viewed as a hostile act. If I leave it open my wife generally respects my privacy, but if I close it she will inevitably find some reason to knock and, in a slightly martyred manner, consult me on some matter of domestic maintenance. A conference seems inevitable after the termite inspection, but in the meantime I make some calls that I am determined to regard as pressing, although everyone I can think of calling turns out to be at lunch.

I sit back and listen for the sounds of munching. Maybe its not such a bad thing. After the house gets chewed up and swallowed I can just walk away from it, let the bank sweep up the sawdust. Leave everything behind, get in the car, and drive. Later for you all. Confronting the notion of a thirty-year note frankly weirds me out. I'm suddenly worried I might still be here in thirty years. Not that its a bad house or a bad place, or even a bad marriage, but the thought of thirty years of the same old same old . . . it's depressing.

After a while I hear them in the living room:

"I can't tell you how sorry I am, ma'am. On the other hand, the good news is your basement seems uninfested so far. So we can lay down a chemical shield that will last for ten years and is odorless and harmless with regard to domestic pets and other creatures."

"We don't have any pets."

"Well, I can understand that. I'm allergic, myself."

Pests, we got, but no pets.

I stare at the computer screen, waiting for the conversation to resume so I will have a reason for not working. "I'm going to give you ten percent off on the chemicals, ma'am, which is a latitude the company allows me."

Suddenly inspired, I type on the screen: . . . just because I like the looks of you folks.

"That's very kind of you," says my wife.

I grab my phone when it rings, but it's just a cold-calling broker trying to convince me that there are great opportunities out there that the big money investors have somehow miraculously overlooked. After I get rid of the broker I hear the termite inspector ask my wife if she likes country music.

"Sure," she lies. It's a common question around here. We both come from back East, and country music is not necessarily one of the things we like best about our adopted home. The twangy, whiny rhythms and wounded tremolo, the cliched lyrics with their prefab dualism of sin and salvation, lust and the Lord. When we chance on a country station on the car radio I always look over at my wife, usually with amusement, occasionally with irritation—it's her job that brought us here several years ago.

"Would you like to hear a song?" he says.

"Do you have a tape?" my wife asks, somewhat querulously, it seems to me.

"I could just sing it for you," he says.

"Oh," she croaks. "Right here, you mean?"

The situation seems hilarious to me until I hear her say, "Why don't we go to my husband's office so he can hear it, too."

I can't believe she's dragging me into this. Of all the shitty things to do. There's no back door to my office, nothing to do but wait.

Mock polite, my wife knocks on the open door, "Honey? I've got a little surprise for you."

The termite man shuffles in, still looking much too fearful and shy to be someone who has just volunteered to sing a song in front of strangers. My wife is wearing a cheerful mask that reads: If you think for one minute that I'm going to let you off the hook while I suffer through this, you're crazy, darling.

The termite man seems to be trying to dig a hole in the floorboards with his toe, perhaps emulating his day-job quarry, still unable to look at either one of us.

I can't believe this: trapped in my own house—my very own crummy home and castle that I will have paid for four and a half times over by the time the goddamned new mortgage is finished—cornered by a fucking munchkin who wants to sing to me against my will. At first I'm indignant at this carrottop geek, and then, seeing his extreme awkwardness, I am simply mortified in general for all of us.

"I guess I should say it's my dream to be a singer-songwriter," he explains, still looking at the floor. "Ever since I was a little boy up to Gallatin that's what I wanted. Well, I been practicing singing in my garage in the dark. On account of I been too shy to sing in front of folks. And then a few months ago I just started leaving the light on when I sang. It was what you might call a big step. Now I'm trying to get past the shyness part by singing direc'ly to folks. But y'all have to pardon me that I still can't look you in the eye."

Hearing this, I'm suddenly a little bit ashamed of myself and my cynicism. I mean, Jesus. I kind of feel sorry for this brave little cracker with his ridiculous dream. And I figure it won't kill me to sit through the song.

He starts to rock back and forth from his waist, striking up a beat with his left foot. Then he begins to sing.

At first I was just relieved that it wasn't really dreadful and then I was surprised that it was actually pretty good and then I began to forget myself as I listened. I don't know shit about music, really, and I don't know how to describe the qualities of his voice, except to say that, high as it was, it was much richer than you would have imagined, hearing him speak, and the words seemed somehow wrapped around a big soulful empty core—like the interior of a hollow tree trunk. In fact, I had to admit he had a beautiful voice. When Karen suddenly looked up at me, I saw before I looked away that she was smiling and that there were tears standing in her eyes.

It was a song about the open road, about a man and a woman and a Cadillac. The lyrics were simple, but later we were unable to agree exactly on the story. Karen said that the singer was driving down the road when he saw a beautiful couple in a Cadillac—an image of the happiness that he was always seeking. Whereas it seemed to me he was looking back on his own life, remembering a time when he'd been happy, driving a car that was long gone, like the girl.

When he finished, Karen said, "That was beautiful." And I actually had to agree.

"You wrote it?" I asked.

His face pink now, the termite man sneaked a glance at me. "Yes, sir. Wrote it with my wife," he said. And I thought he added that they wrote songs together when they were driving in their car, but maybe I was still thinking back on the song, since Karen didn't remember that part. She disagreed with me, too, when I said he must be a newlywed. But the way he said my wife, it was like he was dropping a name. Like he was saying— "I wrote it with Patsy Cline" or "I was discussing it with Kim Basinger over breakfast." Trying to appear modest, saying it with a lack of emphasis, which only serves to underline it. I noticed it again later: This was a man who actually blushed when he said "my wife."

"Would you like to hear another one?" he asked.

I was surprised to hear my own voice answering simultaneously with Karen's.

We were more relaxed listening to the second song, no longer afraid of being embarrassed. I didn't think it was quite as good as the first one, but maybe our expectations, so low at first, had been so far exceeded that we were looking for another quantum leap this time. But I felt very content as I listened to him, and I was almost sorry when he finished.

"What about that guy we met at the Harleys," Karen says. "What's his name?"

"You mean with the bad rug."

"No, that's . . . you're thinking of the television guy. This one was wearing crazy boots."

"They all wear crazy boots."

"We must know somebody. I'm going to call Tricia."

It's late afternoon. We're sitting on the back patio with spritzers, trying to think of people we know in the music business. It seems like everyone in the town is somehow connected to the music business, but now we're having trouble coming up with names.

"I mean, you don't think I'm crazy, do you? Didn't you think he was really incredibly good?"

I say I did. I do.

"I think he could potentially be like professional quality."

"I think maybe so. But what do I know? Call Trish."

Karen stands up and drains her drink, the ice cubes rattling in her glass, then leans down to kiss me.

"I'm sorry about earlier," she says.

"Me too," I say.

She walks through the sliding glass door to the kitchen and lifts the phone off the wall. Did I mention she has great legs?

After the termite man finished his second song we invited him to stay for a cup of tea. He said he couldn't linger; he was "on duty." All he would take was a glass of water. We asked him about his plans for his musical career, and he said he was just singing for anyone who would listen, hoping for his big break. He said he believed that God would help him to find the way. And instead of laughing him out of the house as a simpleton, I found myself admiring his sincerity. It was weird. We both hovered over him as he filled out the estimate sheet. And Karen took his phone number as he was leaving. She was disappointed when he said that someone else would be doing the actual spraying the following week.

Looking through the plate glass at Karen on the phone, I suddenly remember meeting the guy I think she means. A specimen in green lizard boots and a white jacket with silver piping who was bragging about how he'd found some kid in a bar who was now one of the biggest stars in country. And maybe two weeks later I'd read in the "Chatter" section of *People* that the star, I forget his name, was suing his manager, the one with the green boots, and how the star's ex-wife was suing him for additional support, claiming she'd stood by him in the lean years only to be dumped when he hit the big time.

I'm relieved when Karen comes back and says she couldn't reach Tricia.

"Let's go out to dinner," I say when she sits down.

"Whatever you say," she answers sweetly.

About halfway through dinner at the new Italian place we've been meaning to try for months, Karen becomes earnest for a moment: "I don't want to be the kind of person who gets all excited and says they're going to do something and then forgets all about it the next day. Let's not be like that. Let's do something for him."

Twirling a spiral of black linguine, I say, "Maybe he's better off not being discovered. Maybe he's happier as he is with his wife and his religion and his dream."

"That's pretty patronizing," Karen says.

I think about it, and I see her point. Who am I to protect him from what he wants?

The next day, with Karen hanging on my shoulder, I do make a call to a friend of a friend who is a publicist connected with the music business, and he promises to have somebody check the kid out. But we don't exactly follow up on it after Karen gets pregnant. Later she calculates backward and concludes that the child was conceived after we got home from the restaurant that night. I can vouch for the fact that it could hardly have been earlier; before that night nothing had happened in our bedroom for weeks.

It was a big surprise, but Karen's thrilled and I'm happy about it, basically, although sometimes I feel a little stranded, a little claustrophobic, when I lie in the bed beside her as she swells in her sleep; she conks out earlier and earlier lately, exhausted by gestation. And here I am wide awake in a dark and silent bedroom in a small house on a dead-end street. Often when I'm trying to get to sleep now, I think back on that night when I was lying awake after we'd come home from dinner. Happy for the first time in months, I was savoring the slow fall from consciousness; I had reached that state where I was watching a series of images unreel behind my eyelids. Just before I fell asleep I saw a big white finned Cadillac wheeling down the road with its top down beneath a huge blue sky. The highway sliced through a sprawling sand and ocher landscape punctuated with soaring red buttes like exclamation points. A beautiful woman who might have been a young Karen, or possibly Kim Basinger, was sitting in the passenger seat, smiling, her blonde hair whipping around her head trying to escape the pink scarf that she had tied under her chin. And beside her in the driver's seat was a red-headed man, taller and straighter and more robust than the one who had come to our door that day, but clearly the same man, although I felt certain that, despite appearances, the driver was actually me. As we drove down the highway he reached over— or rather, I reached over—and put his arm around the beautiful blonde beside him, and together they began to sing. And as they sang the car lifted off from the asphalt and rose into the vast dome of the sky, gathering speed, growing smaller and smaller until it finally disappeared into the blue.

from "High-Heel Neil"

JOHN BERENDT (1939–)

John Berendt received his A.B. from Harvard University in
1961. He has served as an editor with both *Esquire* and *New
York* magazines. His *Midnight in the Garden of Good and Evil:
A Savannah Story* was a Pulitzer Prize finalist for general nonfiction in 1995. "The Book," as it is called in Savannah, has
been a perennial *New York Times* bestseller and was drama-
tized for the screen by director Clint Eastwood in 1997. His
sketch "High-Heel Neil," excerpted here, first appeared in *The
New Yorker* in 1995.

One evening in late March of 1990, Neil Cargile stepped into his
single-engine Mooney airplane in West Palm Beach and took off
for Nashville. About forty miles southeast of the Nashville airport, the plane started vibrating uncontrollably. Cargile wasn't
sure what had happened, but he suspected that one of his pro-
peller blades had broken off; it had been repaired several months
before. He radioed Nashville to tell them he was having engine
trouble. Because of the vibrations, he said, he couldn't read his
instrument panel. He was losing altitude. His radio was being
shaken apart, and he would soon lose voice contact. Nashville
cleared him for an emergency landing at Murfreesboro
Municipal Airport, three miles from his position, but just at that
moment his plane started clipping the tops of trees. Suddenly, he
saw Interstate 24 spread out before him. He angled the plane for
a landing on a grassy embankment and set it down perfectly, but
at such speed that the plane slid onto the highway, skidding
toward traffic on its belly, its landing gear still up. As he strug-
gled to swerve onto the median strip, three sets of headlights
came at him. Two of the vehicles swung off to the side, but his
right wing caught the third, a van, on its underside and dragged it
onto the median, where they both came to a stop. The plane was

a wreck, but the van was only slightly damaged. Miraculously, no one had been hurt.

Emergency vehicles converged on the scene within minutes, along with television crews, and soon thousands of Nashvilleans were watching coverage of the accident's aftermath on the ten o'clock news: firemen spraying foam on a huge puddle of spilled fuel, bystanders lining the side of the road, traffic backed up for miles. At the center of all this—an island of calm amid the sirens and flashing lights—stood Neil Cargile. At sixty-one, he was impressively handsome, with glinting blue eyes, a square jaw, and white hair that fell casually across his forehead. He was wearing a blue blazer, a dress shirt open at the collar, and gray slacks. Aviation officials inspecting the scene praised his skill in handling the plane. They said his cool demeanor and his more than forty years of flying experience, which included a stint as a Navy jet pilot, had probably averted a disaster. Cargile sipped a soft drink and calmly inspected the wreckage.

"You look as though you're going to a party," one of the reporters remarked.

"That's exactly what I was doing," he growled amiably.

"What was the cause of the crash?"

Cargile smiled. "I like being the center of attention."

There was more than a grain of truth in Cargile's jest, as many of those who were watching the drama at home on television were well aware. Neil Cargile was a celebrated son of Nashville, a dashing figure of privilege and status who was never very far from the spotlight. He had played football at Vanderbilt, driven race cars, sailed yachts, and played polo. He was a man of action and daring—of that there was no question. And yet when his friends saw his dapper image on television that night they were all seized by the same incongruous thought: Thank God he wasn't wearing a dress.

It is common knowledge in Nashville, especially among the social set of Belle Meade, the lush residential preserve of old Nashville, that Neil Cargile—twice married, the father of three, and decidedly heterosexual—likes to "dress up." The first time he ever wore women's clothes in public was at a Halloween party at the Palm Bay Club, in Miami, in the mid-nineteen-seventies; four women had talked him into going to the party as Dolly Parton. They'd dressed him in a blond wig, a red dress, and a pair of Charles Jourdan shoes with four-inch chrome heels. Cargile won first prize that night, and a photograph of him in all his glory was posted on the club's bulletin board, where George and Em Crook, of Nashville, happened to see it some months later. "My God, that's Neil Cargile!" Mrs. Crook exclaimed.

The Crooks assumed that the episode was nothing more than a party prank, and they held to this view for the next couple of years, even when rumors of other cross-dressing episodes began to circulate in Nashville. The other occasions were costume parties, too, and they were always out of town.

But then Cargile began to dress up in Nashville. At first, he did it at private parties and with a degree of subtlety. He'd wear a blazer, a shirt and tie—and a kilt. Instead of the traditional knee-length woollen socks, however, he'd put on black stockings and high heels; or he'd wear the kilt and the heels with a formal dinner jacket. Eventually, he held what he called a Vice-Versa party at his home: guests were required to come dressed as a member of the opposite sex. Cargile was between marriages at the time, and his date that night came as Sir Lancelot; she rode into the house on a pony.

The Vice-Versa party and other sightings of Neil Cargile in drag caused a great deal of talk around town, but it was not until the 1979 Cumberland Caper that Nashville got a good look at Neil Cargile as a cross-dresser. The Caper is an annual costume party that benefits the Cumberland Science Museum. It has a different theme every year, and in 1979 Nashville's moneyed élite were asked to come as their favorite character in history. They arrived that evening in an assortment of decorous disguises—as George and Martha Washington, for example, and Marie Antoinette and Louis XVI. Neil Cargile showed up in a blue dress and a long blond wig. Given the theme of the evening, his choice was strangely inappropriate.

"And what historic character have *you* come as?" someone asked.

"As Neil Cargile in a dress," he replied.

Not since Elvis Presley scandalized Nashville by wearing eye-shadow at the Grand Ole Opry in the early nineteen-fifties had the town been confronted by anything like this. Chet Atkins had said of the youthful Presley's made-up eyes, "It was like seein' a couple of guys kissin' in Key West." Twenty-five years later, Neil Cargile's friends took him aside, one by one, and asked him tactfully (and sometimes not so tactfully) if perhaps he had lost his mind.

Cargile was the antithesis of what people expected in a cross-dresser. Nothing in his life had given any hint that he would become one. He had grown up at Jocelyn Hollow, a large estate in the rolling hills of Belle Meade. As a boy, he showed a talent for mechanical engineering, and for standing out from the crowd. At the age of twelve, he set up a machine shop in his father's garage and made motor scooters out of washing-machine engines. At sixteen, he rebuilt an airplane out of surplus parts from the Second World War and flew it solo from his back-yard. Local newspapers doted on his exploits, calling him a "backyard aviator." In the air, he was a superb pilot and a dare-devil prankster. He flew loop-the-loops, and he once buzzed his father on the golf course of the Belle Meade Country Club—a stunt that got him grounded for two months. He survived so many emergency landings, in fact, that he earned the nickname Crash Cargile. As an adult, he had a helicopter landing pad on the front lawn of his Nashville mansion—one of the few heli-ports at a private residence in Tennessee. He got involved in businesses that required grit and daring—flying crop dusters, for example, and designing, building, and operating mammoth dredges that were used for deepening rivers and harbors and recovering diamonds and gold, often in remote parts of the globe. After his exploit at the Cumberland Caper, Cargile assured his worried friends that he had not turned gay. The only reason he dressed up, he said, was that it was *fun*.

Cargile did appear to be having a rollicking good time when he was in drag. It was almost as if he regarded dressing up as a big joke, and on one level it was, since he made no attempt to pass as a woman. He did not alter his masculine voice or feminize his walk, and it was clear that he got as much pleasure out of shocking people as he did out of wearing the clothes. He especially liked to drop in at the Bargain Boutique to shop for second-hand dresses and pop out of the fitting room to ask dumbstruck ladies what they thought of the dress he was trying on. He did not merely seek the spotlight; he coveted it. When another man won the costume prize at the Cumberland Caper one year by coming as Dustin Hoffman in *Tootsie,* Cargile was incensed. He swore he would never attend another Caper if people were going to horn in on his act. He had no discernible qualms about dressing up in public. He even took delight in the new nickname he'd been given: High-Heel Neil.

By the mid-nineteen-eighties, Nashville had become used to the sight of Neil Cargile in women's clothes. Out-of-towners were about the only people still taken aback by it. One evening, a woman who was visiting Nashville to see her grandparents suddenly leaned across the table at the 106 Club and told her grandfather, in an urgent but lowered voice, that a man had just come into the restaurant in a red dress. Her grandfather shrugged and went on eating. "That would be Neil Cargile," he said without bothering to turn around.

I first heard about Neil Cargile during a visit to Nashville last spring. His second marriage had ended in a divorce, and he was living with a girlfriend in Palm Beach, where some of his dredging operations were located. Even at that distance, he remained the talk of Nashville—most recently because he had won a trophy in the Easter-bonnet contest at the Palm Beach Polo and Country Club, which had infuriated dozens of Palm Beach matrons. They objected that they and their daughters and granddaughters had been exposed to (and defeated by) a grown man in a blazer, a miniskirt, and high heels—not to mention a broad-brimmed, lace-festooned, flowered straw hat. An account of the affair which had been published in the Palm Beach *Daily News* was circulating in Nashville when I passed through in May. It had made Neil Cargile the center of attention once again.

"I suppose he does it, as he says, for the fun of it and for the shock value," Em Crook said. "That's Neil."

Jimmy Armistead, and old Nashvillean, disagreed. "Saying it's fun is O.K. for the first few parties," he declared, "but after twenty years there has to be a better reason."

Frank Jarman, the former chairman of Genesco, thought back over Cargile's lifetime of daring exploits and concluded that cross-dressing was simply another of his adventures: "I think he just got bored." A number of people pointed darkly to a tragedy in Cargile's past—the death of his fourteen-year-old son from a burst aneurysm that occurred in the swimming pool of the Belle Meade Country Club in 1970—as if it might have somehow triggered his compulsion to cross-dress. The Easter-bonnet affair was not, in fact, the first time a Palm Beach paper had featured Cargile in drag. A year earlier, the paper had revealed that he had given his alter ego a name: SheNeil—pronounced "chenille," as in the fabric.

Like Cargile's friends, I had always heard it said that the great majority of transvestites are heterosexual, but I couldn't understand that. Homosexual drag queens made a lot more sense to me. Of course, I had never actually met a heterosexual transvestite. Nor, I thought, was it likely that I ever would. Such people, I assumed, did their cross-dressing in private and, if they went out in public, made every effort to be undetectable.

But here was Neil Cargile—probably the most uninhibited, socially prominent cross-dresser in America since Edward Hyde served, in drag, as the governor of New York and New Jersey in the early eighteenth century. Governor Hyde explained the he wore dresses in order to represent the monarch, Queen Anne, as faithfully as possible. It occurred to me that perhaps Neil Cargile, open as he was, might be willing to shed some light on the mystery of cross-dressing, and, with this in mind, I called

him in Palm Beach in early August. He said that he would be
happy to tell me all he knew, but that it wasn't much. His voice
had a gentle Tennessee twang, and he spoke with the measured
calm of a commercial-airline pilot addressing his passengers
before takeoff. He told me he would be coming to New York in
a couple of weeks to discuss financing for gold-dredging operations he was setting up in South America. We could meet then.
He would be traveling with his girlfriend, Dorothy Koss.

"Will you be bringing your dresses with you?" I asked.

"Hell, yes," he said. "I love wearing that stuff."

"Why I Don't Like Poetry"

A. MANETTE ANSAY (1964–   )

A. Manette Ansay was born in Lapeer, Michigan and was raised in Wisconsin. She received an M.F.A. from Cornell in 1991. Her novels include *Vinegar Hill* (1994), *Sister* (1996), *River Angel* (1998), and *Midnight Champagne* (1999). The title story from her collection of short fiction, *Read This and Tell Me What It Says*, won the 1995 Nelson Algren Prize and the collection itself won the Associated Writing Programs Short Fiction Prize. Ansay was assistant professor of English at Vanderbilt University from 1993–1999, and has been an instructor at the Sewanee Younger Writer's Conference. The following story first appeared in *The Crab Orchard Review* in 1997.

I had done his kind of work before, but never in a Southern climate, and there were all kinds of new things to worry about: chiggers and brown recluse spiders and snakes, things I never thought about up North. Snakes in particular seemed to occupy people's minds. The rattlers, Martin said, liked the cool crawl spaces beneath brick houses, particularly those just south of Nashville, which is where we did most of our work. The moccasins preferred the country estates, especially in spring after the little creeks dividing the fields swelled up and bled into the old cattle wallows. By the end of May, the wallows were filled to brim, shining in the mud like new dimes. To a ol' moccasin, Martin said, once summer comes, it's better than a hot tub is to you and me.

I'd spent some time in that hot tub with Martin, but it was just one of those things that lit up a Saturday night or two and then sputtered out as we sweated our way into June. What we meant by landscaping was mowing lawns and watering them, trimming shrubs and hedges and trees, and now and then planting a few limp petunias the sun would fry up within a week. We sprayed for bag worms and tent worms and such, and in a pinch, we made strained recommendations to those who wanted an aesthetic opinion—Should we go with the white budlia or the pink? Martin and the others were used to the humidity, but it left me feeling reckless, unable to distinguish the wet air from my skin, and sometimes when they took off their shirts, I stripped down to my bra. From a distance, it could have been a swimsuit top, but Martin and Jeremy and Cale were all close enough to see exactly what was what. But they whistled and laughed and let me be. I could toss a roll of sod off the truck as well as anyone, and I brought sweet tea in a thermos which I passed around to share.

That summer we all got on pretty well, in part because there was so much to do. We worked fast and cheap, kept both the radio and our voices low, and each job we finished bred another few calls. Martin started giving us cash bonuses on weekends, and that was Martin for you, a good boss, a generous man. Jeremy was just a pup and money didn't mean as much to him, though he would have squalled at that remark and told you otherwise. But Cale and his wife had one kid and a half, and I was saving up to go to school, though I didn't tell any of them that because I was afraid they'd tease me and say I was too old, it was too late, I had waited too long.

Even now, I can't explain why I had my heart set on an English degree. I had taken one college class back in Ohio, but I hadn't done very well. It was a course on how to interpret poetry, something I'd always been a little afraid of, and it met three nights a week. The man who taught it was a poet himself; I have since read two of his books. From the start he assumed we were stupid, although that isn't quite right because in order to assume you must first expect, and we were invisible to him. We spent one entire week on a poem about a woman being raped by a swan. We spent another week on one about a woman getting peeped by a group of horny Pharisees. The poet told us the diction was *delicious*; it created the *delicious* feeling of watching a beautiful naked girl. Do you have any questions? he asked. Does everybody understand? After several more weeks of raping and peeping and desiring in general, I kind of got numb to it all. I'd had my little girl only two months before and the front of my shirt was always wet; sometimes, during the break, I'd have to change in the ladies room. Most of us in that class were young mothers, single like I am, trying not to let bad luck or happy impulse hold us back.

By July, I'd seen my first rattler, a smooth swervy business cutting through the grass. Jeremy chased it all the way to where it disappeared into a thicket, the rest of us laughing at the way he ran, lifting his knees so high as if he thought it might keep the rest of him safely off the ground. All that talk of snakes, but when you finally see one, it isn't so much. I had chigger bites up the insides of my thighs and a rosy ring of tick bites like a belt around my waist and poison ivy on my wrists where gloves never quite protect the way they promise. I got stung by hornets and fire ants. I slapped on the calamine and bug spray like perfume, but it didn't do much good, just like Martin said.

God, it was hot, it was so damn hot. I was living out in Murfreesboro with a girl named Rose of Sharon, and she said I was worse than a dog with all my scratching and carrying on. At night, she'd make me up a cool bath with baking soda and a splash of vinegar, and then she'd sit on the toilet and push back her cuticles and talk while I popped my poison ivy blisters. Rose thought college classes were a good idea for their own sake, though she wasn't sure they'd help me get a job that paid any more than landscaping did.

There wasn't much you could do with an English degree, she said. But I want it anyway, I said. I want to know more about the world, and it seems like this is a way to live all kinds of different lives.

That's why I like history, Rose said. Especially the battles and politics and strategies. I would have made a good general.

When's the last time you were in a real fight?

I don't get in fights, she said. I get past them. That's why I'd have made a good general.

Rose's little boy, Rodney, was living with her mother in Louisville, and she'd made up her mind not to see him again until she had everything figured out. She drove a truck for Fed-Ex and her checks went directly into her mother's account. Her mother sent back a percentage and sweet color photos of Rodney in a sandbox, Rodney eating ice cream, Rodney running across a green lawn toward the camera, arms spread wide. I'm not good at managing money, Rose said. You would not believe how I used to live.

Don't think about *it*, I told her.

I can't help myself.

It doesn't do a bit of good, I said.

What I liked best about landscaping was that it kept me too busy or else too tired to beat myself up like that. Mornings, we started around six-thirty when the sun still looked cool and far away. There were mosquitoes and gnats and big biting flies; every day I was surprised by the size of the bugs. One day, digging up a couple of dead stumps, I found a nest of slugs, each of them longer than my hand. I palmed a few to Cale and he slipped them into Jeremy's sandwich. It wasn't long before I found a handful of sow bugs in mine. It was this silly stuff that made the days fly. I got friendly with the baby-faced son of one of our clients, let him take me out for a beer after work, let him think it was his idea to put the moves on me afterwards. The next day Martin shook his head, but there are times a person needs to be touched, and it doesn't have to be all wine and roses and choreography. It doesn't have to wear a white dress or use complete sentences. Sometimes its better, it's closer, when it's not. It's more true to life somehow, or at least, more true to mine.

The professor had a word he saved for poems and people beyond his contempt. *Mediocre*, he'd say, and then he'd wait for us to write that down. I guess I'd have to say he was a good-looking man, but you could tell he'd been used to looking much better before middle-age kicked him in the chest. I tried to remind myself he had his pain just like the rest of us, but the poems he assigned us made it clear that his pain was called *art*, while what the rest of us felt was *self-indulgent, insignificant, lacking a larger vision*. None of us had words like that to use against him, so we scribbled in the margins of our notebooks and watched the hands of the clock sweep a circle on the wall. Now, I understand that poet was no different than the people in the meanest backwater church in Ohio. There's right and there's wrong and I'm right and you're wrong and that's that. But it still makes me mad to think about it.

One day, in the ladies, one of the other students turns to me and says, He is so absolutely full of crap.

We were reading a poem called "There is a Garden in Her Face." We'd been taking notes on how the natural beauty of a physical landscape functions as a metaphor for the female body.

I don't know, I said. What I do know is that I don't like poetry.

All those guys think about is getting it on with women, someone else said. Only they aren't real women, they're Playboy bunnies. You know, she said, making a curvy shape with her hands. Air-brushed.

Well, these are not the only poems in the world, the first student said, and the next time the class met, she brought in work by her favorite poets. She asked our poet if she could distribute photocopies, and he said it was fine as long as she did it during the break. Some of these poets had women's names, and the poems were written in all different styles. I saved the ones about giving birth, raising kids, trying to keep your head on straight. The ones about being angry and afraid of what that anger might do. At home, my little girl wouldn't stop crying. She wouldn't take my milk. She had this rash all over her body; my palms stuck to her when I picked her up and made this ripping sound when I tried to let go.

This is mediocre, our poet said. This is body-fluid poetry. This does not transcend the personal to achieve the universal.

The heat in Tennessee was like nothing I had ever seen. I wondered if I was sweating away all the poisonous things I'd carried for years, the things that make you tell yourself you will never amount to anything decent, the things that keep you drunk or high or glued to some man or the front of the TV. I was getting books at the library and reading them on my days off. I was saving money. I imagined myself with that English degree, speaking to a room filled with students. One night, I told Rose about my little girl and how the state of Ohio had finally taken her away. Now the foster parents wanted to adopt her. She'd been with them for three years. The social worker said she was adjusted, she was happy, it would be cruel to tear her away. Rose had a towel waiting for me when I stood up out of the tub, and she wrapped me up inside it like I was a little kid. You could see how she really was a good mother, holding the towel just so to catch me in it, then leading me down the hall to my room and tucking me into my bed. We had a bad wind storm that night, and for several weeks afterwards me and Martin were hanging from the trees like monkeys, passing the chainsaw back and forth, while Cale and Jeremy dragged the fallen limbs away and cut them up. Sometimes, if the owner didn't have a fireplace, we got to keep the wood, and the pile out in back of Martin's house was growing fast. In fall we planned to sell it from the back of the truck and make ourselves a killing—all those nice, dry logs.

I'd started reading poets the librarian recommended— Gwendolyn Brooks, H. D., Muriel Rukeyser, Anne Sexton. After that, I went back to the poets I'd studied in Ohio and read their work again, especially Wallace Stevens, and I realized that poems were mirrors made of words, a place where you looked to catch a glimpse of your own face, whoever you might be. When that happened, the rhythm and the sound shook you up better than music and you felt as big as the world, or bigger, like there was no such thing as loneliness. I even started writing poetry of my own; I figured it was better to be mediocre than silent. Rose teased me a bit, but she was nice about it. Maybe I can be your muse, she said, and I remembered our poet telling us how another poet said that men would always be better poets than women because the muse is a woman. Then he laughed and said, That's bit extreme of course.

I'm my own muse, I said.

August brought thunderstorms every afternoon. We'd sit in the truck, waiting out the rain, listening to Cale tell knock-

knock jokes his kid brought home from school. We talked about the jobs we'd just finished, and the jobs we had scheduled for the week. We talked a lot about snakes. Cale had a dog, a cocker mix, who hated them worse than anything. One night, when Cale and his wife were still renting out near Hermitage, that dog started acting funny. They were all sitting in the living room, and Cale said, Well maybe he's wanting something to eat. He got up and went into the kitchen, but when he tried to open up the cupboard, the cocker went nuts. I thought he was rabid, Cale said. I backed outta there and got the gun, and if he hadn't of been sittin' quiet when I came back I would of shot him. But he isn't movin', he's just starin' at that cupboard, and then I hear those rattles goin' *shhhhhhht!*

In a cupboard? I said. In a house? How can a snake get in a house?

Up the front steps, same as you and me, Martin teased.

Cracks in the foundation, Cale said. Even with his tan he looked pale and sick. His wife was expecting that baby any day.

I still find it hard to believe, I said.

Well you can believe it, Jeremy said. My grandparents' basement was full of them. In fall, when they'd light the furnace, you'd hear them just scuttling away.

God's truth, Cale said, nodding solemnly.

Nashville has changed some, Martin said. But when I was a boy and we played outside, my mama'd sit there watching with the rifle over her knees, there was that many rattlers.

God's truth, Cale said again.

You afraid of snakes getting into this house? I asked Rose;

Good Lord, yes, Rose said. But there's likelier things I am much more afraid of. Don't you watch the news? Put the thing in perspective, girl. It isn't a snake that'll get you.

Just before Labor Day, a certified letter came for me and inside it was the paperwork to sign away my daughter. By then I was on this schedule, reading two books a week and typing out my impressions and saving them in a folder, but suddenly everything seemed like shit and all the old poison was singing in my head. I walked around the apartment, kicking things over, then cleaning up the mess. When Rose came home I met her at the door. I said, I need to get fucked up.

OK, she said, like she was relieved, like I was keeping a promise. We got ourselves dressed and into the car and by sundown we were dancing our way around Printer's Alley with some old friends she'd called up. The hours passed, the way hours tend to do, but things got particularly interesting when the man I'd been talking to invited me and Rose back to his place up in Gallatin. By then the last of Rose's pals had slipped away, so she said what the hell, and we hoisted ourselves into the bed of his truck because the cab was full of dogs. We thought there might be three or four; we couldn't get an exact count because they kept lunging like wolves at the plexiglass. But there was an old couch to get comfy on, and ropes to hang onto, and it was such a beautiful night. There were even a few stars, despite the light pollution which was pretty too in its own way, creamy as orange sherbet. The streets slipped past like pieces of a dream you just assume you'll understand when it's over.

I THOUGHT HE SAID GALLATIN, Rose said. She had to put her mouth to my ear so I could hear.

SO? I hollered back.

SO WE'RE GOING THE WRONG WAY.

NO, I said, but it was true; the truck had passed the ramp to I-40 North and was slowing down to turn south. Panic took us by the throats as if the driver had appeared beside us with a razor. We looked at each other, grabbed hands, let go and jumped out of the truck bed. There was an incredible floating feeling—the word *delicious* slipped into my ear—and then everything was pounding and weeds and dirt and empty beer cans and we were on our backs in the gully looking up at the quarter moon. The truck faded down the ramp, picking up speed. We watched until it cut out of sight onto the highway. Rose sat up first.

He *did* say Gallatin. He was up to something.

Yuh, I said. I'd bit my tongue. I could taste it, like metal in my mouth, like a brand new filling.

You don't take I-40 South to Gallatin. You go straight north.
I go north.

Me too. Unless he knows some other way.

Or maybe he wanted to stop somewhere for beer.

Or pick up a friend or something.

Or let one of those damn dogs out to piss.

It even hurt to think about laughing, and that was just the
beginning. We figured it was twenty blocks back to where we'd
left the car. The neighborhoods weren't bad, but they weren't
good either. Hey, Rose said, shaking out her hair. Tell me truth-
fully, are you worried about some *snake?*

I said I thought we should get out of there in case the truck
came back.

We were crawling back up the embankment toward
Broadway, picking our way through all that broken glass, when
Rose said, It's too bad nobody writes poems about stuff like this.

I'll write one then, I said.

I was kidding, Rose said. Who would ever read it besides people like us?

She didn't say it to be mean but I started crying anyway
because, in the belly of that night, I wasn't sure if there were any
people like us. There were only people like my little girl's new
parents with their college degrees and stable environments, more
than I could bear to hope for. My little girl would have all that,
too. I knew they'd care for her better than I could. But even as I
walked along the dark street, crying and hanging onto Rose for
balance, a quiet part of myself must have been thinking about
the poem I'd write, because the next day I woke up hearing the
sound it made inside my head, and the next day I was feeling like
maybe even I could start over and find a place for myself in the
world. In fact, I still think about my daughter every day, wondering if I did the right thing. And I never went back for that
English degree, either. But what I *did* do was buy Martin out
when he decided to move on to Baton Rouge two years later.
Now I have five people working under me, and I'm thinking of
hiring two more. I still read poetry and go to bookstore readings

and I write poems, too, though I'd never show them to anyone. I belong to our library discussion group and I read the essays asking can poetry matter, is poetry really dead, why don't people read poetry? I think about that poet in Ohio, and if I still believed in God, I'd pray for him.

Sometimes I imagine going back to see him, now that I've got this business of my own and my life has settled down and I have a language for the things I want to say. I imagine knocking on his office door, the two of us standing face to face. Of course, he doesn't remember my name, but he listens to everything I've just said, beginning to end without interrupting, and then he asks, not unkindly, Why are you telling me this? Why should any of this matter to me? And I say, Because it would appear you need me just as much as I need you. I say, Because even though we recognize different truths, I am not unintelligent, and I thought it's time you knew. I say, Because I still am standing without while you have seated yourself within, and I cannot understand why you won't see that I am here.

"History"

DIANN BLAKELY (1957–)

Diann Blakely graduated summa cum laude from the University of the South in 1979, received her M.A. in English from Vanderbilt University in 1980, then studied at New York, Harvard, and Boston universities before finishing her M.F.A in creative writing from Vermont College in 1990. Blakely's first collection of poetry, *Hurricane Walk* (1992), was listed as one of the year's ten best books by the *St. Louis Post-Dispatch*. She was awarded the Poetry Society of America's Alice Fay di Castagnola Prize for her collection *Cities of Flesh and the Dead* in 1999. Now residing in Nashville, she is the poetry editor for *Antioch Review* and the *Nashville Scene*. Her poem presented here was first published in the autumn 1997 edition of the *Southern Review*.

It's blood, and generals, who were the cause,
Shadows we study for school. In Nashville, lines
Of a Civil War battle are marked, our heroes
The losers. Map clutched in one fist, my bike
Wobbling, I've traced assaults and retreats,
Horns blowing when I stopped. The South's hurried
And richer now; its ranch-house Taras display
Gilt-framed ancestors and silver hidden
When the Yankees came, or bought at garage sales.
History is bunk. But who'd refute that woman
Last night, sashaying toward the bar's exit
In cowboy boots to drawl her proclamation?—
"You can write your own epitaph, baby,
I'm outta here—*comprende?*—I'm history."

from "The Past from the Air"

MARK JARMAN (1952–)

Mark Jarman was born in Mount Sterling, Kentucky, and received an M.F.A. from the University of Iowa in 1976. In the 1980s, he edited and published *The Reaper*, an influential journal that advocated the principles of the New Formalism movement in poetry. The young poets of New Formalism promoted the use of meter, rhyme, narrative, and traditional forms in their work. Along with David Mason, he edited *Rebel Angels: 25 Poets of the New Formalism* (1996). Among his six collections of poetry are *North Sea* (1978), *Far and Away* (1985), and *The Black Riviera* (1990), for which he was awarded the Poets' Prize. His latest collection, *Questions for Ecclesiastes*, was a finalist for the 1997 National Book Critics Circle Award in poetry. Jarman has also been awarded the Joseph Henry Jackson Award, three grants from the National Endowment for the Arts, and a fellowship from the Guggenheim Foundation. Jarman is a professor of English at Vanderbilt University, where he lives with his wife, the soprano Amy Jarman, and their two daughters, Claire and Zoë. "The Past from the Air," from which the following excerpt "The Apparition" comes, first appeared in *Crazyhorse* in 1997.

THE APPARITION

The old trees of the neighborhood are dying.
Entire limbs have torn off hackberries.
The redbuds have gone hollow. And the blades
Of tree surgeons are busy. It has been
Two years since we last walked here, looking for
Nothing so much as things to talk about.
The sun and rain have made streets dark and light
In jigsaw patterns. Winter's almost here.

In fact, it is here, has been for two days.
Gulf air, we guess, has pushed Canadian
Out from beneath the mellow Christmas sun.
The barbed cold front has tangled in the tree
Of Tennessee, and rain has turned them green
Where molds and lichens, mosses, sheathe their bark.
White fungus florets dot a twig, rain-black
And broken at my feet, two fingers long.

I pick it up and quote some poetry,
Because it looks like Pound's similitude
For the incandescent faces in the crowd,
"Petal on a wet, black bough," in the subway.
My mother holds the glistening stick of locust
And responds, sighing, that indeed she sees,
But not the pale spring blossoms in Pound's eyes.
She sees the faces only and the darkness.

She sees my face (It's time to change the subject!)
As I came running home across the lawn
One night. The voice and body of her son,
Which as she heard me calling had been separate,
Joined in the porchlight, asking for forgiveness.
What had I done? Only stayed out past dinner.
But what a dark deed then, that distant summer.
How white our faces both were with distress.

from *Nashville 1864: The Dying of the Light*

MADISON JONES (1925–)

Novelist, short-story writer, and critic Madison Jones was born in Nashville and attended the Wallace University School there. Before serving in the military in Korea from 1945–1946, he spent several years farming and training horses in Cheatham County, Tennessee. He earned an undergraduate degree from Vanderbilt University, where he studied under Donald Davidson, before taking a master's degree from the University of Florida, where he studied under Andrew Nelson Lytle. After brief stints at Miami University (Ohio) and at the University of Tennessee-Knoxville, he moved to Auburn University, from which he retired in 1987. He is currently professor emeritus and writer-in-residence at Auburn. Among his ten novels are *The Innocent* (1957), *A Buried Land* (1963), *An Exile* (1967), *A Cry of Absence* (1971), *Season of the Strangler* (1982), and *To the Winds* (1996), among others. *An Exile* was adapted for film as *I Walk the Line* (1970), starring Gregory Peck and Tuesday Weld. *A Cry of Absence* was a *New York Times* bestseller. He has been awarded several fellowships, including grants from the *Sewanee Review*, the Rockefeller Foundation, and the Guggenheim Foundation. The following excerpt is from Jones's 1997 T. S. Eliot Award-winning *Nashville 1864*.

My father, Jason Moore, joined the Confederate army in '62 just a couple of weeks before our troops retreated through Nashville in the face of the oncoming Yankees. I was only ten at the time but I was already a help around the house and in the garden and in a dozen other ways important on a farm. I was even charged with much of the responsibility of caring for my two baby sisters, and so, more and more, my overworked mother came to depend on me. Of course we had slave help, one family with two boys and two girls. But the girls were too young to be of any real help and the older boy, Cice, about sixteen in '62, could not be depended on for much. In fact a year or so later he ran away for good. That left Pompey, the father, his always sickly wife Ella, and Dink who was my age and my companion in most things. So what we had was one man, one able woman and two boys to work and maintain more than two hundred acres of farmland, buildings including our rather big house, and livestock, till the Yankees took it all.

Until then, till '64, we had just managed to hobble along. We had suffered depredation, all right, plunder of our livestock, cornfields, garden, and smokehouse not only by detachments authorized for the job, but also by strays, mere criminals, Yankee soldiers and otherwise. In '63 the better two of our three teams of mules were confiscated and we were left to make out as best we could with a team half crippled by age. There was also the constant feeling of threat, nights when my mother with a loaded shotgun would come out of her bedroom and settle down in the dark at the head of the stairs, watching, listening. One night she fired it, a noise as stunning as a cannon shot just outside my room. She said there had been somebody on the porch trying the front hall door. Nothing else happened, though, the silence after went unbroken. The next morning we had to cover with tow cloth the ragged gap where the window light had been.

As this event may indicate, my mother, Amantha, was a strong woman—strong in the way that I recall as being characteristic of Southern women in those days. Not that she ruled in our family. There was a line she would not cross, or would cross only in rare moments of stress, that was my father's domain where the final word resided. But her domain was large and scrupulously respected by him. Even allowing for the distortions that time can impose on memory, I am sure that it was as harmonious a marriage as fortune has ever permitted me to witness. I recall especially the manner in which they regularly spoke to each other on subjects of any importance: exactly as though in the matter at hand the other one was the true authority.

I have in my memory many vivid pictures of my mother and father, together and separately. But none is more clearly fixed there than the one from that late spring day in '62 just as Father was preparing to set out for the army. All of us were present, white and black, in front of the stable door, half-circled around the horse whose reins my mother instead of Pompey was holding. The horse's name was Windward, a handsome clay-bank gelding that my father had not included among the horses he had earlier donated to the Confederate army. Windward stood saddled and ready, a sheathed rifle in front of the stirrup on his off-side and a pack behind on his cruppers. In my memory Father, like the rest of us, including the horse, abides there frozen out of time, he by much the taller looking gravely down into my mother's face. No movement, no sound. I suspect it may not have been just so in those moments, but always when that picture comes back into my mind it is fused with a kind of despairing sadness engendered by an ancient folk ballad my mother used to sing sometimes. It contained these lines:

All saddled and bridled and gallant to see.
Home came his good horse
But never came he.

I have never since heard that ballad, or read it in a book, that I did not shed a few secret tears.

It was only a single day before Father's departure that his intention was actually voiced in my presence, though the signs of it had been visible to me for a week and more. In those last days he had ceased to be the man of few words I had always known. I would overhear him delivering to Mother or to Pompey detailed and lengthy instructions that would have appeared absurdly unnecessary if I had not already guessed what was about to happen. There was his busyness about small repairs to the house and fences, and his trips by wagon into town for household stores in quantities that in the past would have been deemed excessive. And there was his gentleness, beyond the usual, to Mother, to my little sisters and, in his fashion, to me. Then, on that final day, he spoke to me directly.

Weather in Middle Tennessee is changeable in winter. Suddenly, in the wake of days of bitter rain and sleet, there will come an air like balm on cheek and forehead, a spell like high springtime when men and women shed their coats and children their shoes without discomfort—intervals made half-dreamlike in the slanting rays of the sun. Such was that last day, when Father and I stood side by side with our hands on the rail fence in front of the house, looking down toward the pike and the creek bottom beyond. Breaking a full minute of silence, he said, "You know, Steven, that I leave early tomorrow."

I think I nodded.

"I have no choice any longer. I had hoped . . . I don't know what I hoped. I didn't want this war. But we have it, and they are coming . . . so very many of them. They are not even far away any longer. I'm afraid they will take Nashville."

"But General Johnston'll stop them . . . Won't he?" I said, looking up, up into his bearded face and eyes cold blue in the sunlight.

"It's been badly handled. Our preparation was slow in coming, and clumsy. The fault of too much pride, I'm afraid, in our own strength and valor."

"But won't Johnston keep them from crossing the river?" I said, now finding it hard to speak. "Can't he hold them back, from our side of the river? With cannons and all?"

"That is what people say. I doubt it. I don't think he has the power, not at present. They may cross the river in pursuit of our army, but I don't think they'll pass this way. Straight through Nashville, or farther east, I expect. But we can't be sure. I have given your mother instructions. I wish I had a choice but I don't. Even if I played the coward and stayed here, I would surely be taken prisoner."

Bursting out with it I said, "They couldn't do that to you!" They could not, not to my father, tall and strong and brave as he was. And gallant. In that moment, as I had done before in these last days, I envisioned a bright scarlet plume in the big gray hat he wore.

"War's like that, Steven. That's what happens. That and death and destruction. You will have to take the place of a man, Steven, whatever happens. I have good hopes that, if they do come this way, they will behave like civilized people. I pray they will."

My gaze shifted away from his face, down to where his intent blue eyes seemed fixed. It was the pike at the foot of the long slope, of red clay made redder still by all the recent rain. Then, in my imagination, there at a distance up the pike where it curved from behind the hill was a blue column of Yankee soldiers silently coming on. The vision held for a second, and was gone. But it might be real, might come to be so. Then all this, this house behind us, beautiful with its two white columns and balcony overhead, stable and barn and Pompey's cabin, the rich bottom field stretching out behind the pike for half a mile to the creek, would not be ours anymore. It was a thought that for a few moments eclipsed even my father's voice. He was speaking about Mother and my little sisters, as if committing them solely to my care. Then, after a pause, he said,

"I'm confident you can depend on Pompey. He was brought here as an infant and I'm sure he expects to die here. About Cice, I don't know. Keep your eye on him."

This was the end of that conversation. Unless you could call the minute or two that followed, in which my father did something he had never done before, a silent extension of it. He put his hand and held it there on top of mine on the fence rail. I thought of it as the laying on of my commission, the moment of my resolve to act, as far as I was able at ten years old, the part of a grown man. Even the thought was a heavy burden.

Father was right about the immediate future. General Johnston found that he could not hold at Bowling Green with only fifteen thousand troops and so retreated south and crossed the river at Nashville. But Nashville too was found to be not defendable and the army continued its retreat, on south and west across the

Tennessee River. Almost the next day, as I remember, the Yankees crossed the Cumberland and occupied Nashville. Immediately they gave evidence of intending to stay there. Within days they began fortifying their new and strategically valuable possession. From our distance of a few miles we witnessed this with alarm. It was like having the ground, our ground, violently snatched from under our feet.

But it was some time before we began to feel the material consequences of the occupation. For a couple of months the only visible evidence of Yankee presence was half a dozen detachments of soldiers in blue uniforms, usually mounted, passing by on the pike. None of them ever stopped, but from our places of concealment, which we sought when they came into view, we could see their upturned faces and sometimes a raised hand pointing. Laying plans, we would think, and afterwards go uneasy about our business.

Full springtime had blossomed before we suffered our first actual visit from Yankees. Father had given my mother many detailed instructions, which she scrupulously followed. Among the more important were those concerning our livestock. A good part of our acreage was spread over the hills behind the house, in part wooded, making it possible, up to a point, to hide our mules and cattle. So we did, successfully for a while, making good use of the clever detail which Mother herself had added on: that of leaving the old, decrepit team of mules in the stable lot and declaring to the Yankees that the other teams had been seized by the Confederate army. In extension of this stratagem we plowed and planted only a few acres in the creek bottom across the pike and actually planted most of our corn crop on the back side of two hills where pasture had been before. There was no such way to protect the chickens and pigs. The best we could do was turn them out of their pens, letting them go more or less wild and, so, harder to catch.

It was an afternoon in early May when we got our first chance to test our stratagems. I was in back of the house in the shade by the well pump cleaning a couple of chickens I had killed, when I heard footsteps and then Dink's voice just above a whisper. I looked up into eyes that all of a sudden were mostly white. "What?" I said.

"It's two Yankees 'round front."

I sprang to my feet but could not say anything at first.

"Standing there by the front steps." Dink's face that was normally about the color of an eggplant was a couple of shades lighter now. "What we goan do? Better tell Mistess."

Still I hesitated. Then, my gaze leaping past him, I saw the two Yankees coming around the camellia bush at the corner of the house. Both of them had big pistols stuck under their belts. I just stood there frozen. Without saying anything they came on and stopped about ten feet away from us. They were both shabby-looking in their blue uniforms. One of them, the fat one, wasn't wearing a cap. The other one said, "Nice-looking chickens you got there."

I thought of saying thank you but didn't say anything. Dink stirred beside me, nothing more.

The fat one said, "Maybe you'd like to make a little gift to the Union army."

The other, the lean one with the jagged chin, said, "Who's in the house?"

My mother, I thought, and held it back. Some words of defiance rose but did not reach my tongue.

"Tell me, boy."

"I am." It was my mother, standing on the back gallery. She was not a tall woman, a little under the average height in fact, but standing there in her slimness three feet above ground-level with her arms lying folded and easy beneath her breasts she had a look of confident power I never had seen her wear before. Then, seeing the Yankees faced around and staring gap-mouthed up at her, I felt as if the tables were turned, the Yankees all but put to flight.

"What do you want here?" she said in a flat, not-loud voice.

One of them, the one with the jagged chin, had shut his mouth. I thought he even swallowed before he spoke. "Looking," he said. I saw that now a thought had come into his mind. It was to rest his hand on the handle of the pistol he wore, to call attention to it. "Where's your husband?" he said.

"It is none of your business."

He hesitated but I could see his confidence coming back. "Off with the Rebs, I bet." Then, "You a mighty uppity woman. This here place ain't yours no more. Belongs to the Union army. You Rebs is whupped."

My mother's cool blue eyes seemingly lidless and fixed on this Yankee's ugly face had not wavered a jot. But I could tell that her mind was racing. Maybe three or four seconds went by before she said, "What are you here for? To steal our chickens? I am sure your commander doesn't know what you're up to."

I saw the angry ripple of his jaw. But this time it was the fat one who spoke first. "Our commander, he don't give a hoot in hell what we do to Rebs."

"So just hold your mouth, woman," the first one said, meaner than before, resting his hand on his pistol again. "It ain't nothing to keep us from taking anything we want. Or coming in that house if we want to."

My mother's expression did not change, but she did, just for a split second, lift her gaze from his face. That was when it struck me that she had arrived at some kind of an idea. What she said was, "Don't be so sure about that."

"Yeah," the Yankee said, ugly, "I ain't seen nothing to stop us. Have you, Dan?" This with a leering grin at the fat one.

"I shore as hell ain't."

There was a pause. I knew it was coming now, whatever it was, my mother said, "Perhaps you soon will."

My mother turned (going where?) and walked deliberately to the corner of the gallery from where she could reach the rope to the farm bell on the post there. Her quick hands seized the rope and pulled, and pulled again, and again, while the Yankees stood staring as if the big bell's resonance had stunned them in their tracks. In the last shuddering echo of sound my mother's sudden voice called out, called loud for distance. "Tell them to come quick . . . all of them." Turning toward where her gaze was trained, I saw Pompey was there, at a little distance beyond the yard fence, standing motionless this side of the garden gate.

There was a little interval before I could make sense of it. Maybe it was those blank Yankee faces that jogged my understanding and set me all of a sudden fearing that Pompey might fail to see. In fact it took him another tense second or two. Then I saw his head jerk, his body wheel and lurch into a run that quickly took him out of sight beyond the stable and the cedar thicket where the graveyard was. It was only then that I looked back at the Yankees, both of them were looking at my mother again.

"Calling on your niggers, huh? Yeah."

My mother took his gaze as before, without expression. The fat Yankee spoke to him, words I didn't catch. But the words seemed to make a difference. The ugly one looked away, looked toward the cedars where Pompey had vanished, then back at my mother again. "All right," he said. "But them niggers won't be with you much longer."

"We'll see," my mother said. "I think you should leave right now."

He hesitated, glanced over his shoulder, looked back at her. "All right. This time." He started and, though already several steps behind the fat one, stopped again. "But your time's coming, Miz High-tone Reb. We going to get every last thing you got."

With that he turned away and, to the back of him, my mother said, loud enough to be sure he heard, "You're a little late. The Confederate army beat you to it."

Then they were gone. We, Mother and Pompey and Dink and Cice and I, standing in front of the house watched them go on down the pike on a pair of mules they had surely stolen and meant to sell. I remember thinking that if the Union army was made up of scum like those, we didn't have much to worry about in the long run.

Throughout 1862 and into '63 the situation locally, though hard and often frightening, was bearable. But after General

Rosecrans was appointed Commander of Nashville we began to feel the whole weight and bitterness of Yankee occupation. Together with Governor Andrew Johnson, that envious and mean-spirited son of the East Tennessee mountains, Rosecrans set out to show us the consequences of our wicked rebellion against the sacred Union. The new policies of harassment he executed on us included, for example: a loyalty oath, a card index on every citizen in the county, breaking and entering houses at all hours without pretext, sending people (including women) to the penitentiary and to Northern prison camps because of their politics, confiscating livestock, rocking and shooting of houses, refusing right of burial for killed Confederate soldiers, suppression and confiscation of the press, heavy assessments on citizens, rewarding Negroes for informing, and other policies I could name. Possibly excepting New Orleans, no other occupied Southern city had to endure so much. Living several miles from the city was of some advantage to our family. But as the war drew on, this advantage was less and less. As the number of Yankee troops steadily increased, finally swelling the city's population to three times its pre-war level, the pressure more and more extended to include the countryside around. Yankee soldiers along the pike were now a common sight. And it came to be that some of our unwelcome visitors were there with official sanction to plunder whatever might be thought useful. Several times, without apology or explanation such soldiers entered our house by open force, treating themselves, as it were, to a little tour of all the rooms in search of objects or persons unnamed—and of course to the terror of my two little sisters. Because of my mother's poise and astuteness they were not able to discover much that was a great loss to us, except once. It was a valuable Turkish rug that Mother had somehow failed to hide with sufficient cunning. She cried afterwards, a little, with silent tears.

Simply obtaining food enough for our own and Pompey's family was increasingly a problem. From early '64 on, our staple diet consisted of corn meal, turnips, and yams, the fruit mostly of the garden we had located on the sheltered side of the hill in back of the house. Occasionally we would have some pork, from our now-wild pigs which we had to shoot like game in the woods. But most of this my mother held back for sale or for barter with neighbors, and sometimes with Yankees. In the latter case this usually meant a trip into the city. I remember those trips (they were not very many) as always frightening. And indeed, according to reliable reports, there was good reason to be afraid, especially for a woman. Still, we did it, Mother and I on that battered wagon behind those two decrepit mules.

I will never lose the vivid memory of my mother on that wagon seat with the lines in her hands, stiffly erect in a long, loose gray garment she had contrived to wear, nun-like. Her wide bonnet too was gray and so shaded her face that, as it seemed, only her bright, watchful eyes were entirely visible. The first of our trips was in early spring and most of the once-paved streets, between those somehow desolate brick and clapboard storefronts, were a slop of mud fetlock-deep. They were crowded, though, with a tangle of wagons and caissons and mounted men nearly all in blue, and a din of rattle and splash and clamorous voices. But intermittent along the walkways of boards to either side were little pools of quiet, clusters of still white faces of men in dark clothes of everyday.

Then, turning, into a spacious lot nearly impassible with wagons and the long winding queue of people, citizens, inching and waiting and inching forward into the warehouse door. A tall, black-bearded Yankee soldier wanted to know what was under the straw in our wagon bed. My mother, about to climb down from her seat, settled coolly back. "Yams," she said.

Under the straw in fact were two pigs all cleaned and gutted, but (my mother's ruse) near the surface, overlaying the wrapped carcasses, was a solid heap of yams.

"Let's see them yams," the Yankee said and put his hand into the straw. It came out with a big half-rotten one. He looked at it. "God damn hog food," he said. "Grub for Rebs." He flipped it hard onto the ground. My mother just looked at him till he turned away.

We got good and much-needed money for those pigs and, that time, returned home without incident. We were not always so lucky. Harassment of Rebs seemed to be the favored form of Yankee humor, and though it commonly expressed itself in mere wisecracks it sometimes became more serious, designed to humiliate. Like the day two mounted Yankees, having overtaken us on our way home, rode close along beside our wagon ridiculing the bonnet my mother wore. When they got no response at all, not even the hint of an upward glance, the one riding beside her reached down and snatched it from her head. When this also failed to get a response he decided to keep it, and with mock expressions of gratitude rode off waving it merrily in the air. My mother, just as before except for the bonnet gone, with rays of the late sun illuminating the gray now mingled in her auburn hair, said not a word through the rest of that slow ride home. We never had to suffer molestation more serious than on this occasion, but there were people much less fortunate than we.

Let me say here, however, that behavior of this kind, and much worse, was by no means universal among their soldiers. Often we heard tales of kind and gentlemanly acts on the part of individual soldiers, and one, a Captain Burns from Illinois, went to considerable lengths to have a stolen milk cow returned to us. (Though in less than a month the cow was stolen again.) But such kindnesses diminished in number as the war went on and on.

In April and May of '63 there were two events very damaging, and also disillusioning, to us. As we discovered, they were connected events. The first was Cice's leaving us, without a hint of warning, simply disappearing in the night. He was not a reliable worker, but his help was much better than nothing. There were two causes, I think. One was Mr. Lincoln's Proclamation of January 1 purporting to free all slaves in the rebellious states. It was slow to percolate down, but it did so finally. The other cause was General Rosecrans's policy of rewarding slaves for informing. When a small detachment of soldiers appeared and, without so much as a nod our way, went straight back to and over the hill to where we kept our two good teams of mules, we immediately surmised what had happened. This was confirmed, very reluctantly and with shame by Pompey. Loss of the mules was a blow, but the fact of Cice's betrayal was almost a greater one.

Acknowledgments

Special thanks to the following individuals for their assistance in making *Literary Nashville* possible:

Josh Bowling, Natalie Cheney, Deborah Foley, Patricia Flynn, Jason Kesler, Kelly Kinirons, Jim Knowles, Jane Kobres, Cheri Marquette, Hubert McAlexander, Bridget Moore, John S. Sanders, Jennifer Sotak, Gabriel Wilmoth, and Dan Walker

"Why I Don't Like Poetry" by A. Manette Ansay ©1997 by A. Manette Ansay. Reprinted by permission of the author.

"Triptych 2" by Madison Smartt Bell ©1984 by Madison Smartt Bell. Reprinted by permission of International Creative Management.

"High-Heel Neil" by John Berendt ©1995 by John Berendt. Reprinted by permission of International Creative Management, Inc.

"History" by Diann Blakely ©1997 by Diann Blakely. Reprinted by permission of the author.

"Sources of Country Music" by Alan Cheuse ©1990 by Alan Cheuse. Reprinted by permission of the author.

Selection from *Home to the Hermitage* by Alfred Leland Crabb ©1948 by Leland Crabb.

"False Youth: Two Seasons" from *The Whole Motion: Collected Poems, 1945-1992* by James Dickey ©1992 by James Dickey. Reprinted by permission of Wesleyan University Press and the University Press of New England.

Selection from *The Storyteller's Nashville* by Tom T. Hall ©1979 by Tom T. Hall. Reprinted by permission of the author.

"'Mystery Boy' Looks for Kin in Nashville" from *Words in the Mourning Time* by Robert Hayden ©1970. Reprinted by permission of W .W. Norton & Company.

"Flood on the Mississippi" from *The Big Sea* by Langston Hughes ©1940 by Langston Hughes and renewed 1968. Reprinted by permission of Hill & Wang, a division of Farrar, Straus & Giroux.

Selection from *Milbry* by Bowen Ingram ©1972 by Bowen Ingram.

"The Past from the Air" from *Questions for Ecclessiastes* by Mark Jarman ©1997 by Mark Jarman. Reprinted by permission of the author.